Advances in
Instructional Psychology
VOLUME 3

Advances in
Instructional
Psychology
VOLUME 3

Edited by
ROBERT GLASER

LAWRENCE ERLBAUM ASSOCIATES, PUBLISHERS
1987   Hillsdale, New Jersey   London

Lawrence Erlbaum Associates, Inc., Publishers
365 Broadway
Hillsdale, New Jersey 07642

Library of Congress Cataloging in Publication Data
ISSN 0163-5379
ISBN 0-89859-706-4

Printed in the United States of America
10 9 8 7 6 5 4 3 2 1

Contents

Introduction:
Further Notes Toward
a Psychology of Instruction

Robert Glaser
University of Pittsburgh

The history of psychological science will mark the 1980s as a decade when research relevant to issues of education and training involved searching interactions with an advancing science of human cognition. Much of this effort will be seen to have profited from fundamental investigations of problem solving and higher order cognitive processes, the analysis of performance in specific domains, and research on the patterns and mechanisms of human development. Studies devoted to learning theory and to the instructional interventions that foster the acquisition of knowledge and cognitive skill will seem noticeably fewer; although now, in the mid 1980s, attention to these matters is increasing.

The challenge of this time in the field of instructional psychology is to derive the connection between learning theory and instructional theory more systematically (without sacrificing the inventiveness essential to good design and engineering), so that as learning theories are developed in various domains, they will yield normative principles for achieving knowledge and skill. Instructional intervention studies will test the adequacy of emerging learning theory, not only as scientific descriptions of experimental data, but also as a source of prescriptive principles that can guide the design of instructional techniques and materials. As Collins and Loftus (1975) put it, "It is also important that a theory be sufficiently powerful to produce the behavior it purports to explain" (p. 427).

Two areas of investigation best reveal current progress in instructional psychology. The first, in which recognized advances have been made, is the analysis of the competences (knowledge and skill) that are acquired in different subject-matter domains. The second is more recent research on theoretically grounded approaches to the conditions and activities of learning and instructional interventions. An adjunct area of work, more briefly mentioned here, is study of classroom processes, which now provides an increasingly well-focused picture of the environments where findings from theoretical and experimental work in learning and instruction will be used. The chapters in this volume present important contributions to work in these three areas. In this introduction, we survey some research in each area and then provide a brief overview of the work reported in this volume by John R. Frederiksen and Beth M. Warren, Lauren B. Resnick and Susan F. Omanson, Robert J. Sternberg, and Harold W. Stevenson, James W. Stigler, G. William Lucker, Shinyin Lee, C. C. Hsu and S. Kitamura.

THE ANALYSIS OF COMPETENCE

With its strong emphasis on learning in specific domains, the analysis of the nature of competence has deepened. Theories of task performance for complex behavior have been developed, greatly stimulated by work on problem solving; studies of language, reading processes, and text comprehension; interest in mathematical skill and understanding and in mathematical problem solving; and the expanding study of cognitive structures in children by developmental psychologists. Studies of the characteristics of expert-novice performance have played a catalytic role. Concepts that seem essential in the description of complex human behavior are now available. Theories of performance consider structures of knowledge and issues of knowledge accessibility, the role of representation in problem solving (including the relationships between form of representation and the development of understanding), the development of automaticity and relationships between automatic "unconscious" processing and controlled processing, the influence of the properties of mental models on task performance, and the significance of metacognition and self-regulatory processes.

Most impressive is the overriding influence of structures of knowledge. We now recognize that structures of knowledge entail more than the accumulation of information or simple connections; they are interacting organizations of information that are integral to processes of cognition. The growth and acquisition of intellectual performances become less mysterious when we view them as facilitated by the learner's theories of knowledge, much as knowledge in the various disciplines of human endeavor generates theories that encourage further discovery. How knowledge becomes organized and how the processes that use this knowledge develop with learning and experience are fundamental questions. These questions have been addressed by research on the knowledge structures and cognitive processes that enable the efficiency, judgment, and problem-solving abilities shown by individuals who display competent performance in a subject-matter domain. Efforts devoted to understanding the cognitive structures and abilities of the skilled performer have identified properties of the states of attainment, but we know less about the transformation operations that turn novice learners into increasingly competent individuals. This limitation is similar to that in our knowledge of developmental stages in children, where we have identified stages, to some extent, but need more knowledge about developmental mechanisms. But our understanding of the nature of competence, at the very least, provides us with targets for assessment as learning and instruction proceed.

Instructional psychology today is heavily influenced by the research on the analysis of human competence in complex tasks. Through task and performance analysis and the studies of expertise in a variety of domains of knowledge, we have begun to identify the hallmarks of acquisition and growing competence that can be recognized in the course of instruction. One of the salient and consistent findings of research that speaks to issues of instruction is that proficient individuals develop organizations of knowledge that enable them to perceive meaningful patterns. These patterns allow them to form representations of problems that lead to appropriate, meaningful action. Novices represent problems in qualitatively different, superficial terms that make problem situations more difficult to solve. There are many examples of pattern recognition and problem representation that are associated with competent performance. Evidences of these phenomena range from the classic work carried out on studies of skill in chess to more recent investigations of problem solving in scientific and mathematical domains. Such indices can become instructional targets in designing the conditions of learning and assessments of attained competence. The essential notion is that, at various stages of learning, there exist different integrations of knowledge, different degrees of procedural skill, differences in rapid access to memory, all of which shape the representations of the tasks and differentiate levels of competence. These differences or indicators signal advancing expertise or possible blockages in the course of learning.

On the basis of such current knowledge of human cognition, we can suggest some exemplary dimensions along which changes in levels of knowledge and skill occur in the course of instruction (cf. Glaser, Lesgold, Lajoie, in press). These dimensions, outlined in the following paragraphs, define in a general way components of acquisition or performance criteria of developing proficiency that become objectives for instruction and focal issues in learning theory. They are implicated in recent theoretically grounded instructional approaches, including those discussed in this volume. Many of the ideas expressed below are yet to be worked out, but our accumulating findings indicate the shape of a guiding framework. Consider the following dimensions of performance:

Knowledge Organization and Structure.   As learning occurs and competence is attained, elements of knowledge become increasingly interconnected so that proficient individuals access coherent chunks of information rather than fragments. In various subject domains, beginners' knowledge is spotty, consisting of isolated definitions, and superficial understandings of central terms and concepts. As proficiency develops, these items of information become structured, are integrated with past organizations of knowledge, so that they are retrieved from memory rapidly in larger units; structuredness and accessibility to interrelated chunks of knowledge become targets for instruction.

Depth of Problem Representation.   Certain forms of representation are correlated with the ability to carry out the details of a task or the steps of a problem solution. It is now well known that novices work on the basis of the surface features of a task situation or problem, and that more proficient individuals make inferences and identify principles that subsume the surface structure as they approach a problem or task. Ability for fast recognition of underlying principles is an indication of developing competence and could be assessed by appropriate pattern recognition tasks in verbal and graphic situations. If this is the case, then instruction might concentrate on attaining the understanding and depth of representation appropriate to stages of learning achievement.

Proceduralized and Goal-oriented Knowledge.   Modern learning theory has suggested that the course of knowledge acquisition proceeds from an initial declarative form to compiled procedural form. In the early stage, we can know a principle, or a rule, or a specialized vocabulary without knowing the conditions where that knowledge applies and how it can be used most effectively. Studies of the differences between experts and novices indicate that beginners may have requisite knowledge, but it is not bound to conditions of applicability. When knowledge is accessed by experts, it is usually associated with indications of how and when it is used appropriately. This functional knowledge of experts is closely related to their knowledge of the goal structure of a problem space. Experts and novices may be equally competent at recalling specific items of information, but the experts chunk these items in memory in cause and effect sequences that relate to the goals and subgoals of problem solution and then feedback information for further action. The implication for instruction is that the progression from declarative to tuned procedural and goal-oriented information indicates developing competence in an area of knowledge.

Theory Change.   In the course of learning, people modify their current theories of knowledge on the basis of new information, and develop schemata that facilitate more advanced thinking and problem solving. Recent research on prior knowledge has described the naive theories individuals hold that can enhance or retard learning. Even after a period of instruction, these naive theories often persist; although students have learned problem-solving algorithms, they have little principled understanding. Thus, theories of knowledge become targets for instruction.

Automaticity to Reduce Attentional Demands.   In investigations of competence, it has become evident that human ability to perform competing, attention-demanding tasks is rather limited. When the subtasks of a complex activity make simultaneous demands for attention, the efficiency of the overall task is affected. This effect has particular implications in the interaction between basic skills and advanced components of cognitive performance. For example, in the investigation of reading and text comprehension, where attention may alternate between basic decoding skills of word recognition and higher level skills of comprehension that integrate sentence ideas into memory, automaticity in decoding has been shown to be crucial to good performance. Although such component processes may work well when taught and tested separately, they may not be efficient enough to work together. A slow or inefficient component process in interaction with other processes can lead to breakdowns in overall proficiency. If a task, such as reading, consists of an orchestration of basic skills and higher level strategic comprehension processes, then instructional procedures should be able to diagnose and repair the inefficiencies. In the development of higher levels of proficiency, basic skills should receive enough practice to become automatized, so that conscious processing capacity can be devoted to higher level processes as necessary. One criterion for instruction, then, is the level of efficiency or automaticity required for sub-processes to have minimal interference effect; that is determining whether the automaticity of a basic process has progressed to a point where it can facilitate and be integrated into the total performance—whether it is sufficiently developed for more advanced learning and higher level performance to occur. Specific procedures for developing automaticity and allocating attention in course of instruction are undergoing intensive investigation.

Metacognitive Self-regulatory Skills for Learning.   Self-regulatory or self-management skills are general "executive" skills for approaching problems and for monitoring performance. They are not performance components specific to a particular problem or procedure, rather, they refer to the knowledge that enables one to reflect upon and control one's own performance. Representative self-regulatory skills include: predicting the outcome of one's performance, planning ahead and efficiently apportioning time, checking and monitoring solutions or attempts to learn, and assessing what one knows or does not know about a situation. Research has indicated that these regulatory skills may be less developed in students with performance difficulties, and it is likely that they appear in various forms and at various levels of competence over a wide range of individuals. An especially interesting property of these skills is that they may facilitate transfer of knowledge to new situations. Individuals can be taught a rule or procedure that improves their task performance, but transfer is enhanced when they can oversee conditions of its applicability and monitor its use. Self-regulatory activities are important candidates for instruction, and competence in these metacognitive skills can be important predictors of success with the problem-solving abilities that result in learning.

In summary, the cognitive analysis of human performance has focused attention on outcomes of learning, such as those listed above, that index stages of competence in acquired knowledge and skill. Such goals for instruction need to be further delineated by studies of acquisition like those on math and reading skill assembled in this volume and by the development of assessment procedures in specific subject-matter domains. In essence, our increasing knowledge of human competence signals new orientations for instructional design that will need to rely on relationships between indicators of cognitive abilities and theories of how these abilities are learned.

THEORETICALLY GROUNDED APPROACHES TO INSTRUCTION

At present, we appear to know less about learning than we knew in the 1960s when attempts were made to apply the behavioristic learning theories of the time directly. Since then, however, we have progressed beyond experiments examining the overt surface level of behavior and are investigating the substructures and mental processes of human cognition. Because we are now better informed about the hallmarks of competence, we are in a position to work out the implications of this knowledge for learning and instructional theory. In this section we survey some past attempts to integrate learning theory and instruction and then look at recent examples. The illustrations draw on earlier forms of learning theory and modern cognitive-theoretical approaches, and include research on classroom practices. Overall, they take into account findings that have clarified our conceptions of the dimensions listed earlier. They demonstrate the usefulness of goal structure hierarchies that facilitate the problem solving and procedural knowledge that lead to learning, issues of changes in the representation of subject-matter knowledge, specifications of the conditions of practice that influence automaticity, and concern for the self-regulatory strategies that influence the acquisition of cognitive skill.

Paired-Associate Optimization Studies and Programmed Instruction

With earlier forms of learning theory, quite direct extrapolations to instruction were attempted. For example, stimulus sampling and Markov models of learning led to optimization studies on the conditions of paired-associate learning, including beginning reading (word recognition) and foreign language vocabulary. Transitions between states of learning were assessed by changes in response probability, and the postulation of different (continuous or all-or-none) models of these changes prescribed different instructional procedures (Atkinson, 1972; Atkinson & Paulson, 1972). The programmed instruction paradigm attempted to optimize performance by direct use of the principles of operant conditioning, using techniques of successive approximations of response requirements, the interaction and fading of stimulus supports, and contingent feedback and reinforcement. In general, programmed instruction, like instructional design based on statitistical learning models, made minimal assumptions about cognitive processes and about the structural properties of subject-matter knowledge.

Learning Hierarchies

Behavioral theory also suggested the transfer assumptions inherent in Gagné's learning hierarchy model, where a curriculum is analyzed into ordered skills and the acquisition of a subordinate skill bears a transfer relationship to a superordinate skill. A treelike structure defines a sequence of events where prerequisite knowledge and skills are specified as components integrated into higher order performance. The resulting instructional procedure involves learning a lower order skill that facilitates the learning of higher order skills. Individual differences are manifested in terms of the number of subskills that are learned at any one time—that is, the size of the learning step (Gagné, 1968, 1977).

Rule Analysis

Transition strategies have also been suggested by later cognitive developmental studies identifying rules of performance at successive stages of declarative and procedural knowledge. Once the knowledge state of a learner is identified, then learning activities that foster the acquisition of higher levels of performance are introduced. A first step is to conduct a rational task analysis of performance at the most sophisticated level of competence and, then, to derive either rationally or from empirical findings the rules that govern less sophisticated stages of performance. The second step is to identify the knowledge necessary for individuals to progress from one level of functioning to the use of a more advanced rule. An example of this procedure is Siegler's work with children on balance scale problems (Siegler, 1976, 1978; for a different approach along these lines, see also Case, 1984). Siegler's analysis of performance on these tasks shows how individuals differ in the ability to encode and represent particular features of the problem situation. Given information on these differences, instruction can be designed to focus attention on problem features, thus enabling the individuals to detect and use higher order rules that facilitate the transition to higher levels of performance.

Knowledge Networks

The analysis of information structures in the form of networks of facts, concepts, and procedures has provided another approach to instruction. The theory and techniques involved come from work in artificial intelligence on expert knowledge structures, semantic information networks, and question-answering systems. From a psychological point of view, this approach to instruction begins with an ideal model of the organization of knowledge as it might exist in human memory. Assuming that memory is organized in the form of a semantic network, such a network specified in advance provides the type of organization of knowledge that is to be learned by the student (Carbonell, 1970). Starting with a model of the ideal structure, instruction proceeds by the student's interrogation of this structure and by providing information about errors that reflect differences between the student's semantic structure and the ideal structure. Diagnostic and remedial techniques are employed that eventually enable the student, when interrogated, to give the same answers that would be forthcoming from the ideal model. For example, the semantic network that was first rationally imposed can be redesigned to approximate the student's memory organization more closely, and a pedagogical procedure can be determined that most effectively facilitates acquisition of the desired knowledge structure. This approach is implicit in the tutorial interactions analyzed by Collins and Stevens (1982), which they suggest have application for both teacher training and for the development of intelligent computer-assisted instruction. With this form of tutorial instruction, it is assumed that the model of knowledge organization and the student's acquired knowledge organization result in essentially the same output, even though an exact match may not be implied.

Goal Structure Analysis and Performance Models

Work in progress on intelligent computer tutoring (for teaching programming in LISP and high school geometry) by Anderson et al. (1984) considers an instructional approach based on cognitive theories of problem solving, his ACT theory of cognition (1983), and modeling of the performance of private human tutors. This approach has the following characteristics:

• An initial instructional principle is to identify an ideal model of how successful students solve problems in terms of a hierarchical structure of goal states. This goal structure or the problem solving plan is made explicit for the student, as are the search and inferences processes required to produce it.

• The necessary information is given to the student during rather than before problem solving. Evidence from research on memory and problem solving support the tactic of providing instruction in a problem solving context: memory retrieval is increased when the context of recall matches the context of study; information is more appropriately encoded and understood in a problem context; and presenting information during problem solving attaches knowledge to the condition of its applicability and its relevant goals.

- The knowledge underlying problem-solving skill is represented as a set of if-then goal-oriented production rules. The tutor monitors whether or not a student has carried out each rule correctly, and it responds to any errors or missing rules. The learning theory involved assumes a *knowledge compilation* process, in which, as experience is acquired in a domain, sequences of rules collapse into larger macro rules. This enables the tutor to adjust the grain size of instruction as learning proceeds.

- To reduce errors, working memory requirements are minimized by making updates of partial products and subgoals available for inspection. In accordance with established principles of learning, immediate feedback is given on errors to reduce the time cost and frustration of floundering about in incorrect solution paths.

- The student can approach the target skill by *successive approximation* (a procedure employed in older forms of programmed instruction). The tutor supports a gradual approximation of expert behavior by accumulation of separate parts of the performance. These partially correct solutions are accepted and shaped into more completely correct solutions. In a manner reminiscent of programmed instruction, the student is assisted in solving most of the early problems in a set, and fills in more and more of the steps as progress is made.

- Students are provided directly with descriptions of problem-solving operators relevant to the current problem in the attempt to give them an understanding of generalizeable, transferable principles of performance.

Automatic and Controlled Processing

Another line of recent experimental and theoretical work focuses on the interaction between automatic and controlled processing and their relation to skilled performance and has provided fertile ground for instructional and training studies. We mention two examples here—one in the area of reading and the other in the visual search skills required by aircraft control operators.

Roth and Beck (1986) describe two microcomputer programs designed to enhance the decoding and word recognition skills of less-skilled readers in elementary school. The rationale for the programs is the limited capacity model of the relationship between decoding skill and reading comprehension known as the Verbal Efficiency Theory (Perfetti & Lesgold, 1977) that is also an impetus for some of the research behind the theory of reading ability considered by Frederiksen and Warren in this volume. The Verbal Efficiency Theory (Perfetti, 1985) assumes that reading depends on the interaction of numerous subprocesses and that these processes overlap and compete for a reader's attentional resources. Thus, as has been indicated earlier, if one set of processes such as word recognition skills are slow, inaccurate, and attention demanding, comprehension processes may not receive sufficient attention to occur successfully.

A goal of the Roth and Beck studies has been to assess the implications of the Verbal Efficiency Theory and to remediate the word recognition processes of students whose reading performance is substantially below average when they reach the intermediate grades. The instructional approach assumes that these students have poor word recognition skills because of insufficient knowledge of the orthographic subword patterns of English. The instructional programs provide extensive practice in identifying and manipulating word and subword units, encourage rapid response rates, and offer corrective feedback in gamelike activities that are designed to maintain student interest over long periods.

An intensive program of theoretical and instructional research on automaticity in "high performance" skills, such as visual search and air traffic control and electronic troubleshooting tasks, has been conducted by Schneider (1983, 1985). The skills studied require many hours of training; novice's performance is qualitatively different from the expert's, and substantial numbers of trainees fail to develop proficiency. Schneider's working set of guidelines for training are based upon the proposition that skillfulness with these tasks results from the effective interaction of automatic and controlled processes. As described,

> Automatic processing is a fast, parallel, fairly effortless process that is not limited by short-term memory capacity, is not under direct subject control, and performs well-developed, skilled behaviors. Automatic processing typically develops when subjects deal with the stimulus consistently over many trials. Controlled processing is characterized as a slow, generally serial, effortful, capacity-limited, subject-controlled processing mode that must be used to deal with novel or inconsistent information (Schneider, 1985, p. 296–297; Shiffrin & Schneider 1977).

(The inferencing processes Robert Sternberg discusses in his chapter for this volume are essentially examples of controlled processing.)

Schneider's training programs aim to develop automatic skills through performance of routine, consistent task components as well as to develop strategies to allocate limited controlled processing to inconsistent task components. Schneider's training guidelines include the following (only briefly stated here):

Present information to promote consistent performances of skill that may be automatized in order to develop fast, low-workload processing.

Design the task to allow many trials in short periods of time.

Initially, assist performance so that the trainee need not retain an overload of information in short-term memory.

Vary aspects of the task so that automatic skill components generalize to the class of situations in which they are appropriate.

To insure improvement with practice, maintain active participation and high motivation through extrinsic, nondisputive feedback and mild speed stress.

Present information for a component skill in a context that illustrates the large task goal.

Intermix training of various component skills to facilitate distribution of practice and perception of their interrelationships.

Train "metacognitive" time-sharing skills so that performance can be successful in situations that require different speed and accuracy trade-offs, simultaneous responding of the other component skills, and judgments of task priorities.

Schneider emphasizes that assumptions about skill development that have been generated in experiments and training programs for the subset of high performance skills that he studies may be fallacious when extrapolated to skills that require far longer term training, and that further research must be carried out to understand and test instructional conditions for such skills. Further interesting questions about the role of automaticity in learning in procedural domains come up in the Resnick and Omanson chapter in this volume.

Metacognitive Self-regulatory Processes, Modeling, and Coaching

Another current area of research focuses on teaching students the subject matters of reading, writing, and mathematics by combining apprenticeship methods with modern knowledge of the nature of competence and expert processes (Collins & Brown, in press). As in the work of Andersen et al., emphasis is placed on learning in the context of problem solving, but in addition, emphasis is placed on students' recognizing, finding, and delineating emergent problems that they discover through interaction with their environment. Problems become structured through interactions between loosely defined goals and increasing use of the contextual constraints that help to solve them.

Three model programs based on apprenticeship methods that attend to the development of metacognitive skills are described and compared by Collins and Brown: Palincsar and Brown's (1984) Reciprocal Teaching method in reading, Scardamalia and Bereiter's (1982, 1984) process-oriented instruction in writing, and Schoenfeld's (1985) methods for teaching mathematical problem solving. Each is analyzed in terms of four aspects: content, method, sequence, and social interaction.

Content. The treatment of content in all three programs shows the influences of cognitive analyses of subject-matter competence and of metacognitive self-regulatory processes. The training in reading skills involves learning such strategies as formulating questions and summaries, making predictions, and attempting to clarify difficulties in interpreting the text. The approach to writing requires more than "knowledge telling" by constructing sentences; it presents writing as a recursive task in which goals emerge and are refined as part of the process. This involves developing strategies for planning that focus on what one knows about a topic, thinking about the audience and appropriately organizing one's ideas, framing revision strategies for reviewing and improving what one has written. The instruction in mathematical problem solving involves more than simply applying procedures; it includes learning to use both problem-solving heuristics appropriate to different types of problems, and control strategies such as evaluating which heuristics apply, which get you closer to solution, and which you are best able to carry out. In all three areas, competent performance involves planning, executing, and monitoring.

Method.   Modelling and coaching, keystones of apprenticeship training, are used in the three programs. Learning by observing models of behavior has been extensively studied in psychological research. Recent work in cognition has added to earlier conceptions of modeling verbal elaborations on the rules and on the mental models that underlie performance in order to make the knowledge entailed in understanding more explicit. Coaching procedures raise many long-standing questions in new light and require continued research on techniques for diagnosing conceptual difficulties and performance errors, and on methods for taking corrective action, giving hints, or engineering performance to minimize errors. In general, instruction in all three programs moves back and forth between modelling and coaching activities.

Sequence.   In different ways, these three programs use the instructional procedures of "scaffolding" and "fading." Scaffolding consists of supports the teacher gives to help the student to carry out some parts of the overall task; fading consists of gradually removing these props. As indicated, these techniques, which are also used by Anderson et al. (1984) and by Resnick and Omanson, this volume, were warranted quite explicitly in the older forms of learning theory that informed the work of the 1960s on programmed instruction.

Social Interaction.   All three programs emphasize cooperative learning where students between themselves and with teachers alternatively carry out a procedure, generate questions and solutions, critique courses of action, and monitor progress.

Finally, these programs strongly encourage teaching in the context of goal-oriented problem solving situations. It appears that the extensive investigations of problem solving in modern cognitive psychology have led to an emphasis on learning in task contexts and on the use of problem solving performance as an important mechanism for instruction.

In sum, the findings and theories of modern cognitive science combined with past knowledge of learning, encourage investigations that address learning in the context of subject-matter instruction. We are now waiting to see the forms of learning theory that are constructed, the accompanying methods and technologies of instruction, and the interrelationships between the two. Instructional intervention or training studies of the kind described in the first three chapters of this volume, together with studies of classroom processes, like that presented in Chapter 4, will provide the basis for a cognitive psychology of instruction that integrates current work in the cognitive task analysis of human performance; studies of problem solving, inferencing and reasoning; findings on the progressions and transitions observed in studies of human development; and analyses of classroom environments and effective teaching practices.

Classroom Processes

In considering the status of instructional psychology, it is important to call attention to the growing body of related research that concentrates on *macro*instructional processes. This research is yielding a picture of the environments in which instruction occurs that can inform efforts to apply cognitive research. The term "macro" is used here to contrast the classroom variables with the microprocesses of cognition. Both levels of analysis and their interrelationships need to be rigorously examined in framing useful and effective instruction. Research on classroom teaching processes is becoming increasingly sophisticated through detailed analyses of the conditions under which learning takes place. Studies are now being carried out that help to explain the variation in achievement measures in terms of the initial ability of the student, classroom process variables, the nature of classroom discourse, classroom organization and management, and their interaction (Doyle, 1986; Cazden, 1986). Increased attention is also being given to the development of techniques of causal analysis that apply more directly to school variables and the allocation of educational effort (Brophy, 1986).

Work in this area involves systematic definition of the dimensions of classroom instruction, especially the components of operating programs that actually contribute to or detract from classroom effectiveness. These analyses provide information for practical implementation decisions and also contribute knowledge to potential theories of classroom teaching practices. The development to be anticipated is a growing macrotheory of teaching and instruction that is concerned with such practical variables as the allocation and efficient use of time, the structure of classroom management, the nature of teacher feedback and student reinforcement, the pattern of teacher-student interactions, the relationship between what is taught and what is tested, the degree of classroom flexibility required for adapting to learner background, and the contents of curriculum materials as they relate to teaching practice and student achievement. Such variables should be accommodated by instructional theory in the same way that the large variables of economic theory can be applied to economic change. As theory at this level develops, it will be undergirded by microstudies of human thinking, problem solving, and the learning of school subject matter domains (cf. Leinhardt & Greeno, 1986). In the future, the two levels, macro- and microinvestigations, will become increasingly articulated in studies that attend both to classroom learning and educational conditions and to the development of human cognition, knowledge, and skill.

THE CONTENTS OF THIS VOLUME

The contributions in Volume 3 of *Advances in Instructional Psychology* represent important perspectives on many of the components of instruction described in this introduction. They shed light on fundamental questions in the analysis of competence in mathematics and reading, give compelling examples of theoretically driven instructional interventions, and suggest the utility of analyses of classroom processes for accounting for levels of achievement.

John R. Frederiksen and Beth M. Warren report on instructional research on reading skills that is based on an interactive componential theory of the cognitive processes implicated in competent performance. They have developed three training programs, drawing on analysis that explicates the relations of data-linked and resource-linked components in reading as a basis for the selection of instructional tasks, the design of materials for various levels of learning, and the sequencing of instruction. The training environments aim to bolster skill in encoding orthographic information in multiletter units, in decoding unfamiliar words, and in using semantic information in sentence contexts. Strong performance on these skills is critical in the overall reading process; it increases the data resources in memory that are available for word recognition, and it decreases the demands on attentional resources. The three target skills are underdeveloped in poor readers, whose response latency and errors increase where demands for them are high. Thus, the training programs aim to enable students to meet criteria of speed and accuracy typical of good readers.

As opposed to wholistic approaches, in which sources of difficulty are obscured by the complexity of the overall reading process, Frederiksen and Warren's approach allows the immediate feedback that enables students to adjust their performances as they move toward achieving criteria of speed and accuracy. Each of the training programs focuses on one skill, making its performance mandatory, and eliminating the possibility of reliance on other components as much as is possible. In requiring a close focus on individual components, a componential instructional approach raises issues of skill integration. The authors describe, in theoretical and empirical terms, the relations between the trained skills. They also discuss challenges to the generally accepted view that efficiency in decoding correlates with tests of comprehension, and emphasize the need for research to address questions of component interactions.

As their concluding discussion, Frederiksen and Warren present a model of process interaction in comprehension focusing on the role of semantic memory in mapping reference relations and tracing high-order semantic relations among propositions. The potential of compotential forms of analysis for decomposing task performance into information processes in the complex area of reading comprehension is made clear in this discussion. The authors point out, however, that although the compotential approach promises much for reading instruction at the local levels of word and passage comprehension, "It remains to be shown that discourse processing components can be trained so as to affect global integrated performances in reading."

Lauren B. Resnick and Susan F. Omanson's chapter addresses fundamental questions about the relations between understanding and performance skill and the interaction of understanding and procedural competence in learning. Their discussion focuses on findings from studies of arithmetic learning that are designed to examine the links between children's implicit conceptual knowledge and their performance of multi-digit subtraction with borrowing. The results of the studies are provocative in calling for further research on the role of automaticity in procedural performances. Resnick and Omanson approach the problem of procedural skill by viewing procedures as forms of knowledge that possess structures, and that permit and constrain thinking. Approached in this way, these mental constructs can be seen as implicit theories of the domain where they apply.

The prologue to the chapter's discussion of instructional experiments is a review of the extant research on the nature of errors in subtraction (buggy performances), of the mathematical principles that underlie standard subtraction algorithms and constitute understanding, and of findings of elementary school children's knowledge of these principles. On the basis of the research uncovering the systematicity of errors, the researchers identify disparities between children's performances in which they applied their knowledge in working with concrete materials and written arithmetic, and their performances in mental calculation. Overall, the evidence suggests that although many children develop command of principles before formal instruction, their ability to draw on these principles in the context of written calculations can be quite limited.

Resnick and Omanson designed two pilot instructional intervention programs. The first, *mapping instruction,* aims at linking knowledge of principles to procedural performance with the symbols and notational system of arithmetic; it maintains a step-by-step correspondence between block manipulation and written problem solving. It was hypothesized that mapping instruction would prevent bugs by encouraging planning and checking in performing written routines. The second instructional tactic, *prohibition instruction,* does not use manipulateables, but affords practice with written subtraction in which no incorrect steps. were permitted. This practice was expected to aid performance at specific steps. Although neither mapping nor prohibition instruction was effective in correcting bugs, mapping was found to improve certain children's understanding. Those who benefited took substantial time to verbalize the quantities involved in borrowing. The evidence suggested that they replaced a syntactic representation, in which symbols are transformed, with a more semantic one in which quanitites are operated on. When doing a calculation and focusing on digits rather than quantities, despite their understanding, the children often reverted to their more automatic and buggy procedures. The authors speculate that an early focus on the principles of procedural domains might be the most effective way to secure strong performances, in that it might circumvent emergence of buggy procedures. Another possibility they raise is to design an instructional sequence that elicits reflection on how basic principles apply to each step of a calculation procedure along with attention to automatic procedures.

Robert J. Sternberg's paper presents a two-part theory that accounts for the development of decontextualization skills and for information-processing aspects of skills of verbal comprehension. The subtheory of decontextualization describes the development of ability to learn word meanings from context—particularly the inference skills needed for using contextual cues and word structure—as well as issues of knowledge acquisition. The subtheory of information processing describes critical features of word representation, provides a quantified real-time model of processing, and treats performance components and metacomponents. Sternberg presents data from experiments testing both the subtheory of decontextualization and the model of information processing. He sees this two-part theory as an attempt to close with the inadequacies of three current approaches to analysis of comprehension: those that accord domain or subject-specific knowledge primacy; those that use a bottom-up approach, which attribute differences in verbal ability to variations in information processing; and those that use a top-down approach, which focus on "expectation or inference-driven processing." He acknowledges that each of these approaches picks up on essential aspects of the cognitive process of comprehension. His theory, which is largely top-down in its emphasis on inference skills, is designed to incorporate the strengths of all three.

The results of the sets of experiments on the subtheory of decontextualization indicate its utility as a basis for instruction in vocabulary acquisition skills. The theory specifies the information and task strategies used in reading by people of varying ability to develop alternative definitions of unknown words, and it suggests ways that vocabulary knowledge as well as vocabulary acquisition skills can be influenced. The experiments included training studies aimed at improving decontextualization ability in which gains were obtained. The experiments on the subtheory of information processing in real-time verbal comprehension focused first on evaluating alternative models of word meaning representation. On the basis of the evaluation, Sternberg selected a mixture model of word representation for testing his information processing model. The mixture model allows the analysis of the process of encoding word meaning in terms of identification and accumulation of both defining attributes, which are necessary and sufficient, and characteristic attributes, which are neither necessary nor sufficient. His results offer a systematic picture of the representation of meaning and of the processes used to determine reference to a concept. The theory was also found to give a good account of the metacomponents of time allocation at the word and passage levels.

In his conclusion, Sternberg points out that his theory of verbal comprehension mirrors his general theory of intelligence in examining knowledge acquisition, performance, and metacognition, but adds that it is admittedly no key to the roles of phonics, grammar, and syntax in the development of verbal ability. Its strength lies in specifying the interactions between particular kinds of knowledge and mental processes. It goes beyond psychometric approaches and general notions of verbal ability to offer a coherent account of the domain. Further theoretical and empirical work that attempts to capture the combined roles of bottom-up as well as top-down processes in verbal comprehension are needed for a fuller description.

The work that Harold Stevenson, James W. Stigler, G. William Lucker, Shinyin Lee, C. C. Hsu and S. Kitamura report in this volume examines differences between the educational experiences of American children and Asian children from two cultures, and is part of a larger study that deals with differences in patterns of socialization as well. The American children's levels of achievement by comparison to Japanese and Chinese children, as well as many Western European children has been an appreciable stimulus to efforts to improve American education. With American children's achievement in mathematics especially, but in reading too, registering on the lower ends of the scale in certain international assessments, researchers have debated whether explanations reside principally in factors inside or outside the schools. The disparities between American and Asian children in particular, who rank at the top in these assessments, have been seen as reflecting differences in IQ, or in child-rearing practices, as well as in school experience. Review of the findings on IQ, combined with studies of cognitive functioning, call the first line of explanation sharply into question.

Stevenson's and his colleagues' extensive study of school practices took investigators into 20 first-grade and 20 fifth-grade classrooms in Minneapolis, Sendai, and Taipei, cities that were identified as comparable and yet representative of the three cultures. They collected data on variables directly affecting the percentages of time spent in academic activities, using a time sampling procedure. The objectively coded observational data describe subject matter taught; organization of students into class, group or individual instructional units; leadership of activities by either teachers, other adults, or students; students' classroom appropriate and inappropriate behaviors; and teachers' responses to the students. Differences in these aspects of classroom life were marked, and they provide strong grounds for linking the comparatively lower achievement of American children to aspects of the organization and conduct of classrooms that affect the amounts of time available for academic activities. Although the researchers note that Chinese and Japanese children have a longer school day and year than American children, use of time in American schools, rather than quantity of school time, seems to be critical.

The authors' recommendations for improving American education and closing the gap between American and Asian children's levels of achievement are confirmed by research within the U.S. that focuses on the relationships between teacher behavior and student achievement. Teachers whose classroom and instructional arrangements result in greater amounts of academic learning time and students' better engagement in learning tasks have been shown, by this research, to be most effective in raising student's levels of achievement. The heterogeneity of the American student population by comparison with that of Japan or Taiwan, as well as with those of European countries, make this confirmation of special interest. Given the great range of school characteristics that results from this heterogeneity and the overall decentralization of policymaking in American education, Stevenson et al.'s findings and recommendations suggest enlargement of the scope of research that focuses on schooling processes as a useful approach to clarifying issues of management and organization as they obtain in effective schools.

In conclusion, the chapters in this book display a major influence of cognition on instructional psychology, that is, detailed analysis of the nature of human performance in specific subject-matter domains. The chapters also forecast growing attention to studies of instructional intervention based upon theories of the acquisition of knowledge and skill and on investigation of classroom variables that are linked to student achievement. From diverse viewpoints, these contributions represent advances in instructional psychology that indicate the significance of the study of human behavior to revealing sound bases for instructional practice.

ACKNOWLEDGMENTS

This essay is based in part on work sponsored by the Office of Naval Research and the Office of Educational Research and Improvement of the U.S. Department of Education. I am grateful to Michelle von Koch for her contribution and editorial assistance, and to Sherrie Gott for her suggestions for revision.

REFERENCES

Anderson, J. R. (1983). *The architecture of cognition.* Cambridge, MA: Harvard University Press.

Anderson, J. R., Boyle, F., Farrell, R., & Reiser, B. (1984). Cognitive principles in the design of computer tutors. (Report No. ONR 84-1). Arlington, VA: Personnel and Training Research Programs Office of Naval Research.

Atkinson, R. C. (1972). Optimizing the learning of a second language vocabulary. *Journal of Experimental Psychology, 96,* 124–129.

Atkinson, R. C., & Paulson, J. A. (1972). An approach to the psychology of instruction. *Psychological Bulletin, 78*, 49–61.

Brophy, J. (in press). Research linking teacher behavior to student achievement. *American Psychologist.*

Carbonell, J. R. (1970). AI in CAI: An artifical intelligence approach to computer-assisted instruction. *IEEE Transactions on Man-Machine Systems, 11*, 190–202.

Case, R. (1985). *Intellectual development: Birth to adult.* New York: Academic Press.

Case, R., & Bereiter, C. (1984). From behaviorism, to cognitive behaviorism, to cognitive development: Steps in the evolution of instructional design. *Instructional Science, 13*, 141–158.

Cazden, C. B. (1986). Classroom discourse. In M. C. Wittrock (Ed.), *Handbook of research on teaching.* New York: MacMillan Publishing.

Collins, A. & Brown, J. S. (in press). The new apprenticeship: Teaching students the craft of reading, writing, and mathematics. In L. B. Resnick (Ed.), *Cognition and instruction: Issues and agendas.* Hillsdale, NJ: Lawrence Erlbaum Associates.

Collins, A., & Loftus, E. (1975). A spreading-activation theory of semantic processing. *Psychological Review, 82*, 407–428.

Collins, A., & Stevens, A. L. (1980). Goals and strategies of inquiry teachers. In R. Glaser (Ed.) *Advances in Instructional Psychology.* Hillsdale, NJ: Lawrence Erlbaum Associates.

Doyle, W. (1986). Classroom organization and management. In M. C. Wittrock (Ed.), *Handbook of research on teaching.* New York: MacMillan Publishing.

Gagné, R. M. (1968). Learning hierarchies. *Educational Psychologist, 6*, 1–9.

Gagné, R. M. (1977). *The conditions of learning.* New York: Holt, Rinehart & Winston.

Glaser, R., Lesgold, A. M., & Lajoie, S. (in press). Toward a cognitive theory for the measurement of achievement. In R. R. Ronning, J. Glover, J. C. Conoley, & J. C. Witt (Eds.), *The influence of cognitive psychology on testing and measurement.* Hillsdale, NJ: Lawrence Erlbaum Associates.

Leinhardt, G., & Greeno, J. (1986). The cognitive skill of teaching. *Journal of Educational Psychology, 78*(2), 75–79.

Palincsar, A. S., & Brown, A. L. (1984). Reciprocal teaching of comprehension-fostering and comprehension-monitoring activities. *Cognition and Instruction, 1*, 117–175.

Perfetti, C. A. (1985). *Reading Ability.* New York: Oxford University Press.

Perfetti, C. A., & Lesgold, A. M. (1977). Discourse comprehension and sources of individual differences. In M. A. Just & P. A. Carpenter (Eds.), *Cognitive processes in comprehension.* Hillsdale, NJ: Lawrence Erlbaum Associates.

Roth, S. F., & Beck, I. L. (1985). Theoretical and instructional implications of the assessment of two microcomputer word recognition programs. Manuscript submitted for publication.

Scardamelia, M. E., & Bereiter, C. (1982). Assimulative processes in composition planning. *Educational Psychologist, 17*, 165–171.

Scardamelia, M. E., & Bereiter, C. (1985). Fostering the development of self-regulation in children's knowledge processing. In S. F. Chipman, J. W. Segal, & R. Glaser (Eds.), *Thinking and learning skills: Research and open questions (Vol. 2).* Hillsdale, NJ: Lawrence Erlbaum Associates.

Schoenfeld, A. H. (1985). *Mathematical problem solving.* New York: Academic Press.

Schneider W. (1985). Training high performance skills: Fallacies and guidelines. *Human Factors, 27*(3), 285–300.

Schneider, W., & Shiffrin, R. M. (1977). Controlled and automatic human information processing: I. Detection, search, and attention. *Psychological Review, 84*, 1–66.

Siegler, R. S. (1976). Three aspects of cognitive development. *Cognitive Psychology, 8*, 481–520.

Siegler, R. S. (1978). The origins of scientific reasoning. In R. S. Siegler (Ed.), *Children's thinking: What develops?* Hillsdale, NJ: Lawrence Erlbaum Associates.

The contributions to *Advances in Instructional Psychology* benefit from the critical reading and comments of colleagues in the areas of work represented in each volume. The reviewers for this volume were Isabel Beck, Ann Brown, Mary Beth Curtis, Gaea Leinhardt, Charles Perfetti, Robert Siegler, Bernhard Treiber, and Margaret Wang. Michelle von Koch aided me in bringing the book to completion, with the assistance of Susan Craft. Throughout, work on this volume was facilitated by the resources of the Learning Research and Development Center of the University of Pittsburgh.

1 A Cognitive Framework for Developing Expertise in Reading

John R. Frederiksen
Beth M. Warren
BBN Laboratories, Inc.

I. INTRODUCTION

Our major concern in this chapter is to explore the relationship between cognitive theory and instruction in the domain of reading. Our goal is to identify aspects of a domain-specific cognitive theory that set constraints on the form of instruction aimed at developing reading expertise. A well-developed theory of expert performance specifies not only the skill components and knowledge that must be acquired, but also the way in which components interact in the performance of particular tasks. It is our belief that principles governing the form of instruction and the performance criteria for gauging and reinforcing students' progress follow naturally from such an interactive componential theory. In particular, theoretically specified interactions among components determine the choice of instructional tasks, materials that are introduced at each stage, and the sequencing of tasks.

Our work on remediation of skill deficits in reading has explored these issues. To establish the usefulness of a componential approach to reading skill improvement, a number of training studies have been carried out (Frederiksen, Warren, & Rosebery, 1985a/b). These studies have examined the effectiveness of component-specific training systems in developing the components that are the focus of training. In addition, we have been able to study the functional relations among components by examining the transfer of training effects to other components with which, in theory, the trained components interact. In the process, important issues of instructional design and skill integration have been addressed.

In this chapter, we characterize an interactive theory of reading, outline some of the key issues in applying the theory to the design of instruction, and describe both our approach to improving reading skills and its implications for reading and instructional theory. Finally, we propose an extension of the theory to the understanding of component interactions in text comprehension.

II. PROCESS INTERACTIONS IN READING

Prompted in part by Rumelhart's (1977) proposal for a general interactive model of reading, recent theories of reading have emphasized process interactions as the means by which knowledge from multiple sources can jointly determine the interpretation of textual information. Within this interactive framework, considerable attention has been given to understanding the role that context plays in letter perception, and in word and meaning identification (Perfetti & Roth, 1981; Rumelhart & McClelland, 1982; Stanovich, 1981), as well as the effects of prior knowledge of theme and discourse structure on text and story comprehension (Mandler & Johnson, 1977; Spilich, Vesonder, Chiesi, & Voss, 1979; Stein & Glenn, 1979; Thorndyke, 1977). In our research, we have sought to investigate sources of process interaction at multiple levels, with the aim of identifying component processes that are critical to the acquisition of expertise in reading (Frederiksen, 1981a; Warren, 1985). Critical skills are those that have a broad impact on the performance of other reading processes.

Our approach has been to identify processing skills in reading for which low-ability readers show substantial deficits and to investigate the interactions among those skill components through training studies (Frederiksen, 1982; Frederiksen, Warren, & Rosebery, 1985a/b). Earlier studies (Frederiksen, 1981a) have shown that as the processing demands of a component-specific task increase, less skilled readers typically show marked increases in response latencies and, in some cases, produce more errors (see Table 1.1). Skilled readers do not show these marked changes in performance. The view of the expert reader that has emerged from these studies and others (Perfetti & Lesgold, 1979; Perfetti & Roth, 1981) emphasizes the importance of automaticity in skilled performance. The skilled reader has developed a number of highly automatic integrated components. In contrast, the less skilled reader's processing is typified by its controlled, attention-demanding character.

We have proposed elsewhere (Frederiksen, 1982) that functional process interactions in reading are principally of two types: resource-linked and data-linked. Resource-linked interactions arise from competition among components for shared processing resources. Data-linked components interact by virtue of their joint effects on a common memory store.

Resource limitations come into play in the performance of composite tasks that require the concurrent execution of multiple components, as in reading for comprehension (Perfetti & Lesgold, 1977, 1979). When one or a number of those components are not performed automatically, they compete for processing

TABLE 1.1
Processing Characteristics of Skilled and Less Skilled Readers

Processing Characteristics	Poor Readers	Good Readers
Efficiency & accuracy in perceptual encoding of orothographic information within words; distributed attention (Frederiksen, 1982)	Inefficient encoding of orthographic units; performance poor for embedded units	Automatic recognition & encoding of orthographic units larger than a single letter embedded within a stimulus array
Efficiency & accuracy in translating orthographic information into a phonological representation (decoding) (Frederiksen, 1982)	More errors in pronouncing pseudowords and low-frequency words; pronunciation latencies were greatly affected by variations in orthographic complexity	Fewer errors in pronouncing pseudowords and low-frequency words; performance less dependent on orthographic complexity
Efficiency & accuracy in word recognition (Frederiksen, 1981a)	More dependent on decoding processes in the recognition of high-frequency words (smaller sight vocabularies)	Able to reduce reliance on decoding processes for high-frequency words (larger sight vocabulary)
Use of frame-based activations to prime conceptual categories in semantic memory (Frederiksen, 1981a)	Retrieve only most typical word that is predictable in context; contextual priming restricted to high-probability words only	Use context to prime categories of meaning; show equal degrees of priming for high- & low-probability words that are contextually appropriate
Efficiency in locating referents in memory for discourse (Frederiksen, 1981b)	Tracing referents more difficult, particularly when referent is not topicalized	Efficient assignment of referents; not dependent on topical status of antecedents

resources, with the result that performance on the composite task declines. When two processes are in competition for the same resources, therefore, the automatic operation of one will free resources for the other.

Data-linked components enter into functional interaction through their operation in parallel on a shared data base from which they derive input data and to which they deposit results of their operation. Products of one component can thus serve to modify inputs of other components and may therefore influence their efficiency of operation. These functional interactions may be categorized on the basis of the temporal relations between the components involved. They may be strictly sequential (or hierarchical) in the sense that the exhaustive operation of one component produces data structures that are needed by or enable the timely execution of the other component. Alternatively, two data-linked components may run concurrently in cascading fashion (McClelland, 1979), with the second process improving in efficiency and quality as the first runs further to completion. Another possibility is that concurrent processes may be mutually facilitating in that changes in the data structures brought about by the operation of each one facilitate the operation of the other.

One of the interesting tenets of the interactive componential theory is that skilled and less skilled readers differ not only in the efficiency of operation of various components, but also in their manner of interaction. For the domains of word recognition and comprehension, we illustrate component interaction due to data and resource linkages, emphasizing differences in both the manner and nature of such interactions for skilled and less skilled readers.

A. Context-Free Word Recognition

Interaction Due to Data Linkages.   In the word analysis domain, skilled readers are known to have larger sight vocabularies than less skilled readers. This eliminates the need for active decoding when sight words are encountered, because lexical information becomes available before decoding processes have run to completion. It also allows text interpretation to take place at an earlier stage, because word recognition processes operate in parallel with decoding processes, and the outputs of each become available to higher level processes for text interpretation in a cascading fashion.

In addition, when skilled readers do not recognize words on sight, they decode them on the basis of perceptual units larger than the single letter. The automatic recognition of multiletter perceptual units is another example of a process that alters the data base for subsequent components, in this case, decoding processes. Assuming that processes of perceptual encoding and phonological decoding operate in cascade, efficient perceptual encoding alters the quantity and quality of the orthographic information on which decoding is based. Without multiletter unit encodings, decoding must proceed on the basis of single letters. Principles for decoding from single letters are known to be complex (Venezky, 1970). Readers who encode larger multiletter orthographic units can base their decoding on a smaller number of units whose pronunciations are more invariant across orthographic environments. Thus, there is a tradeoff between increased demands on a perceptual component (e.g., a larger unit vocabulary) and reduced demands on a decoding component (e.g., substitution of knowledge of phonological mappings of multiletter units for complex decoding rules).

Interaction Due to Resource Demands.   Use of sight vocabulary and efficient perceptual encoding, as we have seen, enable the skilled reader to identify or decode words with less effort. A consequence of this increase in efficiency of word analysis is a reduction in resource demands and, therefore, in cost to concurrent processes involved in sentence and text understanding. For example, processes involved in selecting referents for pronouns operate concurrently with processes of decoding and word recognition and compete for the same limited processing resources. The effect of high levels of automaticity in processes of word recognition is, in theory, to reduce the resource demands of those processes, allowing attention to be focused on analysis of the semantic content of a text. Perfetti and Lesgold (Lesgold & Perfetti, 1978; Perfetti & Lesgold, 1977, 1979; also, Perfetti & Roth, 1981) suggest that this explains the high correlation between decoding latency and reading comprehension ability.

B. Text Comprehension

In addition to being more efficient than less skilled readers at context-free verbal encoding, skilled readers are better able to use the semantic information they derive from sentences to recognize words and extract contextually appropriate word meanings. The use of contextual information also allows them to reduce their reliance on word analysis processes when making lexical identifications (Frederiksen, 1981a). The heightened availability of appropriate semantic information also facilitates text comprehension in ways that we outline later. These benefits of context-induced facilitation, again, appear to extend principally to the skilled reader (cf. Perfetti & Roth, 1981; Stanovich, 1981). This "top-down" influence of text interpretation processes on word identification processes is an example of process interaction through data linkages. At the same time, use of context in recognizing words and their meanings reduces the demand for decoding processes in word identification and thus decreases the resource demands of word recognition.

The analysis of functional interactions among component processes can be extended to processes involved in analyzing the cohesive features of texts, such as mapping referents for pronouns and understanding high-order relations among propositions. In a later section of this chapter we explore this possibility in some detail. In broad outline, we argue that the semantic analysis of contextual information and its use in activating related concepts in semantic memory (hereafter referred to as frame-based activation) have a significant impact on processes of text comprehension, including the tracing of referential relations and the analysis of high-order semantic relations among text propositions. Briefly, we propose that frame-based activation of concepts facilitates identification of referents for anaphoric words, such as pronouns or lexical substitutes, by increasing the accessibility of antecedents in semantic memory. Residual activation resulting from the processing of antecedents also provides a basis by which anaphoric terms that are lexically related to the antecedents (such as lexical substitutes) can be "sensed" as anaphoric.

The analysis of component interactions can be extended still further. There is reason for believing that the mapping of anaphora to their antecedents leads to the reinstatement into working memory of earlier occurring propositions within which the antecedents are embedded (cf. Kintsch & van Dijk, 1978). Reinstatement of antecedent propositions is a necessary condition for analyzing high-order semantic relations among earlier and current propositions. Processes that contribute to efficient tracing of referential ties (such as processes involving activation of concepts in semantic memory) can thus be expected to contribute, through their effect on processes of reference tracing, to the thoroughness with which high-order semantic relations among text propositions are analyzed.

This outline of interactions among component processes in word recognition and text comprehension can be viewed as a plan for training component skills of comprehension. It suggests skill components that may be critical to the operation of other components and lines of functional interaction that can serve as a framework for instruction aimed at improving reading skills.

III. INSTRUCTIONAL APPROACH

A. Overview

Our general approach to instruction is based upon an analysis of performance on composite reading tasks into skill components and their functional interactions. The components selected for training are those for which subjects who have low levels of general reading ability show demonstrated skill deficiencies. These components are sufficiently comprehensive to have a potentially broad impact in facilitating the performance of other components, by virtue of their functional relations, either through data linkages or the demands they make on processing resources.

Training activities we have developed focus on individual components, so that immediate and direct feedback concerning improvement in performance is possible. Training proceeds until criteria of speed of performance (automaticity), as well as accuracy, are met. In addition, functional relations among components are exploited in the sequence of training activities. For example, training on an enabling or facilitating component precedes training on the facilitated component. In this way, improvements in performance of lower order components can contribute to the acquisition of higher order components either by: (1) improving the quality or the availability of data structures required by the higher order components, or (2) reducing competition for shared processing resources. Integration of skills is promoted by having the later occurring training tasks incorporate the earlier trained components. Successful completion of the training sequence therefore demonstrates mastery not only of the individual component skills, but also of their joint application in the performance of high-order skills such as inferential comprehension.

With this outline of our instructional approach in mind, we address principles for analyzing components of skill, developing component-specific training systems, and sequencing training activities.

B. Analyzing Components of Skill

The identification of skill components on which training can focus derives from a cognitive process model for the domain that takes into account individual differences in skill. The functional elements in a reading model are processes that operate on certain data structures, resulting in their transformations. The resultant data structures then serve as the basis for or input to other processes. For example, perceptual processes yield identified multiletter units that then serve as input to an efficient phonological decoding or word recognition process. Taking a second example, a process for analyzing the propositional content of clauses or sentences, in theory, may provide the input data structures required for processes involved in mapping high-order semantic relations among text propositions. The skill components that constitute the focus of training are, therefore, processes that yield functionally useful data structures and that, consequently, are likely to have a broad impact on the operation of other processes. Finally, of the set of skill components meeting this requirement, those for which there are clearly demonstrated deficits among low-ability readers are chosen as the focus of training.

C. Design of Training Systems

The difficulty a reader has in processing a text is jointly determined by characteristics of the text and the skills of the reader. Because texts make multiple skill demands on a reader, failure in comprehending a text can be due to many factors and typically goes unnoticed until a subsequent test of comprehension is administered. Even then, the source of the difficulty is likely to remain obscure. Attempts to foster improvements in reading skill through practice on the "whole task"—that is, practice in reading texts—are therefore likely to have limited results because efficient development of component skills appears to depend on the contingencies that are established between skill performance and feedback. The key notion here is that, for students to be able to make the necessary on-line adjustments in performance of a target skill, on-line feedback is required. Information concerning the efficiency and accuracy of performance of a particular skill component must therefore be extracted from the subject's responses while he or she is performing the training task.

A number of factors reflecting these ideas have governed the design of training systems.

The Focus of Training is Component Specific. Each training system is designed to focus on a particular skill component. The design of the training task ensures that performance of the component is mandatory. Alternative strategies employing other components are precluded insofar as that is possible.

Measurability of Component Performance.   The training task allows assessment of not only the accuracy of performance, but also its speed or efficiency. The measurement of component-specific performance also allows direct and immediate feedback to be delivered to the student.

Development of Automatic Skill Performance.   Developing automaticity of component processing is a prime objective of training. To this end, feedback must stress the chronometric aspect of processing as well as its reliability.

Compatibility With Whole-Task Performance.   For each training task, it is desirable to maintain compatibility with other tasks that are representative of the domain so as to facilitate integration of components. In general, it is important that the skills and strategies required in performing the training tasks be compatible with skills and strategies known to be applied by domain experts. However, the first two design factors, component specificity and measurability, may in some cases require the construction of training tasks that, strictly speaking, cannot be regarded as meeting the compatibility criterion. Among tasks in the domain of reading that violate the principle of compatibility are those that focus on lower order perceptual or decoding skills where the student may be required to detect letter units within words or pronounce words in isolation aloud. An important question in such cases is how readily the newly acquired, lower order skills are applied in tasks that more fully represent the complexity of the domain. In contrast, training tasks dealing with higher-order comprehension skills, while maintaining a focus on a particular processing component, will also elicit performance of additional components. Successful performance in such tasks will require not only mastery of the skill that is the focus of training, but also integration of the multiple skills involved.

Instruction Is Indirect and Adaptive.   Instruction in a component skill is indirect in that the procedures and rules for performing the required skill are not presented to the student for study. Instead, the training environment enables it to be developed progressively through the deliberate structuring of task materials and conditions. Students begin training with less difficult materials that require only subsets of the final rules and procedures. After mastering them, students move on to more difficult materials and conditions. At each stage, the training exercises are adaptive both in the setting of starting levels of difficulty and the goals to be met. Starting levels are selected to reduce time spent working with materials or conditions that do not reflect the trainee's current level of proficiency. Goals for a training trial are set to represent a challenging but attainable performance objective.

Training Systems Are Gamelike.   To achieve the objectives of training, several thousand practice trials or instances of component performance must be elicited while motivation and effort are maintained at high levels. To this end, the training exercises are designed as games. As such, they involve *competition*, either with a computer player or simply against a clock. They place strong *time pressure* on a student's performance, with the student's current level of performance having an immediate influence on the progress of the game. In this way, feedback is felt in the pace of events within the game. In addition, there are *explicit scoring rules* that incorporate the joint criteria of efficiency and accuracy, and goals are set according to these rules. A *game motif* allows the student to track his or her progress in terms of a fantasy. The training game is *adaptive,* presenting degrees of challenge that are contingent on the student's score. Motivation is further promoted by having the student progress through a sequence of subgoals, representing successively higher levels of expertise.

Hierarchical Goal Structures.   The degree and type of challenge within the training tasks are adjusted at several levels: (1) by the efficiency goals set at each stage of training for materials of a given level of difficulty, (2) by the difficulty of the materials themselves, and (3) by progress through a sequence of training exercises, each of which focuses on a different reading component. This series of challenges reflects a hierarchy of goals. At the topmost level, the goal is the successful completion of the sequence of training games. At an intermediate level, the student has the goal of mastering increasingly difficult sets of materials while engaged in a particular training game. And, at the most local level, the student has the goal of completing the current trial on the training game, which involves competition with the computer in meeting both speed and accuracy criteria. Because the games are designed to have face validity as indicators of skill performance and progressively involve the integration of skill components, the student has a sense of developing a general mastery of the domain as well as mastery of each particular activity.

D. Principles Governing the Sequencing of Training

Principles used in establishing the organization and sequencing of the instructional games are based on a set of *process models* developed for each of the training tasks. These models detail the skill requirements for each game. They enable us to describe each game not only in terms of the skill component that is the focus of training, but also in terms of the full set of components that are applied concurrently in performing the task. Training games may then be related hierarchically in two senses: (1) the component that is the focus of training in the first game is functionally linked to and facilitates the component that is the focus of training in the second, and (2) the component developed in the first game, even if not functionally linked to that developed in the second, may still be among the set of components required for performing that game.

On the basis of these hierarchical relations among training tasks, the critical problem of *integrating* skill components can be addressed. On the surface, a component-based approach to instruction would appear to foster principally the development of individual skills at the expense of their coordination in tasks that reflect the full complexity of the domain. Integration of skill components thus becomes an important requisite for a component-based system that is concerned with developing a skill as complex as reading. By integration, we mean specifically the ability to use information developed or encoded by particular components during the operation of other components and in the performance of composite tasks requiring the concurrent application of multiple components. Our view is that it is possible to foster the integration of skill components through attention to the nested skill requirements of hierarchically related instructional games. Specifically, training tasks can be sequenced to exploit the types of interactions among skill components we have discussed, either through changes to the internal data representations on which skills operate or through the reduction of resource requirements.

Exploiting Data Linkages Among Components.   When components are functionally linked through shared data bases, it is possible to alter the manner in which one component functions by first training a component to which it is linked. This provides a strategy for changing the mode of operation of one component by changing the internal data structures on which it operates. For example, reaction time studies of good and poor readers indicate that the good readers tend to decode words on the basis of large, multiletter units such as "ance." A strategy that exploits the functional linkage between multiletter encodings and word decoding would first involve training subjects to "chunk" orthographic strings into letter groups and then, when that skill has reached a high level of automaticity, beginning training in phonological decoding. This strategy is precisely the one we adopted in evaluating two word-analysis-skills training systems (SPEED and RACER). In theory, performance of the automatic "perceptual" component will persist in the context of the decoding training task, thus transforming the data base on which the decoding component must operate and facilitating its acquisition.

Reducing Competition for Processing Resources.   Training tasks that focus on developing higher order skills in a domain generally require the concurrent application of multiple components. For students to concentrate on the skill that is the focus of training, they should be able to perform the concurrent components with as little effort as possible. For this reason, training that focuses on the concurrent components should precede training of the higher order components. In reading, this strategy would be exemplified by a sequence of training activities in which decoding training preceded training in particular components of comprehension.

Finally, within a comprehensive sequence of training tasks for a given domain, tasks should increasingly come to involve the full complement of skills that characterize expertise in that domain. Mastery of the later, more multicomponent tasks would therefore imply an ability to execute the multiple components required by these tasks in an integrated, mutually facilitating manner.

IV. STUDIES OF COMPUTER TRAINING ENVIRONMENTS

To date, we have developed three microcomputer training environments and have carried out training studies (focused on the performance of individual students) to evaluate their effectiveness (for complete details and results see Frederiksen, Warren, & Rosebery, 1985a/b). In this work, we have viewed component-specific training as a vehicle for studying functional interactions among reading components. As indicated, the research plan was to develop microcomputer-based training environments that focus on individual components of reading and, for each environment, to evaluate transfer of training effects to other processing components that, in theory, are functionally related to the trained component. To evaluate transfer effects, a set of component-specific tasks representing the related components was administered before and after training on a given system.

In this section, we begin by briefly describing the methodology of the training studies and the three instructional systems by way of providing background information. We then discuss the training results by briefly examining the acquisition of skills that were the focus of training. Then, we present an analysis of the patterns of transfer among the trained components, followed by a discussion of instructional issues relating to the design of instruction and integration of skill components. Our overall purpose in this section is to address issues relating to the usefulness of an approach that emphasizes the analysis of functional interactions among components, both for understanding a complex domain such as reading and for developing instructional principles aimed at improving skill in the domain.

A. Methodological Overview

Three training environments have been developed, each of which focuses on a particular component of reading. The first environment, SPEED, focuses on developing efficiency in encoding orthographic information of words in multiletter "chunks" rather than single letter units. The second environment, RACER, focuses on developing students' skill in decoding words that they are unable to recognize on sight. The third environment, SKIJUMP, is designed to develop skill in using the semantic information in sentence contexts to retrieve and integrate word meanings.

Subjects.   A total of 10 subjects participated in the training studies. They were students from a local public high school in Cambridge, Massachusetts. Four of the 10 subjects participated in the evaluations of all three instructional systems. Of the remaining six, 1 participated in the SPEED study alone, 2 in the RACER study, and 3 in the SKIJUMP study. Subjects were chosen for participation on the basis of teacher recommendations and percentile ranks corresponding to raw total scores achieved on the Nelson–Denny Reading Test (Brown, Nelson, & Denny, 1973). Percentile ranks for the 10 subjects ranged from the 4th to the 13th.

Transfer Measures.   A set of component-specific transfer instruments was administered before and after training on each system. These included three tasks directly related to the skills trained: a unit detection task, pseudoword and word pronunciation tasks, and a context priming task. In addition, the study included an inferential comprehension task that focuses on assessing students' ability to select an appropriate conjunction for a three-sentence passage. The context priming task was administered during the SKIJUMP evaluation only. The inferential comprehension task was administered during the RACER and SKIJUMP studies only.

B. Instructional Systems

SPEED.   In the SPEED game students are required to detect whether or not a target multiletter unit (e.g., por, ance) is present in each of a series of words that are presented in rapid succession on the screen of a video monitor. The game involves 60 training units. The screen display for a SPEED trial is shown in Fig. 1.1. The game simulates a car race in which each correct unit detection or rejection leads to an increase in the car's speedometer, representing the rate at which words are presented. Errors, which also include failures to respond, are represented in a set of five error lights. Each time an error occurs, a reduction is made in the rate of word presentation. The subject's goal is to accelerate the speed of word presentation until a goal speed, represented by the maximum value on the speedometer, is reached. Thus, the student must be both fast and accurate. The scoring rules are designed to serve as an incentive to the student to minimize runs of errors but to permit the student, in a limited way, to trade off accuracy for speed in order to maintain a high rate of unit detection. Each time an error occurs, a light is turned on. When all five lights are on, the next error results in a "crash," and the run is terminated. However, each time a correct response is made, an error light is extinguished and a previous error is "forgiven."

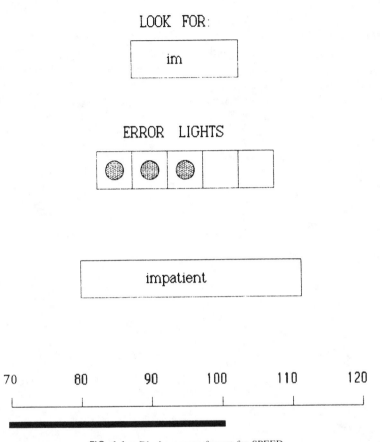

FIG. 1.1.   Display screen format for SPEED.

RACER.   In RACER, students are required to *pronounce* a series of 20 words quickly and accurately as they are briefly displayed in windows on the screen. Time pressure is created by the use of a race motif in which the student races against the computer, which represents the student's current level of performance. Stimulus words are presented in successive windows corresponding to the cells of a matrix, as shown in Fig. 1.2. The progress of the race itself is portrayed above the matrix. The critical time interval is the student's pronunciation latency, or the time that elapses from the presentation of the stimulus word to the onset of vocalization. The student, represented by a sailboat, moves forward a constant one twentieth of the distance to the finish line for each word pronounced. The computer, represented by a horse, moves at a constant rate during the interval between the display of a word and the student's pronunciation of that word. Thus, if the student takes a long time to decode a word, the horse

13

will advance ahead of the sailboat and lead in the race. In order to win the race, therefore, the student must exceed his or her own performance—have an average response latency that is faster than the horse's pace (in msec per word). To have the opportunity to run against faster horses (and consequently increase the level of challenge), the student must win the race.

Accuracy is monitored in a second phase of the game called the Sound Trap. In the Sound Trap, the student *listens* to pairs of words, one member of which is

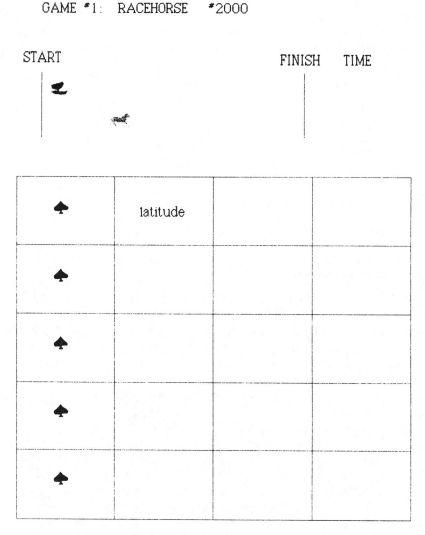

FIG. 1.2. Display screen format for RACER.

drawn from the set of words presented in the Race and the other a similar sounding foil. The student's task is to choose, on the basis of its sound, the word that appeared during the Race. In order to advance to a faster computer-opponent, the student must not only win the Race, he or she must also be accurate on at least seven of the eight Sound Trap word pairs. Through these techniques, there is an incentive to maintain both response accuracy and speed in the game.

Students begin RACER by practicing with words of one and two syllables representing consistent phonic principles. As students progress, they build up to three and four syllable words of mixed frequencies.

SKIJUMP.   In SKIJUMP, the student first reads a sentence from which one of the final words has been omitted. The student is then presented with a series of target words, in order of increasing probability, with the least likely words preceding the most likely. The student must judge whether each is semantically appropriate or inappropriate in the context of the sentence.

The game is built around the theme of a ski jumping competition, where one heat is represented by the responses associated with a single sentence context. The game screen is shown in Fig. 1.3. A team of skiers, one for each of the target words for a sentence, skis down a slope that leads to a jumping platform. When the skier reaches the jumping platform, the display of the target word begins. Each target word is displayed on the screen with pre- and postexposure masks in a sequence of flashes, starting with a flash duration of 18 msec. The duration of each successive flash is increased by an additional 18 msec. The length of each skier's jump (and, by analogy, the student's game score) is determined by the number of target word exposures that the student requires before making a judgment. The student's final score for a heat is based on the average number of feet jumped by the team of skiers. This score determines the level of challenge in the next heat. Early recognition leads to a longer jump, and later recognition to a shorter jump.

The scoring rules encourage accuracy as well as speed. Incorrect rejection of a target word counts as a jump of zero feet. In addition, semantically anomalous foils are randomly mixed with the semantically appropriate targets. Foils are treated differently in the scoring system. Correct rejections of foils are not counted in the student's final score. However, errors on foils are costly, counting as a jump of zero feet. Students are thus highly motivated to respond as quickly as they can, but not before they have enough information for judging a word's appropriateness.

The level of challenge in the game is reflected in the length of the interval between successive flashes of a target word. This provides a way of varying the time a student has for retrieving the word meaning, integrating it with context, and judging its contextual appropriateness. Early in training, this interval is fairly long. As students gain in skill, it is shortened. In addition, students begin SKIJUMP by practicing with sentences that strongly constrain the domain of

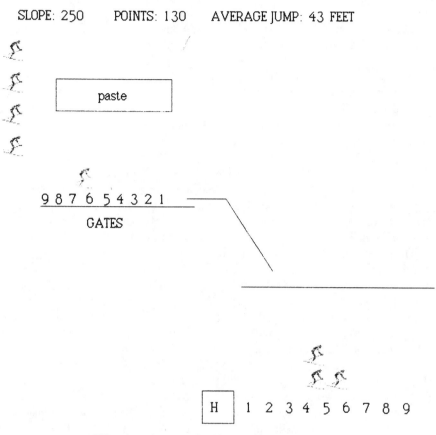

FIG. 1.3.   Display screen format for SKIJUMP.

semantically appropriate target words and progress to sentences that only weakly constrain the target domain. Successful acquisition of the skill is demonstrated when students show comparable performance for low- and high-probability target words.

C. Acquisition of Components

Our purpose in this subsection is to present brief summaries of the evidence on skill acquisition from our training studies. Evidence in support of skill acquisition provides us with a basis for examining transfer of skill to functionally related processing components and is a first step in evaluating the usefulness of an interactive componential approach for improving reading skills.

SPEED.   A representative summary of performance during training is presented in Fig. 1.4 for one student whose Nelson–Denny Reading Test score was

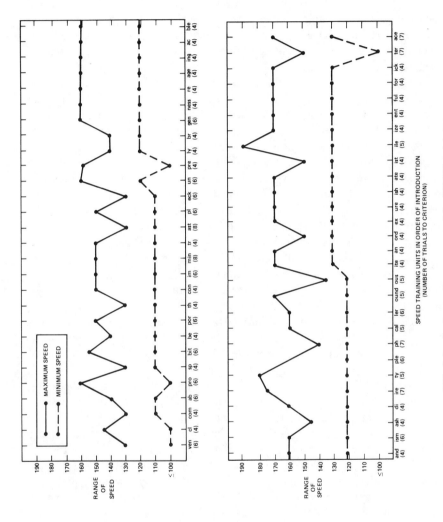

FIG. 1.4. Student performance record for SPEED training.

17

at the 14th percentile. In the figure, the units are listed along the abscissa in the order in which they were introduced, although runs for a unit were generally not presented consecutively. The number of runs on each unit is noted below the unit name and the bottom graph is a continuation of the top one. In addition, minimum and maximum speeds in words per minute for each unit are plotted. The minimum speeds were those at the beginning of training on a unit, whereas the maximum speeds were those attained at the end of training on the unit.

Several features of this training record are characteristic of the group of subjects as a whole. It is clear that over the course of training there were substantial increases in speed for each of the units presented. The training environment is one in which, over a series of four to eight runs, the subject was able to markedly improve her ability to detect a unit when it occurred in unpredictable locations within target words. Her minimum speed ranged from 100 wpm early in training to 130 wpm late in training, whereas her maximum speeds ranged from 130 wpm early in training to 170 wpm later in training. This improvement in efficiency was due in part to a transfer of skill to new units— units that had not yet been presented. The initial speeds for units introduced near the end of training are substantially higher than those for units introduced earlier. Thus, it appears that the skill developed in mastering SPEED is more general than learning to detect particular units and involves general perceptual and attentional skills that can facilitate the rapid encoding of orthographic units, whether or not they have actually been trained.

Each of these observations was further substantiated by a more formal experiment in which subjects' mean detection latencies for units appearing in unpredictable positions within words were measured before and after SPEED training. There were significant effects of training on latencies for detecting units, and there were significant reductions in the effects of a unit's position within a word and in a unit's length or frequency as a result of training. After SPEED training, subjects could recognize low-frequency units or units embedded within words as readily as high-frequency or prefix units. And, the reductions in overall latencies for detecting units were as great for *untrained* control units as they were for units actually trained. We have concluded that training using the SPEED game helps students to develop automatic processes for efficiently encoding multiletter orthographic units, regardless of whether they are common or uncommon in printed English or whether they are embedded within words or occur at word boundaries.

RACER.   Figure 1.5 contains a representative performance record for one RACER subject whose score on the Nelson–Denny Reading Test was at the 4th percentile. The subject's mean RT in seconds is plotted for the first five and final five races, for word sets at different levels of decoding difficulty. (The arrow indicates the direction of change from the starting to the ending level.) The word sets are listed in the order in which they were introduced. The composition of

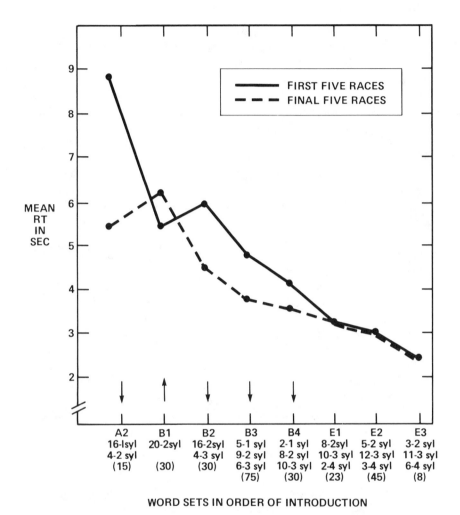

FIG. 1.5. Student performance record for RACER training. Mean RT in seconds is plotted for the first five and final five races for word sets at a given difficulty level.

these word sets is noted along the abscissa. For example, the first set of words contained 16 one-syllable items, and 4 two-syllable items, whereas the last set contained 3 two-syllable, 11 three-syllable, and 6 four-syllable items. The number of races run at each level of difficulty is also noted in parentheses. Before examining the record more closely, a word of explanation is in order about the RT value that is plotted. The mean RT in seconds for the first and final five races within a word set is that for the *sum* of the vocalization onset latencies for the 20 words in each of those races.

The training record illustrates a number of important points. First, it shows that over the course of training the subject made steady gains in decoding efficiency, even as the difficulty of the words he was required to pronounce increased. The student completed training with a mean RT for matrices composed primarily of three- and four-syllable words that was markedly lower than his mean RT at the start of training for matrices composed largely of one- and two-syllable words. These gains were achieved without a sacrifice in accuracy, which remained between 80 and 90% throughout training. Note also the close correspondence between the decoding speed that the subject achieved at the end of a word set at a given level of difficulty and the starting level for the next most difficult word set. This improvement in efficiency of decoding for the more difficult orthographic forms when they are introduced is evidence for a general transfer of skill. It suggests that it is possible, without any explicit instruction in the rules of decoding, for subjects to develop automated procedures for applying decoding rules effectively to words at increasing levels of orthographic complexity.

This observation is further supported by an evaluation of the effectiveness of RACER training on subjects' speed and accuracy in pronouncing test lists of pseudowords and words. For pseudowords, there were significant reductions in vocalization latencies. Following training, subjects were as efficient in decoding the more difficult, two-syllable pseudowords as in decoding those of one syllable. And these increases in efficiency were not achieved at the expense of accuracy; subjects' accuracy in pronouncing pseudowords actually showed improvement. Subjects' performance in the word pronunciation task showed similar effects of training. Pronunciation latencies were significantly reduced and effects of syllable length were also eliminated. Subjects also showed improved accuracy in pronouncing words following training.

SKIJUMP. A representative SKIJUMP training record for a subject who scored at the 30th percentile on the Nelson–Denny test is presented in Fig. 1.6. Plotted are the mean RTs for each training session, as measured from the onset of the first exposure of a target word to the subject's response. Separate plots have been made for : (1) high-probability target words presented as the last or next-to-last item of a given context sentence, (2) low-probability target words presented as the *first* item, and (3) foils, or words that are semantically unrelated to the context. The data for high-probability targets occurring after the subject has been exposed to a whole family of words related to the context provide a "lower bound" on mean RT. Even low-ability readers can be expected to profit from context and show priming effects at the start of training when the words are presented in a context that strongly constrains the target domain. In evaluating the effectiveness of training, the critical targets are low-probability words presented as the first item following the context sentence, because it is these items that distinguish skilled from less skilled readers in context priming effects.

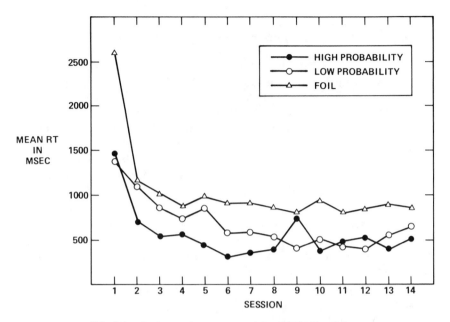

FIG. 1.6.   Student performance record for SKIJUMP training.

Finally, performance on foils provides a control for the effects of practice on factors other than conceptual priming, such as recognizing masked stimulus words and understanding the context sentences. Because each of these skills contributes to performance in recognizing and responding to both foils and target words, the difference in performance provides a measure of the subject's use of contextual information.

Referring to Fig. 1.6, it can be seen that at the beginning of training the subject showed contextual priming for high-probability targets but not for low-probability targets. As practice continued over the first eight sessions (in which context sentences were restricted to those of high constraint), performance for low-probability targets approached that for high-probability targets. This level of performance was maintained when weakly constraining contexts were introduced later in the ninth session. Aside from an initial reduction in mean RT over the first few sessions, there was no improvement in performance on foils over the course of training. It thus appears that training in the SKIJUMP game resulted in a specific improvement in the targeted skill component, namely, the use of contextual information to gain access to meanings of words that are conceptually appropriate in the given context. These performance improvements were independently assessed using a context priming task that is directly analogous to the training task, except that it tests different sentence sets. Results for this task were similar to those obtained with the SKIJUMP training task itself.

D. Functional Interactions
Among Trained Components

Given that the three training environments have been shown effective in developing the target components, we now have the opportunity to study the effects of the improvements in component performance on tasks that require other components for their performance. For these transfer tasks, improvement in the trained component will affect performance only indirectly, through functional interactions among components involved in the training and transfer tasks.

Our general hypothesis is that patterns of transfer among components will follow the lines of functional interaction outlined earlier in our discussion of process interactions in reading. Specifically, in cases where there are hypothesized functional interactions between processes, we expect that development of a component will influence performance of other components that utilize the information coded by the trained component. This positive transfer will be due to changes in the availability of information, resulting in an increase in the thoroughness or efficiency of processing for the facilitated component. Such transfer can take the form of an increase in efficiency of processing or an increase in accuracy of processing. If performance of the transfer task is, at the outset, highly inaccurate and those inaccuracies are due to nonavailability of information, then developing a component that can supply the needed information will result in improved accuracy. If, at the outset, the transfer task is performed accurately but inefficiently, then training an enabling component will lead to increased efficiency.

A second source of skill transfer derives from consideration of the resource demands of a component before and after training. If the effect of skill development is to reduce substantially the resources required for processing, then improvement should also be found in the performance of transfer tasks that require the concurrent application of the trained skill component. Such improvement will occur even when there are no data linkages between the components that are addressed in the training and transfer tasks. Across a series of transfer tasks, the degree of transfer will depend on the difficulty of the task and the degree to which the trained component is concurrently involved in its performance.

In the remainder of this section, we briefly summarize the results of transfer experiments carried out for each of the three instructional systems and evaluate the evidence for functional interactions among components.

E. Transfer Following SPEED Training

On the basis of a cognitive theory of enabling relations among reading components, we have hypothesized that efficient encoding of orthographic information should lead to improvements in accuracy and/or efficiency of students' decoding. This is due to increased efficiency in decoding based on the availability of multiletter orthographic units.

To examine this issue, we carried out two tests. In one test, subjects were asked to pronounce pseudowords (which are pronounceable, English-like items such as "brench"). Their reaction times to the onset of vocalization were measured, and their accuracy of pronunciation was judged by an experimenter. This pronunciation task was administered before and after SPEED training in order to assess the effects of improvements in perceptual and attentional skills on speed and accuracy in decoding unfamiliar items. SPEED training brought significant increases in decoding accuracy. Subjects who were initially very inaccurate in their pronunciations of pseudowords showed the largest increases in accuracy as a result of SPEED training, accompanied by increases in reaction times. For these subjects, training presumably had the effect of increasing the availability of efficiently encoded orthographic information. However, it remained for these subjects to develop more efficient decoding processes. Other subjects, who were initially more accurate in their decoding of pseudowords, showed decreases in reaction times for decoding as a result of SPEED training. These subjects were apparently able to employ the more efficient processes for encoding orthographic information that are developed through SPEED training in their decoding performance. Two subjects were also given a word pronunciation task before and after SPEED training. Both of these subjects showed reductions in vocalization onset latencies and increases in accuracy of word recognition. It thus appears that subjects are capable, even before engaging in extensive training on a higher level skill such as decoding, of applying the perceptual information they have learned to encode in the performance of a higher level reading process.

F. Transfer Following RACER Training

The theory of process interactions among reading components proposes that improvements in decoding efficiency and accuracy should substantially reduce the resource demands of the decoding component. The effect of such a reduction should also be felt in the performance of other reading tasks requiring the concurrent application of other components. This argument, elsewhere referred to as the verbal efficiency model of reading skill (Lesgold & Perfetti, 1978; Perfetti & Lesgold, 1977, 1979), did not receive support in our evaluation of the effects of RACER training on a task involving inferential comprehension.

The purpose of the task was to assess subjects' ability to select from a choice of two conjunctions the one that fit the intended meaning of a three-sentence paragraph. Subjects read three-sentence passages, presented under their control, one sentence at a time. A blank field at the beginning of the third sentence represented the position of an omitted connective expression marking the relation between sentences one and two and sentence three (e.g., "as a result"). After reading the third sentence, the subject is presented with the choice of two conjunctions. Finally, the subject must answer a multiple choice comprehension question. The subject's accuracy in selecting the correct connective and in answering the comprehension question are measured, along with his or her reading speed, which is the average reading time per word for the third sentence of each passage.

In general, RACER training had no effect on accuracy of performance on the inference task or on reading speed. On this basis, we have tentatively concluded that decoding efficiency, although clearly critical to expertise in reading, does not provide a complete explanation for the correlation between decoding efficiency and tests of comprehension, at least for a test that focuses very explicitly on a particular aspect of inferential comprehension.[1] The broad implication of this finding is that a theory of process interactions in reading must also address component interactions in text comprehension processes in order to account as fully as possible for the sources of skill difference in reading. We take up this issue in the final section of this chapter.

G. Transfer Following SKIJUMP Training

The theory of component interaction also leads to predictions concerning the effects of SKIJUMP training on the task of inferential comprehension. In this case, the mechanism of transfer involves lines of functional enablement: Activation of concepts in semantic memory resulting from SKIJUMP training has been hypothesized to be functionally related to comprehension of high-order text relations, indirectly through its effect on the thoroughness and efficiency of reference analysis, and directly through semantic constraints on the meaning of the relation linking text propositions. There was an overall improvement in subjects' accuracy in selecting appropriate connectives in the inference task following SKIJUMP training, from an average of 58 to 79% correct. These improvements in accuracy occurred for subjects who were initially the least accurate in performing the task. Those subjects who were initially most accurate instead showed decreases in time for reading the final sentence of the paragraph and for choosing the most appropriate conjunction representing the high-order relation linking sentences one and two with sentence three. We attribute these improvements in performance on the inference task to functional interactions among reading skills. We believe that the activation of concepts that are related to context contributes to the reinstatement of prior text propositions and, as a result, has an effect on understanding high-order text relations of the kind probed

---

[1]Charles Perfetti (personal communication, March, 1985) has pointed out, quite correctly, that the inference task may be too demanding to expect transfer from word-level improvement. It may require too many components that are not affected by word-level processing.

in the inference task. These ideas are discussed in more detail in the final section of the chapter.

H. Instructional Environments and Their Sequencing

In addition to hypotheses regarding functional interactions among components that derive from the interactive theory of reading, we are also seeking to test several hypotheses concerning the effectiveness of computer training environments that focus on individual components. These hypotheses derive from a number of the basic tenets that underlie a component-centered instructional design:

1. Can component skills be developed more efficiently when a training environment provides explicit feedback concerning component performance?

2. When feedback in a training task is focused explicitly on a particular component, will other concurrently applied component processes nonetheless show improvement due to practice?

3. If they do, is the improvement dependent on how reliably the concurrent components can be performed in the context of the training task?

4. When training tasks are nested to reflect enabling relations among component processes, can later trained components be readily integrated with earlier trained components?

The answers to these questions will enable us to begin to formulate, at least for the reading domain, a componential theory of instruction. Questions one and two lie at the heart of the rationale for developing a component-centered instructional environment. They examine the relative efficiency of instruction that does or does not focus explicitly on particular components, both for developing those skill components themselves and for effecting transfer. Questions three and four are important if we are to deal with the problem of skill integration. Question three, in particular, addresses the possibility that if components can be trained so that they are reliably executed, they will continue to show improvement while the student is engaged in other reading activities. If this were found to be the case, it would not be necessary to train lower level components to the point of maximum efficiency, because that improvement could come in the context of other training tasks that required the component. The last question represents a second side to the transfer issue: Can students learn to use the information made available by a lower level, earlier trained component in developing components that underlie higher level reading operations? If the answer is affirmative, then a hierarchically structured series of training environments focusing on individual skill components represents a promising method for promoting skill integration in a complex skill such as reading.

I. Component-Specific Instruction

One of the general questions we are raising is whether or not a component skill is most effectively developed using a training environment in which feedback is explicitly focused on that component. Alternatively, can other components that are not the explicit focus of training also be developed efficiently if they are involved in the performance of the training task? The results of training with RACER allow us to examine this issue with respect to development of the perceptual encoding skill: How effective was RACER training, which itself involves the perception of orthographic units but does not provide any explicit feedback relating to perceptual efficiency or accuracy, in improving students' perceptual encoding skill?

To answer this question, we evaluated the effects of RACER training on subjects' mean unit detection latencies before and after training. Subjects who had not had prior SPEED training showed some improvements in speed and accuracy of unit detection as a result of RACER training, but these improvements fell far short of those achieved as a result of training within the SPEED environment, which explicitly focused on the perceptual component. Thus, these results suggest that component-based training is more effective in developing individual components of reading than training that may elicit performance of a skill but does not provide explicit feedback concerning that skill. We also examined the degree of improvement in performance on the unit detection task following SKIJUMP training because SKIJUMP requires subjects to recognize words under visually masked conditions. On the unit detection task, subjects who were not trained in SPEED showed a significant improvement in RT as a result of SKIJUMP training, but the reductions were modest in comparison with those shown by subjects after SPEED training. This again supports our conclusion that, although a component can be developed in the context of a training environment focused on other components if it is elicited within that environment, skills that are the explicit focus of training and feedback will show the greatest benefit.

Additional evidence we have obtained suggests that, in training environments in which a skill is not explicitly required or elicited, that skill may yet show improvement if it has been developed to high levels of automaticity. In theory, automatic skills will be reliably executed even in environments that do not explicitly call for them and thus may show benefits from such training. In our analysis of effects of SKIJUMP training on word and pseudoword pronunciation latencies, we found that subjects who had received prior training in word decoding using RACER showed further improvement in decoding efficiency as a result of training using SKIJUMP. Subjects who had no prior training in decoding showed no such improvement. Because the SKIJUMP game is a silent reading comprehension task and emphasizes recognition of words on the basis of visual and contextual cues, word decoding is not an overt requirement of the task. It appears, however, that readers who have developed automatic decoding skills through training with RACER will continue to execute them within the SKI-

JUMP environment and will therefore continue to show improvement in decoding efficiency.

J. Sequencing of Training Environments

The componential approach to reading instruction is based upon two general hypotheses about learning: first, that skill components can be most effectively developed in instructional environments that focus on one component at a time and, second, that students will be able to integrate skills developed in earlier training environments as they acquire additional skill components. To explore the question of skill integration, four subjects were given, in sequence, the SPEED, RACER, and SKIJUMP training environments. This allowed us to study the effect of prior SPEED training on performance during RACER training, and the effects of prior SPEED and RACER training on performance during training using the SKIJUMP environment. Subjects who were given prior SPEED training performed at significantly higher levels at the beginning of RACER training than subjects with no prior training. This suggests that subjects can use the information encoded as they apply earlier trained components in the performance of training tasks that focus on other components. However, there were no effects of prior training using SPEED and RACER on subjects' initial or subsequent performance on SKIJUMP. This suggests that in SKIJUMP the resource demands of decoding words are relatively low.

A second source of evidence on skill integration is the effect of training on a general measure of reading performance, that is, subjects' reading time for a difficult comprehension task. The measure we used is the average number of words per minute for reading the third sentence in the inference task, which involved constructing a linking relation with the initial two sentences of the paragraph. While reading these sentences, subjects had to infer high-order relations among propositions in the text in order to later select an appropriate connective expression for introducing the third sentence. Although there were no significant changes in reading rate for subjects who had had training with SKIJUMP only, the reading rates for subjects given all three increased by 28%. This suggests that when a number of critical reading skills have been trained in a sequence that encourages their integration, readers can apply the skills they have developed in performing difficult inferential comprehension tasks.

V.   PROCESS INTERACTIONS
IN UNDERSTANDING DISCOURSE

A. Overview

In this final section we propose a model of process interaction in text comprehension, focusing on the effects that parallel, frame-based activation processes in semantic memory have for processes involved in interpreting cohesive features of texts. These include mapping of reference relations and tracing high-order semantic relations among propositions. Each of these components is essential for reading a text with understanding, and the evidence suggests that each poses particular difficulties for poorly skilled readers (Frederiksen, 1981b; Warren, 1985). As a first step towards remediation, we propose an interactive componential model, which can also be viewed as a plan or prescription for training components of text understanding. By training components that interact with higher order components and evaluating transfer of performance to those components, it will be possible in the future to analyze the hypothesized interactions among processing components specified by the theory.

B. Critical Components in Understanding Discourse

Within the framework of the interactive componential theory, our interest is in examining how particular processing components may *enable* other functionally linked components that are critically involved in the analysis of cohesive features of texts. Two critical problems for text comprehension are (1) the analysis of referential terms within a text, and (2) the interpretation of conjunctive expressions, which signal the presence and nature of the high-order semantic relations among text propositions. Each of these problems has been emphasized by Halliday and Hasan (1976) as an important feature of cohesive text. Sentences containing referential terms (e.g., pronouns, lexical substitutes) cannot be understood within a discourse context without mapping the referential expressions to their referents. Likewise, high-order semantic relations between propositions (such as those of causality, temporality, and conditionality) depend for their interpretation, at least in part, on an analysis of the meaning of the conjunctive expressions representing those relations. For a theory of text comprehension to have some generality, it must include as one of its goals the identification of skills that enable readers to deal with the multiple and often subtle ways objects are referred to within the language and relations among propositions expressed.

Our approach to this problem emphasizes the interaction of comprehension processes and text characteristics, focusing on the processing demands that particular properties of texts make on the skills of expert and nonexpert readers. For example, the presence of pronouns in a text requires that referents be traced. If the references are the topic of the text, then a reader who is sensitive to—or in the extreme case, dependent on—topical structure will have little difficulty in locating the referent (Frederiksen, 1981b). If, however, the referential expressions are lexical (e.g., synonyms, near synonyms, superordinates, general nouns, collocative expressions), as they often are in natural text, then the anaphoric character of the referring term—that is, the presupposition of something that precedes it in the text—will be less clear. The reader who does not readily recognize such terms as anaphoric will encounter difficulty in resolving the reference problem.

Texts also vary in the ways in which semantic relations of causality and temporality, to name just two, are marked. Readers who do not understand conjunctions or who are not fluent in the variety of resources within the language for expressing high-order semantic relations (e.g., through conjunctions, prepositions, verbs, or adverbs) will have particular difficulty in reading texts that contain relations marked in these ways. For example, it is possible to express causal relations among propositions as readily through verbs as through conjunctions. However, if the reader is not sensitive to the relational character of verbs, for example, then he or she may have difficulty in constructing an appropriate representation for the intended relation and integrating the related propositions into a coherent model of the text's meaning (Warren, 1985).

Our concern in this section is to sketch a theory of process interaction in text understanding focusing on processes that enable the reader to manage particular cohesive forms in the language in building an integrated text model. More particularly, our concern is with processes that enable the reader to gain direct access to concepts and knowledge in memory that are related to the context frames being read and to use the resulting patterns of activation in memory to build data structures for the efficient operation of other functionally linked processing components.

C. Functional Interactions among Components

The model that we propose is sketched in Fig. 1.7, in which hypothesized lines of enablement among the three processing components under consideration are illustrated. In addition, the model includes other aspects of skill in mapping anaphora and tracing high-order relations that contribute to the effectiveness of these processes. In the discussion that follows, we first characterize the nature of expertise in using frame-based activations to gain direct access to specific meaning categories, as this process mediates the operation of the other two in important ways. We then examine the nature of the enablements that hold among the three processing components and discuss the implications for instruction. Finally, we consider other aspects of skill in mapping anaphora and analyzing high-order relations that might be required in effectively interpreting problems of reference and conjunction.

Frame-Based Activation of Concepts. In an earlier study (Frederiksen, 1981a), we investigated the ability of readers to use semantic information derived from a context frame in gaining access to conceptual categories in semantic memory. Results from this study have led to the following characterization of reader skill differences: skilled readers are able to use semantic information derived from a sentence frame to activate *in parallel* a broad band of contextually relevant words and concepts in memory, whereas less skilled readers are able to gain access *only* to the most likely completion, that is, the most common word or meaning. For example, we found that in the presence of a highly constraining

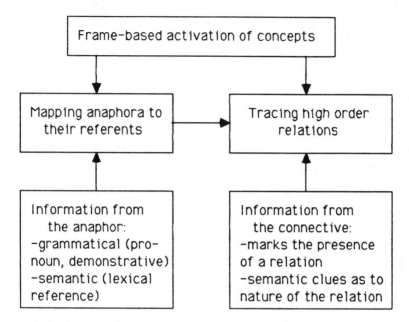

FIG. 1.7.   Proposed model of functional interactions among components of text comprehension.

context, skilled readers were able to use context frames to prime all words within the semantically appropriate set, whatever their frequency. Less skilled readers, however, showed facilitation in highly constraining contexts only for high-frequency words such as those that are typically chosen by subjects to complete the context. The nonadditive effects of contextual constraint and word frequency typical of low-ability readers suggests that they lack a parallel, automatic process for using frame-based activation to gain access to specific categories of meaning in memory.[2]

What are the implications of skill in using frame-based activation for processes involved in mapping referential relations? At the moment an anaphor is encountered, a number of kinds of information are potentially available to the reader. These are illustrated in the following example, taken from Frederiksen (1981b): "The congressman's early struggles were a subject about which he

---

[2]The sources of difficulty that underlie this component may be manifold and may include impoverished knowledge of word meanings, ineffective skills for analyzing the semantic content of texts, and lack of thoroughness in processes of semantic integration (C. A. Perfetti, personal communication, March, 1985; also cf. Curtis, Collins, Gitomer, & Glaser, 1983; Rosebery, 1985). This complexity may have implications for the contents of a training program directed at improving overall reading ability.

reminisced in two candid interviews. *They* were pieces of a past still clearly alive and very much part of the current picture."

To begin with, there is information from the anaphor itself ("they") relating to grammatical features of number and gender in the case of pronominal reference and demonstratives, or semantic features in the case of lexical forms of reference (e.g., if "they" in the text were replaced with "these happenings"). In the example, the pronoun "they" tells us that its referent is a plural noun representing animate or inanimate entities or objects. In addition, there is semantic information from the local context frame in which the anaphor occurred. A superordinate category "pieces of a past" is used, suggesting memories, events, traumas, and the like. And lastly, there are two forms of information from the reader's memory for prior text. One is a text model containing a representation of the text's propositions and relational structure, and the other is patterns of activation within semantic memory resulting from the retrieval of concepts in reading the prior context. In the example, "early struggles" is the subject noun of the paragraph (is *foregrounded*) and is likely to receive activation. The concept is also the *theme* of the processive verb "reminisced" and occupies that role in the case structure. We assume further that there are linkages between these two forms of information. Semantic information concerning concepts is not unpacked within the text model; rather, there are bidirectional pointers or links between concept markers in the text model and their referents in the knowledge base.

At the time an anaphor is encountered, the reader accesses the appropriate category in memory on the basis of the grammatical markers and semantic features contained in the anaphor itself (if the anaphora is a lexical substitute) and the local context frame. In addition, when the anaphor is a lexical substitute such as "these happenings," residual activation in memory resulting from activation of conceptually related words during the processing of earlier occurring sentences serves to "signal" its anaphoric status. Once a lexical category meeting the grammatical and semantic constraints is found in memory, a pathway becomes available back to the referent. This parallels the mechanism proposed by Kintsch and van Dijk (1978) and studied by Lesgold, Roth, and Curtis (1979) for automatic reinstatement of antecedent propositions that are linked to a currently processed proposition through shared arguments (i.e., lexical repetition). The mechanism we are proposing for mapping anaphora covers more subtle forms of pronominal and lexical reference that occur in texts, including synonymy, superordinates, and collocation, lending our proposal some generality.

The consequences of inadequate skill in frame-based activation of concepts for processes of reference tracing are fairly straightforward. In theory, failure to activate frame-related concepts will result in low levels of activation in semantic memory, thereby diminishing the likelihood that referential terms other than pronouns and demonstratives will be "sensed" as anaphoric. Further, differential activation of antecedent concepts in semantic memory will be lacking so that mapping of references must involve a search of the prior text model. A failure to map reference relations involving forms of lexical cohesion will lead as well to loss of activation for related, earlier occurring propositions.

Use of frame-based activations may also facilitate the analysis of high-order relations among propositions, as indicated in the model, although less directly than in the case of reference tracing. The precise nature of the enablement can perhaps be best captured through examination of a second illustrative text, as in the following:

> The worker *failed to solder* a critical connection in assembling *the guidance computer*. (As a result), *the guidance system malfunctioned* at a critical point in the mission.

In this example, the case system for "failed to solder" involves or entails the associated result, "malfunction." In addition, there is a referential linkage between the lexical terms *guidance computer* and *guidance system,* providing a basis for the reinstatement of the earlier occurring propositions and the integration of propositions containing the common referent. The noteworthy point here is that propositions that enter into high-order semantic relations may be successfully integrated on the basis of frame-related activation patterns without relying on the additional support from an explicit marker such as a conjunction.

Propositions entering into high-order relations are typically linked by referential relations whose analysis will lead to reinstatement of the earlier propositions to which the currently encountered propositions are related. This creates the possibility of a direct enabling relation between processes involved in tracing referential ties and those involved in analyzing high order relations among propositions. Again, a sample text best illustrates the point:

> The strategic advantage of undetected missile-launching submarines may not be fully realized unless a perplexing problem in underwater communication is solved. Because conventional radio frequencies can penetrate only a few feet of water, the submarine antennas must remain near the surface when receiving radioed instructions from headquarters. Consequently, some of the submarine's value as a concealed missile-launching platform is lost.

The propositional content of this text is represented structurally in Fig. 1.8, loosely following the analytic scheme of Carl Frederiksen (1975). This schematic representation illustrates how the text content can be coded at the lowest level (the bottom nodes of the structure) as a set of *identifications of concepts and actions,* corresponding roughly to noun groups and verb groups. These are linked together at the next level through a system of *case relations* representing the roles of various identified objects and actions within the case system for an event or process. Finally, case frames and, less frequently, identifications can be interconnected through a *system of high-order relations* expressing semantic relations of causality, temporality, additivity, comparison, and their subtypes (cf. Halliday & Hasan, 1976).

Figure 1.9 illustrates the number and kinds of referential ties present in the text. These vary in kind from the simple repetition of lexical items ("submarine"), to synonymy ("concealed," "undetected") and reference through a superordinate term ("communication," "radio," "antenna"). Of particular note in this figure is the overlap between propositions that participate in a high-order

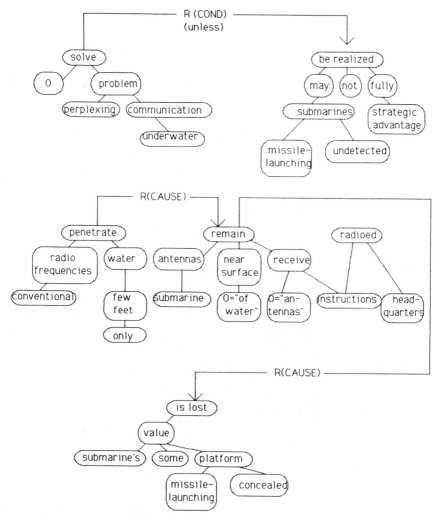

FIG. 1.8.   Schematic representation of the propositional structure of the sample "submarine" text.

relation (R_{COND}, R_{CAU}) and the presence of referential links among those propositions. The generalization that we draw is that propositions that enter into high-order relations are likely to have a number of traceable referential paths between them. This correlation has important implications for understanding the linkage between processes of reference tracing and those involved in analyzing high-order relations among propositions.

As described earlier, anaphora are mapped to their referents partly on the basis of patterns of residual activation in the knowledge base. Through this

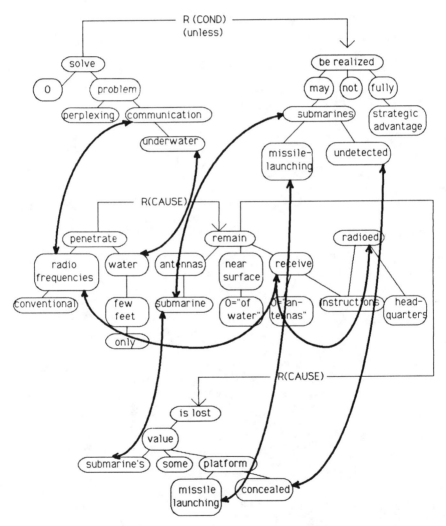

FIG. 1.9.   Schematic representation illustrating the number and kinds of referential ties between text propositions.

mapping process, antecedent propositions that are related to the anaphor are reinstated in working memory. Following Kintsch and van Dijk (1978), we postulate that this reinstatement is a necessary, although by no means sufficient, condition for analyzing high-order relations among antecedent propositions and those currently processed. It is through the mechanism of reinstatement, therefore, that reference tracing enables high-order comprehension processes. Here we have an excellent example of process interaction whereby one component—retrieval of antecedent propositions containing referents—serves to support another level of textual analysis, namely, the analysis of high-order text relations.

D. A Proposal for Training

We have characterized the nature of the enablements that hold for three processing components. In the work on word analysis processes described in the preceding section, training of perceptual encoding skill served as a wedge for improving the quality and the quantity of the data structures on which decoding processes operate. Similarly, in comprehension, one of our aims has been to demonstrate that parallel, frame-based activation of concepts in memory—as an enabling process—can serve to improve the operation of processes involved in the cohesive analysis of texts through its effects on the data structures available to those processes. But, in addition to enablements of this kind, which we have defined as necessary for improving the operation of functionally related processes, there are aspects of skill in mapping anaphora and analyzing high order relations that can only be adequately addressed through training systems explicitly designed to develop those aspects of skill to expert levels.

Reference Tracing.   Focusing for the moment on reference tracing, we can illustrate what we mean by aspects of skill that require focused instruction of the kind described earlier in this chapter. In addition to information that can be derived from local and more distant context frames, the anaphor itself contains information that is useful in resolving problems of reference. In the case of pronouns, this information relates to grammatical features of number and gender, although in the case of lexical reference, the information is also semantic in nature. Both types of information can provide a basis for recognizing the anaphoric status of referring terms as well as for selecting a referent from the set of possible antecedents. If, therefore, readers are not aware of the anaphoric status of, for example, lexical substitutes in a text, then such items will not be seen as involving a problem of reference. In that event, references will remain unmapped and subsequent processing of relations among propositions will be inhibited. To remedy this insensitivity to the anaphoric status of lexical forms of reference, training would have to involve the student in dealing *explicitly* with multiple instances of lexical reference and *require* that such references be traced back to their referents. Difficulties with forms of pronominal references could also be addressed in this way.

Our proposal for training involves constructing a task in which subjects will be required to supply referents for anaphoric words rapidly and accurately when they are probed. Earlier experience with this task (Frederiksen, 1981b) has shown that under certain conditions readers differ in speed and accuracy in supplying referents. These differences are greatest when the reference training problem is made more difficult by, for example, making the referent something other than the topic of a passage. It is important to the goals of training that students *generate* for themselves the referent on the basis of their own processes for search and retrieval. Thus, the task will require the actual performance of the target skill, the analysis of anaphora. Successful skill acquisition will be demonstrated when a student shows efficient and accurate retrieval of referents for anaphora of various types within textual environments representing varying levels of difficulty as suggested by the theory.

If training is to develop subjects' ability to use current activation states within semantic memory in solving problems of referential analysis, it is important that subjects be given prior training in using context frames to activate concepts in semantic memory, as is done in SKIJUMP. Our instructional plan is to train subjects using SKIJUMP prior to beginning training in tracing referential relations so as to exploit the functional interaction between these skill components.

Analyzing High-Order Semantic Relations.   Processing high-order relations among propositions likewise may involve aspects of skill that, in combination with enabling processes, contribute to the thorough interpretation of relational links among propositions. Thus, reinstatement of antecedent propositions is not necessarily sufficient for analyzing high-order relations. Analysis of the relational link for its semantic character may, in many cases, also be necessary. Thus, in contrast to the "guidance computer" example in which the resultant relation is strongly entailed through the event frames for "failed to solder" and "malfunction," there are many cases in which a connective is not simply redundant with context. Take the following example (from Warren, 1985):

(a) Mrs. Verrant had avoided Basil for three months. (. . . . .) she treated him during their interview as if those three months had made him an old friend.
(b) Mrs. Verrant had avoided Basil for three months. *Yet* she treated him during their interview as if those three months had made him an old friend.
(c) Mrs. Verrant had avoided Basil for three months. *As a result,* she treated him during their interview as if those three months had made him an old friend.

Without explicit marking of the connection, as in (a), it is possible to infer a linkage of the type shown in (b) on the basis of the relationship of negated expectation that naturally holds between avoidance and friendship. The conjunction of these two facts leads further to the inference that Mrs. Verrant's motives in treating Basil as an old friend should be viewed with some suspicion. Compare this with the text as written in (c). The force of the connectives in these two cases is markedly different. In (c), the connective "as a result" implies a different set of inferences: more guilt than calculation in this case. Clearly, then, connectives do not serve merely to mark the presence of a high-order semantic relation; nor do they serve simply as an instruction to the reader to search memory for prior text (cf. Halliday & Hasan, 1976). Rather, they carry semantic force of their own, specifying the meanings of relations between propositions and, as in the example, constraining the kinds of inferences that may be drawn.

For these reasons, developing readers' skill in understanding high-order text relations implies the need for an instructional system in which they are required to interpret the full complement of relational types, as well as the variety of linguistic guises in which these relations are expressed. As future research elucidates the particular sources of difficulty students have in analyzing coherent text structures (cf. Warren, 1985), the exact requirements of an instructional system will become apparent. We expect that, following the model of skill interactions we have proposed, there will be demonstrable effects of training in use of context and analysis of referential relations on subsequent development of skill in inferring relations among propositions. Beyond that, we expect that training focused on particular difficulties subjects have in inferring relations among propositions and that follows the prescriptions used in the development of our earlier component-specific training environments will prove an effective way to develop these high-order comprehension skills.

The extension of the interactive componential model to the comprehension domain and to instruction in components of that domain represents an important step in demonstrating the feasability of a component-centered approach to training. The evidence developed thus far suggests that, for readers who have been unable to develop adequate reading skills over the course of 10 to 12 years of schooling, components can be effectively trained using a carefully developed componential approach. The evidence also suggests that newly acquired components can be integrated in performing other, more complex reading tasks that involve the concurrent operation of a number of components. It remains to be shown that discourse processing components can be trained so as to affect global integrated performance in reading.

ACKNOWLEDGMENTS

The research reported in this chapter was principally supported by the Personnel and Training Research Programs, Psychological Sciences Division, Office of Naval Research under Contract No. N00014-80-C-0058, Contract Authority Identification Number, NR 154–448. Additional support was provided by the National Institute of Education under

Contract No. HEW-NIE-C-400-81-0030. No endorsement of the content of this chapter by either ONR or NIE should be inferred.

We wish to thank Charles Perfetti for his thoughtful comments on an earlier draft of this chapter.

REFERENCES

Brown, J. I., Nelson, M. J., & Denny, E. C. (1973). *The Nelson–Denny Reading Test*. Boston: Houghton Mifflin.

Curtis, M. E., Collins, J. M., Gitomer, D. H., & Glaser, R. (1983, April). *Word knowledge influences on comprehension*. Paper presented at the meeting of the American Educational Research Association, Montreal.

Frederiksen, C. H. (1975). Representing logical and semantic structure of knowledge acquired from discourse. *Cognitive Psychology, 7*, 371–458.

Frederiksen, J. R. (1981a). Sources of process interaction in reading. In A. M. Lesgold and C. A. Perfetti (Eds.), *Interactive processes in reading*. Hillsdale, NJ: Lawrence Erlbaum Associates.

Frederiksen, J. R. (1981b). Understanding anaphora: Rules used by readers in assigning pronominal referents. *Discourse Processes, 4*, 323–347.

Frederiksen, J. R. (1982). A componential theory of reading skills and their interactions. In R. J. Sternberg (Ed.), *Advances in the psychology of human intelligence* (Vol. 1). Hillsdale, NJ: Lawrence Erlbaum Associates.

Frederiksen, J. R., Warren, B. M., & Rosebery, A. S. (1985a). A componential approach to training reading skills: Part 1. Perceptual units training. *Cognition and Instruction, 2*, 91–130.

Frederiksen, J. R., Warren, B. M., & Rosebery, A. S. (1985b). A componential approach to training reading skills: Part 2. Decoding and use of context. *Cognition and Instruction, 2*, 271–338.

Halliday, M. A. K., & Hasan, R. (1976). *Cohesion in English*. London: Longman.

Kintsch, W., & van Dijk, T. E. (1978). Towards a model of text comprehension and production. *Psychological Review, 87*, 329–354.

Lesgold, A. M., & Perfetti, C. A. (1978). Interactive processes in reading comprehension. *Discourse Processes, 1*, 323–336.

Lesgold, A. M., Roth, S. F., & Curtis, M. E. (1979). Foregrounding effects in discourse comprehension. *Journal of Verbal Learning and Verbal Behavior, 18*, 291–308.

Mandler, J. M., & Johnson, N. S. (1977). Remembrance of things parsed: Story structure and recall. *Cognitive Psychology, 9*, 111–151.

McClelland, J. L. (1979). On the time relations of mental processes. *Psychological Review, 86*, 287–330.

Perfetti, C. A., & Lesgold, A. M. (1977). Discourse comprehension and sources of individual differences. In M. A. Just & P. A. Carpenter (Eds.), *Cognitive processes in comprehension*. Hillsdale, NJ: Lawrence Erlbaum Associates.

Perfetti, C. A., & Lesgold, A. M. (1979). Coding and comprehension in skilled reading and implications for reading instruction. In L. B. Resnick & P. A. Weaver (Eds.), *Theory and practice of early reading* (Vol. 1). Hillsdale, NJ: Lawrence Erlbaum Associates.

Perfetti, C. A., & Roth, S. F. (1981). Some of the interactive processes in reading and their role in reading skill. In A. M. Lesgold & C. A. Perfetti (Eds.), *Interactive processes in reading*. Hillsdale, NJ: Lawrence Erlbaum Associates.

Rosebery, A. S. (1985). *Semantic and syntactic bases of text comprehension*. Unpublished doctoral dissertation, Harvard University, Graduate School of Education, Cambridge, MA.

Rumelhart, D. E. (1977). Towards an interactive model of reading. In S. Dornic (Ed.), *Attention and performance VI*. New York: Academic Press.

Rumelhart, D. E., & McClelland, J. L. (1982). An interactive activation model of context effects in letter perception: Part 2. The contextual enhancement effect and some tests and extensions of the model. *Psychological Review, 89, 1,* 60–94.

Spilich, G. J., Vesonder, G. T., Chiesi, H. L., & Voss, J. F. (1979). Text processing of domain related information for individuals with high and low domain knowledge. *Journal of Verbal Learning and Verbal Behavior, 18,* 275–290.

Stanovich, K. E. (1981). Attentional and automatic context effects in reading. In A. M. Lesgold & C. A. Perfetti (Eds.), *Interactive processes in reading.* Hillsdale, NJ: Lawrence Erlbaum Associates.

Stein, N. L., & Glenn, G. G. (1979). An analysis of story comprehension in elementary school children. In R. O. Freedle (Ed.), *New directions in discourse processing.* Norwood, NJ: Ablex.

Thorndyke, P. W. (1977). Cognitive structures in comprehension and memory of narrative discourse. *Cognitive Psychology, 9,* 77–110.

Venezky, R. (1970). *The structure of English orthography.* The Hague: Mouton.

Warren, B. M. (1985). *Aspects of skill in understanding high order semantic relations.* Unpublished doctoral dissertation, Harvard University, Graduate School of Education, Cambridge, MA.

2 Learning to Understand Arithmetic

Lauren B. Resnick
Susan F. Omanson
University of Pittsburgh

I. INTRODUCTION

We are concerned in this chapter with the nature of understanding in procedural domains, with the ways in which understanding is related to performance skill, and with how both understanding and procedural competence are learned. Arithmetic offers a particularly convenient arena in which to explore these questions of general interest to cognitive instructional psychology. It is a domain in which procedures are codified and directly taught. At varying levels of transparency, these procedures all reflect general principles of mathematics. Furthermore, our culture values both procedural competence and understanding sufficiently that efforts are made to help children acquire both, and considerable thought has been devoted to how this can best be done.

Prompted sometimes by concern over weaker than desired computational skill among schoolchildren, sometimes by concern for mathmatical understanding as a goal of education in its own right, mathematics educators have long sought ways of demonstrating to children the underlying logic of standard arithmetic algorithms (cf. Resnick & Ford, 1981, chap. 5). A contrast of recent elementary school mathematics textbooks with those of the turn of the century shows that there has been a long-term trend toward increased attention to the relations between performing arithmetic and understanding it. Despite a retreat from the theoretical emphasis of the "new math" texts of a decade or two ago, today's textbooks all include some effort to explain and justify written arithmetic procedures.

In current discussion among mathematics educators two different rationales are offered for teaching the conceptual bases of arithmetic algorithms. The first is the possibility that procedural learning would be more successful if it were well-grounded in mathematical principles. The second is a more recent claim—born of the increasing availability of calculators and the replacement of many calculation functions by computerized systems—that there will be little need for highly practiced computation skill in the future, and that an instructional focus on procedural competence is therefore misplaced. It is argued that what is needed instead is more "number sense," better ability to estimate and judge the reasonableness of calculations, more knowledge of what kinds of calculations to do rather than how to do them—in short, more understanding of mathematics and less procedural skill altogether.

The research we will discuss here is addressed most directly to the first argument. It is concerned with whether and how understanding may enhance procedural skill. However, it is capable of addressing the second concern as well because it forms part of a body of research on mathematics learning that is leading us toward a clearer formulation of what it means to understand a procedure. This, in turn, seems likely to yield fruitful ideas for instruction that treats procedures as expressions of fundamental mathematical principles. Procedures may thus become interesting objects for study, not because computational skill is sought, but because their manipulation or analysis engages deep levels of mathematical understanding.

We are able to move in this direction because cognitive science now offers the constructs that allow development of a theory of procedures apart from their performance. Procedures are now seen as possessing structures, as obeying constraints, as being related to one another in systematic ways. Furthermore, procedures are recognized as mental constructions. Someone invented every procedure, and individuals often invent variants of procedures they may have been taught. It therefore makes sense to ask what knowledge enters into these constructions, what people know that permits and constrains the particular procedural variants they invent. These permissions and constraints can be thought of as individuals' implicit theories about the domain in which the procedures operate. An analysis of preschool children's counting knowledge as an expression of their understanding of certain fundamental principles of number (Greeno, Riley, & Gelman, 1984) is the most thorough and formal statement to date of this way of thinking about procedures.

In the present chapter we use several kinds of empirical data, including evidence from attempts to teach the principles underlying an arithmetic procedure, to examine actual and potential relationships between procedural competence and understanding in a domain central to the primary school curriculum. The domain is place value; its procedural expression is multidigit subtraction with borrowing. By focusing our research on subtraction, we have been able to build upon the extensive theoretical analyses and experimental investigations that are available for this domain. However, our concern is not for subtraction as such, but rather for the more general principles of learning and understanding that the case of subtraction illustrates.

We begin by considering the nature of errors in subtraction and what these errors tell us about the relationships between procedural and conceptual knowledge. Next we outline a set of principles that provide the mathematical justification for a large number of different subtraction algorithms, including the standard school algorithm that we are studying empirically. These principles constitute the *implicit* conceptual knowledge that constitutes understanding of subtraction procedures in our notational system. We claim that they are known by people who understand subtraction, although not necessarily in axiomatic form. Thus, although our analysis is compatible with traditional mathematical analyses, it is not identical to them. Having completed this initial theoretical analysis, we examine several sets of empirical data. First, we look at data that provide some rough evidence of the extent to which elementary school children know the principles. Next, we describe a set of instructional experiments in which we attempt to establish both understanding of the principles and procedural skill. In one treatment, instruction acts directly on children's procedural errors. In the other, instruction is aimed at establishing higher levels of conceptual understanding linked to the procedures. We examine detailed protocols of the learning sessions in an effort to account for the wide individual differences in learning observed and to reconsider how children may develop theories about procedures. In our concluding section we consider the implications of our findings for a general theory of the relationships between conceptual and procedural learning and for approaches to instruction in elementary mathematics.

II. THE NATURE OF ERRORS IN SUBTRACTION

One of the recurrent findings in research on children's arithmetic is that children who are having difficulty with arithmetic often use systematic routines that yield wrong answers. This observation has been made repeatedly by investigators concerned with the learning of arithmetic, and a number of studies have attempted to describe the most common errors. Buswell (1926) used a combination of eye movements and primitive solution-time measures, pencil and paper tests constructed for diagnostic purposes, and what we would now call thinking-aloud protocols to determine the most common sources of errors in calculation with whole numbers. Brownell (1935, 1941, 1964) conducted similar studies in his many years of work on the psychology of mathematics education. These investigators were seeking to put into the hands of teachers tools that would help them discover the basis of individual pupils' arithmetic difficulties, so that appropriate remedial instruction could be offered. The work of Buswell, Brownell, and other early psychologists and mathematics educators clearly was guided by a recognition that children's errors were systematic. Their research, however, and the methodology of the period, did not attempt to describe individual strategies of calculation but concentrated instead on identifying the most common errors among groups of children.

Recent research has focused more on the analysis of individual children's errors. Lankford (1972), for example, using a diagnostic interview procedure with seventh graders, made it clear that students' computational strategies were highly individual, often not following the orthodox models of textbook and classroom. Some of the unorthodox strategies were successful, others were not. Most recently, investigations of "buggy algorithms" (Brown & Burton, 1978) have not only documented the existence of consistent error-producing algorithms, but have resulted in automated diagnostic programs capable of reliably describing the particular errorful algorithms used by a child on the basis of responses to a very small but carefully selected set of problems. Brown and Burton's diagnoses of buggy algorithms provide the starting point for our investigations.

Our initial question concerns the potential sources of buggy algorithms. We know they are inventions by children—because no one teaches incorrect procedures. But what is the process of invention and on what specific knowledge—or lack of it—are bugs based? Why do children tend to independently invent the same buggy algorithms? It is only when we can answer questions such as these that we will be in a position to address in a principled form the question of how to instruct in a way that will limit buggy inventions and perhaps more effectively link procedural and conceptual learning.

Figure 2.1 shows some of the most common subtraction errors that have been identified by Brown and his colleagues in their extensive work on buggy algorithms in subtraction. This is a very small set of the known and demonstrated subtraction bugs, but it is sufficient to allow us to consider the possible sources of buggy procedures in this domain of arithmetic. Two theories of the origin of subtraction bugs have been proposed. One, by Young and O'Shea (1981), suggests that the simpler bugs arise when children either forget or have never learned the standard school-taught subtraction algorithm (see Fig. 2.2 for this algorithm). The second, by Brown and VanLehn (1980, 1982), proposes more complex processes of "repairing" algorithms when forgetting or failure to learn leave children with incomplete or inappropriate procedures. According to repair theory, buggy algorithms can arise when the child, trying to respond, reaches an impasse, a situation for which no action is available. At this point, the child calls on a list of repairs—actions to try when the standard action cannot be used. The repair list includes strategies such as performing the action in a different column, skipping the action, swapping top and bottom numbers in a column, and substituting an operation (such as incrementing for decrementing). The outcomes generated through this repair process are then checked by a set of "critics" that inspect the resulting solution for conformity to some basic criteria, such as no empty columns, only one digit per column in the answer, only one decrement per column, and the like.

Together, the repair and critic lists constitute the key elements in a generate and test problem-solving routine. This is the same kind of intelligent problem solving that characterizes many successful performances in other domains (cf.

1. **Smaller-From-Larger.** The student subtracts the smaller digit in a column from the larger digit regardless of which one is on top.

$$\begin{array}{r} 326 \\ -117 \\ \hline 211 \end{array} \qquad \begin{array}{r} 542 \\ -389 \\ \hline 247 \end{array}$$

2. **Borrow-From-Zero.** When borrowing from a column whose top digit is 0, the student writes 9 but does not continue borrowing from the column to the left of the 0.

$$\begin{array}{r} 6\,\cancel{0}\,{}_12 \\ -437 \\ \hline 265 \end{array} \qquad \begin{array}{r} 8\,\cancel{0}\,{}_12 \\ -396 \\ \hline 506 \end{array}$$

3. **Borrow-Across-Zero.** When the student needs to borrow from a column whose top digit is 0, he skips that column and borrows from the next one. (Note: This bug must be combined with either bug 5 or bug 6.)

$$\begin{array}{r} \cancel{8}\,0\,{}_12 \\ -327 \\ \hline 225 \end{array} \qquad \begin{array}{r} \cancel{8}\,0\,{}_14 \\ -456 \\ \hline 308 \end{array}$$

4. **Stops-Borrow-At-Zero.** The student fails to decrement 0, although he adds 10 correctly to the top digit of the active column. (Note: This bug must be combined with either bug 5 or bug 6.)

$$\begin{array}{r} 7\,0\,{}_13 \\ -678 \\ \hline 175 \end{array} \qquad \begin{array}{r} 6\,0\,{}_14 \\ -387 \\ \hline 307 \end{array}$$

5. **0 – N = N.** Whenever there is 0 on top, the digit on the bottom is written as the answer.

$$\begin{array}{r} 709 \\ -352 \\ \hline 457 \end{array} \qquad \begin{array}{r} 6008 \\ -\ 327 \\ \hline 6321 \end{array}$$

6. **0 – N = 0.** Whenever there is 0 on top, 0 is written as the answer.

$$\begin{array}{r} 804 \\ -462 \\ \hline 402 \end{array} \qquad \begin{array}{r} 3050 \\ -\ 621 \\ \hline 3030 \end{array}$$

7. **N – 0 = 0.** Whenever there is 0 on the bottom, 0 is written as the answer.

$$\begin{array}{r} 976 \\ -302 \\ \hline 604 \end{array} \qquad \begin{array}{r} 8\,\cancel{5}\,{}_16 \\ -409 \\ \hline 407 \end{array}$$

8. **Don't-Decrement-Zero.** When borrowing from a column in which the top digit is 0, the student rewrites the 0 as 10, but does not change the 10 to 9 when incrementing the active column.

$$\begin{array}{r} \cancel{7}\,0\,{}_12 \\ -368 \\ \hline 344 \end{array} \qquad \begin{array}{r} {}^12\,0\,{}_15 \\ -\ \ \ 9 \\ \hline 1106 \end{array}$$

9. **Zero-Instead-Of-Borrow.** The student writes 0 as the answer in any column in which the bottom digit is larger than the top.

$$\begin{array}{r} 326 \\ -117 \\ \hline 210 \end{array} \qquad \begin{array}{r} 542 \\ -389 \\ \hline 200 \end{array}$$

10. **Borrow-From-Bottom-Instead-Of-Zero.** If the top digit in the column being borrowed from is 0, the student borrows from the bottom digit instead. (Note: This bug must be combined with either bug 5 or bug 6.)

$$\begin{array}{r} 7\,0\,{}_12 \\ -3\,\cancel{8}\,8 \\ \hline 454 \end{array} \qquad \begin{array}{r} 5\,0\,{}_18 \\ -4\,\cancel{5}\,9 \\ \hline 109 \end{array}$$

FIG. 2.1. Descriptions and examples of Brown and Burton's (1978) common subtraction bugs. (Adapted from Resnick, 1982. ©1982 by Lawrence Erlbaum Associates. Reprinted by permission.)

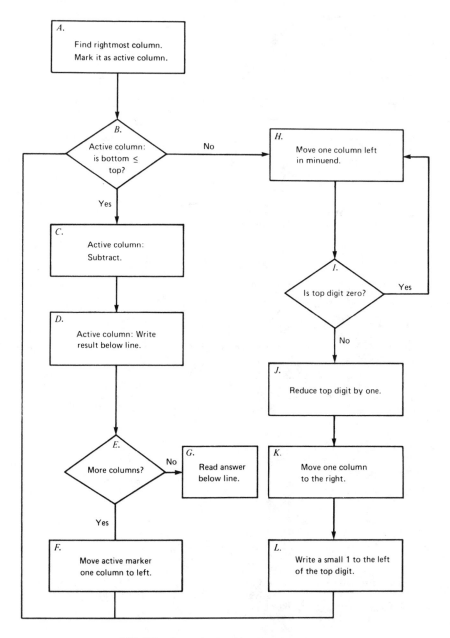

FIG. 2.2. Syntactic algorithm for subtraction.

Simon, 1976). With buggy algorithms, the trouble seems to lie not in the reasoning process but in the inadequate data base applied. Inspection of the repair and critic lists makes it clear that the generation and the test rules in this particular system all operate only on the numerical symbols themselves, without reference to the quantities that they represent. Put another way, they all concern the surface structure of the procedure and do not necessarily reflect the mathematical principles involved in subtraction, or even the conventions of the place value system of numeration.

This distinction between symbols and the principles becomes clearer when we consider some of the individual bugs. Inspection of the bugs in Fig. 2.1 shows that they tend to "look right" and to obey a large number of the important rules for manipulating symbols in written calculation: There is only a single digit per column, all the columns are filled, there are increment marks in some columns with (usually) decrements to their left, and so forth. In the sense of being an orderly and reasonable response to a problem situation, the buggy algorithms look quite sensible. On the other hand, each of the bugs violates fundamental mathematical principles.

These violations are best understood by considering the bugs in Fig. 2.1 individually.

1. Smaller-From-Larger. Repair theory suggests that this very common bug results from switching arguments to respond to a situation in which the system cannot make its normal move of subtracting the bottom from the top number in a column. In other words, the system makes the test at step *B* in Fig. 2.2 but doesn't know how to borrow and decides that the subtraction should be done in the opposite direction. By inverting the numbers, the bug violates the principle of noncommutativity of subtraction. Even more fundamentally, by treating the columns as if they were a string of unrelated single-digit subtraction problems, it violates the understanding that the bottom quantity *as a whole* is to be subtracted from the top quantity *as a whole*.

2. Borrow-From-Zero. Repair theory suggests that this bug derives from forgetting the part of the written procedure that is equivalent to the loop initiated by a "yes" response at step *I* in Fig. 2.2 (moving the borrow marker left) and proceeding directly to step *J*, which leads to the problem of trying to reduce zero by one. The child solves this problem by changing zero to nine, which is a familiar result of borrowing when zeros are present. At a strictly symbolic level, this seems a reasonable response to encountering a zero in the course of borrowing. The bug respects the syntactic requirement that in a borrow there must be a crossed-out and rewritten numeral next to the active column. It also respects the syntax of the special case of zero, where the rewritten number is always 9. However, the bug violates the fundamental principle that the total quantity in the minuend must be conserved during a borrow. Interpreted semantically—that is, in terms of column values rather than simply manipulations on symbols—a total of 100 has been added to the minuend, 10 to the units column, and 90 to the tens column, with no compensating decrement.

3. Borrow-Across-Zero.   In repair theory, this bug arises from the child's search for a column in which to do the decrementing operation with the condition that the column not have a zero in the top number. This would happen when the child doesn't know how to handle zeros and thinks they have no value and thus can be skipped—an interpretation that fails to respect place value conventions. This solution respects the syntactic rules for symbol manipulation, which require that a small 1 be written in the active column and that some other (nonzero) column be decremented. However, like the previous bug, it violates the principle of conservation of the minuend quantity. In this case 100 is removed from the hundreds column, but only 10 is returned to the units column.

4. Stop-Borrow-At-Zero.   Repair theory interprets this bug as omitting steps *H* through *K* of Fig. 2.2 and proceeding directly to step *L*. This bug violates both symbol manipulation rules and the conservation principle. It produces the increment part of the borrow operation—the 1 in the active column—but does not show a crossed-out number or the change of a 0 to a 9. The result is that 10 is added to the tens column with no compensating change in another column.

5. Don't-Decrement-Zero.   The change of 0 to 10 in this bug is the proper symbolic move after borrowing from the hundreds column. But the failure to continue and change the 10 to 9 results in a violation of the conservation principle. A total of 110 is added to the tens and units columns, but only 100 is borrowed from the hundreds column.

6. Zero-Instead-Of-Borrow.   Like Smaller-From-Larger, this bug simply avoids the borrowing operation altogether, although observing all of the important symbolic rules for operating within columns, writing only one small digit per column, and the like. This bug, however, does not violate quantity principles or the structure of decimal notation as blatantly as the Smaller-From-Larger bug. Furthermore, the zero answer may come from an interpretation of decrementing (subtracting) that is not unreasonable in the absence of a concept of negative numbers. In this interpretation, when a larger number must be taken from a smaller, the decrementing is begun and continued until there are no more left—yielding zero as the answer.

This brief consideration of the most frequently observed buggy algorithms for subtraction reveals an interesting set of regularities. First, it appears that the bugs are sensible constructions to deal with special situations for which a known procedure is inadequate—as long as we define what is sensible within the limits of a set of rules for operating on symbols, those symbols being the written numbers. In most cases, the invention represents a dropping of a constraint imposed by the quantitative meaning of the symbols but maintenance of constraints that derive from the rules of symbol manipulation. The results, as we have seen, usually produce a set of notations that look sufficiently familiar and correct that it is easy to imagine that a child who examined his or her own written work would not quickly detect the error. Indeed, teachers looking at children's work often fail to perceive the regularity in the performance or the specific buggy algorithms that children are using. This is why the research on buggy algorithms to date has been of so much immediate interest to educators.

On the other hand, if we look beyond the symbol manipulation rules of written arithmetic to what the symbols represent, the buggy algorithms look much less sensible. All the bugs violate basic principles of quantity and conventions of place value notation. If children had these principles in mind as they inspected their work, or as they attempted to deal with impasses during calculation, we would not expect these types of inventions to occur. It seems reasonable to suggest, then, that a major reason that children invent buggy algorithms so freely is that they either do not know or fail to apply to calculation problems the basic principles relevant to the domain. If so, instruction focused on the principles and on their application to calculation ought to eliminate or at least substantially decrease buggy performances. Those are the hypotheses we explore in the remainder of this chaper. We begin by first describing in detail the set of principles relevant to the domain of subtraction. These are the principles we shall be trying to establish in our children.

III. PRINCIPLES UNDERLYING WRITTEN SUBTRACTION

In this section we outline a set of principles that, taken together, provide the mathematical justification for the subtraction algorithm taught in American schools.[1]

A. Additive Composition of Quantities

The first and most basic principle in our set is the notion of additive composition. This is the principle that all quantities are compositions of other quantities. Thus, for example, 7 is not only a cardinal that describes a set of a given size; it is also a composition of 3 and 4, of 1 and 6, and so forth (even of -3 and $+10$, although this adds complications that are unnecessary if our goal is simply to understand

---

[1]We indicate what would be needed to expand the principles to justify some alternative procedures that are taught in some other countries or are invented by some children, but we do not develop these in detail.

school-taught algorithms). Mathematically, there is no limit to the decompositions or recompositions of quantity. However, the decimal place value system,
which we discuss next, imposes a restriction in order to build a convention for
representing large quantities. It requires that written numbers be composed of
only certain kinds of parts: units, multiples of 10, multiples of 100, and so forth.

B. Conventions of Decimal Place Value Notation

All operations in written arithmetic, if they are to have meaning beyond rules for
manipulating the symbols themselves, must be interpreted in terms of the values
conferred by the conventions of decimal notation. In our decimal system of
notation, numbers greater than 9 are symbolized as compositions of quantities.
The decimal place value conventions are thus *permitted* by the additive composition principle. In the decimal system, each position in a multidigit number
represents a successively higher power of ten. Digits in the rightmost column
have a units value—that is, the digit is multiplied by 1 to find its value. Digits in
the next column to the left have a tens value, digits in the next column after that
have a hundreds value, and so on indefinitely. In this notational system, zero
plays the special role of "place holder." Although the zero itself has a null value,
it cannot be ignored, for its presence in effect determines the value of other
digits. For example, in 604 the 6 is worth 600, but in 64 it is worth only 60. The
zero in effect "pushes the 6 into a higher value column." (These words are
sometimes used by children describing how place value notation works.)

It is the place value conventions that constrain the decompositions used in
representing quantity. The conventions limit the number of units or groups of ten
(hundred, etc.) in each column to 9 or fewer. To return to our example, 604 is a
composition of 6 hundreds, 0 tens, and 4 units. It is the decimal place value
system that requires that 604 be decomposed in this particular way (which will
sometimes be referred to as "canonical form").[2] In certain contexts, however,
the rules of decimal place value notation are augmented to allow more flexibility
in representing quantities. For example, in multidigit subtraction, borrowing
notation is permitted in order to show that there are temporarily more than nine in
a column, and that the number has been *recomposed*. For example, the notation,
$\overset{5}{\cancel{6}}\,\overset{9}{\cancel{0}}14$ means that the quantity, 604, has been recomposed from (600 + 0 + 4) to
(500 + 90 + 14). (Numbers which have been recomposed such that they have
more than 9 in a column will sometimes be referred to as being in noncanonical
form.) The principle constraining this recomposition will be discussed later in
more detail.

---

[2]A base-five system would allow decomposition into groups of five, so that 604 could be written
as 4404 in base 5. Or, in a system without place value, but with units, tens, and hundreds symbols,
such as the Egyptian numeration system, 604 could be written with 14 units, 9 tens, and 5 hundreds,
or in any number of other combinations of units, tens, and hundreds.

C. Calculation Through Partitioning

The fact that quantities are composed of other quantities permits calculation to proceed through partitioning, that is, by recomposing the problem into a set of convenient subproblems and cumulating partial results. For example, the partition principle allows one to convert the problem $3 + 5$ to a perhaps more easily soluble problem, $(3 + 3) + 2$. In the case of multidigit subtraction, a difference can be found by making any partitions of the subtrahend and minuend that are convenient, subtracting all subtrahend parts from a minuend part, and then adding all of the partial results.

Algebraically, this permission to subtract by partitioning can be expressed as:

If $X = x_1 + x_2 + x_3 + \ldots + x_n$ and $Y = y_1 + y_2 + y_3 \ldots y_n$, then
$(X - Y) = (x_1 - y_1) + (x_2 - y_2) + (x_3 - y_3) + \ldots + (x_n - y_n)$.

This is the principle that permits written subtraction to be done column-by-column. In this case, the partitions are determined by the conventions of place value notation. Expressed in expanded notation, common in schools, a partition-based solution might be the following:

$658 - 232 = (600 + 50 + 8) - (200 + 30 + 2) = (600 - 200) + (50 - 30) + (8 - 2)$.

In subtraction through partitioning, an important constraint that must be observed is that all parts of the subtrahend be subtracted from some part of the minuend. Further, the conventions of place value imply that each part will be subtracted from a part of equivalent value (i.e., units parts from units, tens from tens, etc.).

D. Recomposition and Conservation
of the Minuend Quantity

In the course of subtraction by partitioning, it will often be useful to *recompose* the minuend quantity. This is needed when the standard decimal partition leads to one or more partial subtractions in which a larger number would have to be subtracted from a smaller number.[3] For example,

$832 - 267 = (800 - 200) + (30 - 60) + (2 - 7)$,

would yield some negative within-column results.

To avoid negative partial results (which primary school children are taught are impossible), the minuend can be recomposed. For example:

---

[3]If negative numbers are admitted to the system and negative partials accumulated, recomposition of the minuend quantity is not needed. A number of algorithms calling on negative numbers exist.

$$832 - 267 = (700 + 130 + 2) - (200 + 60 + 7) =$$
$$(700 + 120 + 12) - (200 + 60 + 7) =$$
$$(700 - 200) + (120 - 60) + (12 - 7).$$

This recomposing is permitted by the additive composition principle, subject to the important constraint that the total quantity in the minuend be conserved.[4] There are two basic ways that the conservation constraint is met in doing written subtraction. One is by making all recompositions on the basis of exchanges of quantity between adjacent columns. The decimal notation structure automatically conserves quantity in such exchanges. When there is a zero in the top number, this requires a sequence of exchanges. For example,

$$
\begin{array}{ccc}
5\ 0\ 2 & \overset{4}{\cancel{5}}\,{}^{1}0\ 2 & \overset{4}{\cancel{5}}\,{}^{9}\cancel{10}\ 2 \\
\quad\;\rightarrow & \qquad\rightarrow & \\
-\ 1\ 7\ 9 & -\ 1\ 7\ 9 & -\ 1\ 7\ 9
\end{array}
$$

Decrementing the hundreds digit by 1 produces a reduction of 100; the 1 placed before the tens column digit changes the quantity 0 into 10 tens, equivalent to 100. Next, the decrement in the tens column reduces that column by 10; and the increment in the units column adds the 10 to that column. The second way to think about conserving the minuend quantity is to think about directly distributing a large borrowed quantity. For example,

$$
\begin{array}{cc}
5\ 0\ 2 & \overset{4}{\cancel{5}}\ \overset{9}{\cancel{0}}\,{}^{1}2 \\
\quad\;\rightarrow & \\
-\ 1\ 7\ 9 & -\ 1\ 7\ 9
\end{array}
$$

In this example, 100 is borrowed from 500, 90 is directly distributed to the tens column and 10 to the units column.

IV. CHILDREN'S KNOWLEDGE OF THE PRINCIPLES OF SUBTRACTION

We turn now to the question of what children in early elementary school know about the principles just outlined. Our analysis has suggested that children who invent buggy algorithms do so without proper attention to the principles. Furthermore, we argued that buggy inventions occur because children attend only to the

---

[4]Actually, conservation of the minuend quantity is only one way of satisfying a higher level constraint, namely that the difference between the minuend and subtrahend not be altered. A widely used algorithm (the "equal addends method") meets this constraint by adding equivalent amounts to both quantities. For example,

$$
\begin{array}{ccc}
8\ 3\ 2 & 8\ 3\ {}^{1}2 & 8\,{}^{1}3\,{}^{1}2 \\
\quad\;\rightarrow & \qquad\rightarrow & \\
-\ 2\ 6\ 6 & -\ 2\ \overset{7}{\cancel{6}}\ 6 & -\ \overset{3}{\cancel{2}}\ \overset{7}{\cancel{6}}\ 6
\end{array}
$$

written symbols and operations on them, not to the quantities to which the symbols refer. We do not know, however, whether the failure to apply mathematical principles derives from a lack of knowledge of the principles or a failure to access and apply knowledge that is present. Perhaps children know a great deal about the principles of decimally organized arithmetic in the context of nonwritten systems, such as money or other decimally coded tokens, but do not understand how to apply this knowledge to the symbols of written arithmetic. In this section, we report research aimed at establishing the nature and extent of primary grade children's knowledge of the principles of subtraction in both written and nonwritten systems. We first describe two interview studies that examined children's knowledge of the principles in the context of written arithmetic and of arithmetic using decimally coded blocks. Then we describe a reaction time study that examined children's use of decimal knowledge in the context of mental arithmetic.

A. The Principles Applied to Concrete Materials and to Written Arithmetic

The interview studies focused on differences between children's knowledge about written arithmetic operations and their knowledge and understanding of concrete arithmetic. The studies were exploratory in nature. We used semistructured interviews to explore children's knowledge and sometimes pursued avenues of questioning that we had not planned in advance but that were suggested by the child's responses. In addition, at the time that we conducted these interviews, we were just beginning to formulate the analysis of the principles of subtraction. In fact, the results of the interviews along with our subsequent training studies, played a role in this formulation. Our interviews were, therefore, not always structured in ways that optimally probed for the principles we have outlined here. Nevertheless, they yielded rich information about the range and character of children's knowledge and provided some evidence of discrepancies between children's ability to interpret decimally coded concrete tokens in principled ways and their inability to interpret written arithmetic notation in the same ways.

The Pilot Interview Study

A pilot interview study was conducted in a university laboratory school. The four children in the study, selected as average or typical math learners by their teacher, were all in a nongraded, individualized mathematics curriculum. Three were second graders and one was a third grader. They were studied between November and May of the school year in which they first learned addition and subtraction with regrouping. In November the children had recently passed the criterion test for a unit in which they were required to read and write numerals up to 100 and to interpret these as compositions of tens and units. We reinterviewed the children twice: in February, after each had encountered instruction in addition and subtraction with regrouping but had not yet passed the criterion test for those skills; and again in May, when all had passed the curriculum test for addition and subtraction with regrouping.

All interview sessions were individually administered and semistructured, with a planned sequence of problems presented in a standard format. Probes by

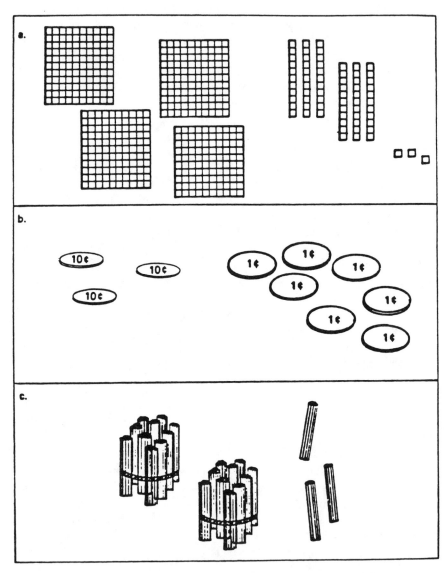

FIG. 2.3. Examples of displays used in research on decimal knowledge.

the experimenter and some attempts to explain or even demonstrate a procedure were permitted. Learning obviously took place in the course of the interviews—sometimes in response to the experimenter's informal teaching, sometimes as a result of spontaneous inventions by the children. We have used the speed and character of these learning incidents, along with stable responses to interview questions, to infer the children's knowledge base.

The content varied over the three interview periods. In November, we focused on the children's understanding of decimal numeration in concrete forms. Most of the tasks required the children to represent written numerals (10 through 99) in concrete forms and to add and subtract in the concrete representations. Dienes blocks, color-coded chips, bundles of sticks, or pennies and dimes were used for the representations. Figure 2.3 shows examples of these concrete materials. In February, most of the tasks were addition and subtraction problems, presented in both written and concrete form. We paid particular attention to the extent to which the child made correspondences ("mappings") between written and concrete representations of these processes. The May interviews replicated those of February and also included a special session in which the children were asked to teach a hand puppet to add and subtract. This allowed the children to give explanations and justifications for their addition and subtraction procedures in a less self-conscious way than when they explained to an adult why certain routines were used. The kinds of tasks set and questions asked are described in the following paragraphs, which report patterns of knowledge for each of the principles in the context of concrete materials and of written numbers.

Conventions of Place Value: Concrete Materials.   Beginning in November, three of the four children showed in various ways that they had attained strong knowledge of the decimal system for units and tens in concrete representations.

1. When asked to represent a two-digit number with concrete materials, they immediately used the designated color chip, bundle, or block shape to represent tens.
2. When interpreting concrete displays or counting out objects to construct those displays, they counted by tens and then by units.
3. When comparing the quantities in two concrete displays, they sometimes counted only the tens—thus assuming a canonical display (no more than nine tokens of each denomination) in which the representation of the higher number will necessarily have more tens.
4. When counting large numbers of units, they grouped them into piles of ten in order to count by tens.
5. They recognized the conventionality of the codes. For example, one of the children said that the bundles of sticks might have nine or eleven sticks each, but, "Let's say they all have ten."

By contrast, the fourth child acquired this knowledge only over the course of the year in which we studied her. In November, she often counted all tokens as units, if the experimenter did not remind her of the convention. With the Dienes blocks she used a compromise solution, in which each of the individual squares on the ten bar was counted. She thus respected the conventional coding, but did not really benefit from its "ten-ness."

Recomposition and Conservation: Concrete Materials.   Aspects of the children's performance on problems in which they added and subtracted using decimally coded tokens allow us to infer their knowledge of recomposition and related principles. For example, when doing addition, children would accumulate more than the canonical 9 units tokens. In November, none of the children ever initiated a trade of pennies for dimes in this situation. However, when the experimenter said, "The store won't accept so many pennies," each child traded 10 pennies for a dime without further prompts. Thus, the children initially saw no need to recompose the quantity, but when the need was presented, they did show that they knew the recomposition-by-exchange procedure. And because their trades were "fair" (i.e., 10 units for 1 ten), it is possible that they knew the implicit constraint of conserving the whole recomposed number.

There was some evidence that exploration of noncanonical representations of quantity is characteristic of children with good understanding of the meaning of the place value system. For example, the child whose mental arithmetic performance and general facility with the various concrete representation tasks suggested a very early and strong command of the base system seemed to have the *least* preference for canonical displays. She instead seemed to be experimenting with the various ways in which a given number could be represented. She often recomposed block displays, from canonical to noncanonical form and vice versa, making far more exchanges than any of the other children. By contrast, the child who was still counting by units in May and not using the decimal features of the system adopted the experimenter's rule of "no more than nine per column" without reference to its rationale. It became an arbitrary constraint to be followed at all costs. This created difficulty for her on subtraction problems, where (in an analog of borrowing) it is sometimes necessary to have more than 9 tokens of a given denomination.

Subtraction provides more direct evidence of children's understanding of recomposition than does addition, because exchanges to noncanonical form are required. The problem initially posed to the children in November was to take 61 cents (which all of the children did by taking six dimes and one penny) and then give the experimenter 37 cents. There are two critical aspects of this performance. The first is whether the child initiates a trade down or needs to be prompted. The second is whether the trade is fair—i.e., whether the child always makes a one-for-ten trade. In November, only one child both initiated the trade and made a one-for-ten trade with no prompting or explanation. All others required at least some prompting to trade and made some unfair trades. The weakest of the four children needed to be explicitly told to trade on almost every trial. When the children made unfair trades, they almost always followed a pattern of trading the dime for exactly as many pennies as were needed to give the experimenter the number she requested. For example, in the 61–37 problem, a dime would be traded for six pennies that together with the penny already in hand, makes it possible to give seven pennies to the experimenter. The children improved between November and May, so that by May all but one were initiating trades and all were making only fair trades. We see, then, that the idea of recomposition was developing slowly over the year in which addition and subtraction with regrouping were taught.

Conventions of Place Value: Written Numbers.   All the children, beginning in November, could interpret written numbers as "*x* tens and *y* units." Performance on other tasks that tapped knowledge of the writing code, however, suggests that this performance—which is heavily drilled in most schools—may not reflect a very rich knowledge of the referents of written numerals. We observed the following:

1. Although three of the children correctly represented two-digit numerals with concrete tokens and could also write the numerals when shown a display in one of these concrete representations, they did not seem to link mentally the different tokens to the digits. For example, instead of counting the tens tokens and writing a numeral to represent them, then doing the same for the ones tokens, it was common for the children to count all the tokens, say the numeral aloud, and then write this numeral without matching its digits to the concrete display.

2. Three of the four children were able to use expanded notation cards to construct numerals. For example, 98 was constructed from 90 and 8, with the 8 placed on top of the 0. However, it did not appear that the solutions to these expanded notation problems were based on an analysis of the compositional structure of the numbers and numerals. Instead, the children seemed to be trying different ways of putting the cards together until they found something that looked right. Further, all the children demonstrated some difficulty with zeros (as in the number 708) when using these cards.

Recomposition and Conservation: Written Arithmetic.   We do not have very direct evidence in this study for children's understanding of how the principle of recomposition and conservation applies to written arithmetic. Written addition and subtraction problems were first presented to the children in February and were repeated in May. Except for a few special probes, only two-digit problems in subtraction were used, so we could not observe most of the bugs described earlier. However, we can comment on the emergence of written carry and borrow competence and its relation to understanding of the principles as expressed in performances with the concrete tokens.

The most striking feature is the lack of association between the two. The child who was weakest in understanding the base system as represented in concrete materials performed the carry procedure perfectly in February. Meanwhile, the child with the strongest understanding avoided written procedures altogether, relying instead on the mental computation strategies she had invented. Another child who showed considerable understanding of the blocks almost completely avoided carrying in February by counting on his fingers and then writing the answers, and he continued to show some difficulty with carrying in May. Thus, strong semantic understanding (as shown by appropriate manipulations of the concrete representations and use of mental arithmetic) in no way guarantees ability to use the carry procedure in written addition. The carry procedure can, however, be learned as a symbol manipulation routine on the basis of school teaching.

The same general pattern was repeated for borrowing in subtraction. However, as might be expected, this procedure was harder to learn than carrying and was mastered later in the year. The child with the strongest understanding first performed the borrow procedure in May, with many false starts and bugs. Another child who showed good understanding of the principles in the blocks repeatedly stated that he was supposed to borrow, but even in May he had some difficulty remembering the exact procedure. On the other hand, by May the children with weakest understanding of the concrete materials were using the correct, school-taught written algorithm with ease, notating both increments and decrements. It is of some interest that all of the children at some point displayed the Smaller-From-Larger bug, although each overcame it in the course of the year. This is important because it indicates that the children were not initially thinking of the column-by-column operations of written arithmetic as a partition-based strategy for taking one quantity from another.

The Formal Interview Study

These initial findings allowed us to construct a more formal interview technique for the following study. This study was an attempt to replicate and extend in a less educationally privileged population the major findings of the pilot study. The interviews were somewhat more systematic, although the interviewers were still free to explore lines of reasoning suggested by the child's responses. We also probed somewhat more systematically for the children's understanding of the written symbols.

The school where we worked was a Catholic parochial school serving a largely black population. Ten third-grade children—five boys and five girls— participated in the study. In this school, subtraction with borrowing was taught during third grade. The children were selected by their teacher as being neither particularly advanced nor particularly backward for their age in mathematics. However, their performance in this study indicated there was considerable vari-

TABLE 2.1
Description of Tasks Given in the Formal Interview Study

I. *Tasks Assessing Knowledge of Blocks*

A. Conventions of decimal coding
1. NAME THE VALUE OF INDIVIDUAL BLOCKS OR TOKENS. For example, the interviewer would hold up a long Dienes block and ask, "How much is this block worth?" The child was expected to say, "ten."
2. "READ" A DISPLAY OF ONE OF THE CONCRETE REPRESENTATIONS (I.E., BLOCKS, STICKS, OR CHIPS), TELLING WHAT NUMBER IT REPRESENTS. For example, the experimenter would put eight bundles of 10 sticks and 3 single sticks on the table and ask, "What number do we have here?" The child would then count the sticks and say, "eighty-three."
3. CONSTRUCT A DISPLAY OF BLOCKS, CHIPS, OR STICKS TO REPRESENT A CERTAIN NUMBER. The interviewer would say, for example, "Would you use the blocks to show the number two hundred fifty-six?" and the child would get 2 hundreds, 5 tens, and 6 ones.
B. Principle of recomposition
4. SHOW A QUANTITY IN TWO WAYS—i.e., with all units and with both tens and units. In this task the experimenter would give the child a pile of ones, ask him or her to count it, and then to show that number in another way. The child then rebuilt the number using tens and ones.
5. SPONTANEOUS USE OF TRADE PROCEDURE IN SUBTRACTION WITH BLOCKS. In subtraction with blocks the experimenter set up the problem for the child by asking him or her to show the top number in blocks and then to give away the amount shown by the bottom number. For example, to do the problem $34 - 19$ in blocks, the child got out 3 tens and 4 ones and had the goal of giving away 19 from the pile of blocks. The problem confronting the child in examples like these was that of getting enough units to enable him or her to subtract the required number. We were interested in whether or not the child initiated a trade of 1 ten for 10 units.
6. REBUILDING A DISPLAY WITH MORE OF A DENOMINATION. For example, we asked the child to show 34 with more than 4 ones.

II. *Testing Knowledge of Written Numbers*

A. Conventions of decimal coding
7. COMPARE THE VALUE OF THE SAME DIGIT APPEARING IN TWO DIFFERENT COLUMNS. For example, we asked the child to compare the 3s in 32 and 73 and say which was worth more.
8. SHOW THE VALUE OF A DIGIT USING BLOCKS. For example, given the number 473, the child was asked to show the 7 with the blocks and was expected to put out 7 tens.
B. Arithmetic procedures
9. ADDITION WITH CARRYING. Children were asked to do several two- and three-digit addition problems using paper and pencil.
10. SUBTRACTION WITH BORROWING. Again, children were given several two- and three-digit problems.
C. Principle of recomposition/conventions of decimal coding for noncanonical numerals
11. NAME THE VALUE OF THE CARRY MARK. The experimenter pointed to the small 1 that was written as the carry in an addition problem and asked the child to say how much it was worth. The child was expected to say, "ten."
12. NAME THE VALUE OF THE BORROW MARK. The experimenter pointed to the small 1 written next to the units digit of the minuend (e.g., the 1 in $\overset{2}{\cancel{3}}{}^{1}4$) and asked the child to say how much it was worth. The correct response was "ten."

---

ability in their knowledge of base-ten numeration and arithmetic. The interview tasks concentrated on three main aspects of arithmetic knowledge: the conventions of decimal coding, the principle of recomposition, and procedures of addition and subtraction. Three kinds of concrete materials were used: Dienes blocks, bundles of sticks, and colored chips. Table 2.1 describes each of the tasks given in these three areas.

TABLE 2.2
Performance on Tasks in the Formal Interview Study

	Proportion of Children Responding Correctly on All Trials		
	Nov.	*Feb.*	*May*
BLOCK TASKS:			
A. Conventions of Decimal Coding			
1. Name value of individual blocks			
a. ten block	8/10	5/6	9/9
b. hundred block	8/9	7/7	9/9
2. Read a display			
a. all units	10/10	—	—
b. tens and units	4/10	9/10	10/10
c. hundreds, tens, and units	4/10	6/10	9/10
3. Construct a display			
a. tens and units	6/10	9/10	10/10
b. hundreds, tens, and units	8/10	7/10	10/10
B. Principle of Recomposition			
4. Show a quantity in two ways	8/9	—	—
5. Spontaneous trade in block subtraction			
a. 1 ten for 10 units	—	3/8	6/10
b. 1 hundred for 9 tens, 10 units	—	—	6/7
6. Rebuilding a display			
a. with more units	—	—	9/10
b. with more tens	—	—	9/10
WRITTEN NUMBER TASKS:			
A. Conventions of Decimal Coding			
7. Compare value of digit	1/10	—	—
8. Represent digit with blocks	—	1/7	2/3
B. Procedures			
9. Addition with carrying	—	9/10	9/10
10. Subtraction with borrowing			
a. from adjacent column	—	6/10	9/10
b. across zero	—	2/5	4/7
C. Principle of Recomposition/Conventions of Decimal Coding for Noncanonical Numbers			
11. State value of carry mark	—	0/7	6/9
12. State value of borrow mark	—	3/6	4/7

As in the pilot study, each child was interviewed individually three times during the school year—in November, February, and May. The November interview was designed to introduce the children to the materials and then to test their understanding of the conventions of decimal coding in these concrete forms. The February interview further tested their understanding of the conventions of decimal coding in both concrete and written forms, repeating many of the November tasks, and then probed their knowledge of addition and subtraction with blocks and in writing. The May interview focused mainly on addition and subtraction procedures and on the principle of recomposition.

Table 2.2 shows the proportion of children responding correctly to each of the tasks used in the interviews. Denominators show the number of children who were given the task; numerators, the number who were successful on 100% of the trials. Because there were no reliable differences in difficulty among the three concrete representations (blocks, chips, and sticks) the data were collapsed across the different media in Tasks 2 and 3. In all of the other tasks only Dienes blocks were used.

Conventions of Place Value: Concrete Representations of Number.   The tasks of identifying blocks and reading and constructing displays (Tasks 1 through 3) were concerned with conventions of decimal coding in the blocks. Virtually all of the children, even in November, could identify the value of a single block shape (Task 1) and read a display consisting only of the units denomination (Task 2a). When working with displays of more than one denomination, the children had more difficulty. It was not until February that almost all children could reliably read two-denominational displays, and not until May that they could do the same for three-denominational displays. Reading displays of objects appeared to be more difficult than constructing them. Only four of the ten children read three-denominational displays correctly in November, but eight of the children were able to construct these displays reliably.

One factor in the comparative difficulty of reading displays was the children's lack of competence in coordinating counting strings with blocks when several denominations were present. Figure 2.4 gives examples of the difficulties children had in reading three-denominational displays. Alice used the units counting string to count tens blocks. Jane continued with the hundreds counting string when she switched to enumerating tens blocks. Both children showed that they knew and could use the tens string when the experimenter isolated tens blocks from the rest of the display. Thus, there seems to be a period during which the child knows the individual strings well enough to use them separately for quantification but cannot coordinate the use of several strings within a single quantification task. When constructing block displays, it was not necessary to coordinate counting strings because the child could just count out the number of blocks in each denomination separately. For example, to show the number 423, the

a)   Alice
     E: Shows:

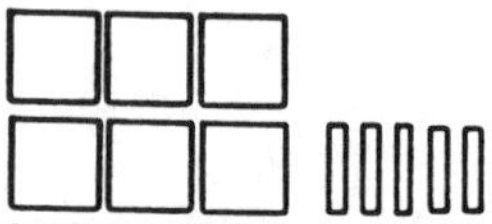

     S: (Touching the hundreds) 100, 200, 300, 400, 500, 600 . . . (touching
          the tens) 7, 8, 9, 10, 11 . . . 611.
     E: Let's try one more like this. How about this one?

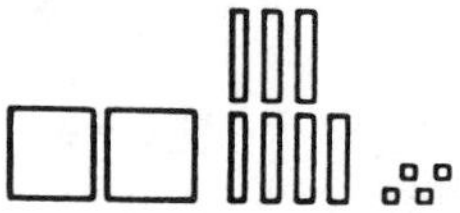

     S: (Touching the hundreds) 100, 200 . . . (touching the tens) 201, 202,
          203, 204, 205, 206, 207 . . . (touching the ones) 208, 209, 210, 211.
     E: Hmm. Let's count them again. This time, why don't you count these (tens
          and ones).
     S: (Touching the tens) 10, 20, 30, 40, 50, 60, 70 . . . (touching the ones)
          71, 72, 73, 74.
     E: How much is this (hundreds)?
     S: 200.
     E: Okay. How much is that altogether?
     S: 200 and . . .
     E: I have 200, and I add this much (a ten block) more. How much is that
          worth?
     S: 201.

b)   Jane
     E: Good. So how much do you think this would be?

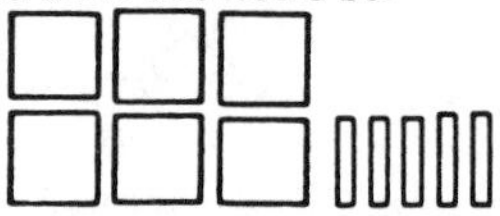

     S: (Touching the hundreds blocks) 100, 200, 300, 400, 500, 600 . . . (touching
          the tens blocks) 700, 800, 900, ten hundred, eleven hundred.
     E: Are these (tens) worth 100?
     S: I count them all together.
     E: But these (tens) aren't hundreds.
     S: I am counting these like tens.
     E: OK. But how much would these (tens) be worth then?
     S: Oh. 10, 20, 30, 40, 50 . . . 50 dollars.
     E: How much would this (entire display) be worth altogether?
     S: 600 . . . wait! It's 5 and 6.
     E: But how much is it altogether? This (hundred) is 6, right?
     S: Eleven hundred.

FIG. 2.4. Examples of children's difficulties with 3-denominational displays.
(From Resnick, 1983. ©1983 by Academic Press. Reprinted by permission.)

child could count "100, 200, 300, 400," then "10, 20," and finally, "1, 2, 3" without having to link denominations by saying "410, 420, 421," and so forth.

Recomposition and Conservation: Concrete Representations.   Knowledge of recomposition, as reflected in the ability to represent a quantity in several ways (Tasks 4 and 6) was apparently present in most children even in November. At that time eight of nine children counted the number of units blocks in a pile that the experimenter constructed and then showed the same quantity using a combination of tens and units. This ability was confirmed in May, when nine of ten children first represented a number such as 34 with 3 tens and 4 units and then rebuilt it using more than 4 units (e.g., 2 tens and 14 units). The same children also were able to rebuild a display such as 245 using more than 4 tens. However, although they knew how to do this recomposition, most children did not use this knowledge spontaneously in the course of doing subtraction with blocks (when an exchange was required in order to have enough units to subtract as in Task 5). After a prompt, most children did apply this knowledge in May, even when a double trade—1 hundred for 10 tens, then 1 ten for 10 units—was required (Task 5b).

Conventions of Place Value: Written Numbers.   Taken together, the results just described show that by the end of their 3rd year in school these children had quite a strong command of the decimal structure as coded in blocks or other tokens, and that they could relate the blocks to standard number names. However, when we look at their ability to analyze written numbers in terms of decimal structure, we see a much weaker performance. In November, the children were asked to compare the value of the same digit appearing in different columns (Task 7). Only one child could reliably do so. The other children either said that the digits were equal (e.g., in 73 and 31, the 3s were both worth 3), or were unable to separate the digits from the whole number, saying that, for example, the 3 in 73 was worth more because 73 is larger than 31. In February and May, some of the children were given a different version of this task. Instead of comparing digits, they were asked to show the value of a single digit within a multidigit number using the blocks (Task 8). Only one of the children could do this reliably in February. Most of the children used only unit blocks to show the digits. For example, when asked to show the 4 in 642, they put out 4 units instead of 4 tens.

Recomposition and Conservation: Written Arithmetic.   The idea that all digits are worth only units also appeared in most of the children's responses to our questions about carrying and borrowing (Tasks 11 and 12). In February all the children said that the carry mark written in the tens column was worth just one, rather than ten. Similarly, three of the six children who were asked said that the small 1 written next to the units digit in the top number of a subtraction problem was worth just one. In the May interview there was considerable improvement in identifying the value of the tens carry mark (Task 11) and some improvement in naming the value of the borrow mark (Task 12). Nevertheless, correct quantitative interpretation of borrow and carry marks remained a problem for many children even at the end of third grade.

What is more notable is the facility in performing the written addition or subtraction did not guarantee that a child understood the value of the carry and borrow marks. When asked to do written addition that required carrying (Task 9), all but one child could do the algorithm correctly, as early as February. All but one did simple borrowing (i.e., from adjacent columns) correctly by May (Task 10). Of the four children who did borrowing over zero correctly in May, only two were among those who gave the correct values for borrow marks (Tasks 11 and 12). Thus, procedural skill and understanding do not seem to develop in conjunction under the school instructional program to which these children were exposed.

Summary.   Of the principles of place value arithmetic described in the previous section, only the value conventions and recomposition were directly tested in this study. We can see that this group of children was in far better command of the value conventions in block representations than of those in written representations. Furthermore, although they could use blocks to represent two- and three-digit total quantities, they could not use them reliably to represent individual digits. We take this to mean that there was very weak mapping between the individual elements of the two representational systems. It is not surprising, in light of this, that children's capabilities for doing arithmetic with blocks was not reflected in a comparable ability for doing written arithmetic procedures.

The children showed good understanding of the recomposition principle in blocks in the course of the various multiple representation tasks. They seemed to know that the total value was not changing—which would correspond to the constraint to conserve the total quantity—but we did not question them directly on this point. On the other hand, their failure to assign appropriate values to written carry and borrow marks suggests that the regrouping and compensation principles were not being applied in written arithmetic—even though the procedures were sometimes performed correctly. Children did seem to know that they could decompose *numerals* and operate column-by-column (at least they performed that way), but they did not appear to understand that in doing this they were actually decomposing *quantities*.

Perhaps the strongest violation of the recomposition/conserve minuend principle is seen in the Smaller-From-Larger bug, which three of these children displayed in the February interview and one child (the slowest of the group) developed in May (he could not do written subtraction at all in February). When a child is willing to invert the numbers within a column in order to subtract in that column, we can infer that he does not think of the digits as representing parts of a larger quantity. By May, these three children were no longer doing smaller-from-larger, but buggy routines in borrowing over zero persisted. As we have shown, these bugs violate the constraint to conserve the minuend quantity because they fail to preserve the total quantity in the top number; but they do respect the notion of composition because they represent an effort to recompose the top quantity.

B. The Principles Applied to Mental Arithmetic

Another potential indicator of children's understanding of the principles of subtraction is the kinds of procedures they invent for doing mental arithmetic. Because American schools do not specifically teach mental arithmetic procedures, children must construct these procedures for themselves. As a result, children's ways of performing these tasks often reflect more clearly than do their written procedures what they understand about the principles of the number system.

Occasional episodes in the interviews from the two studies just described gave us reason to believe that at least some children were applying principles of partition and recomposition to solving addition and subtraction problems even when they were still having difficulty with the school-taught written algorithms. For example an 8-year-old, Amanda, in the pilot study avoided the problems of carrying and borrowing by doing two-digit problems in her head. She solved 37 + 25 as follows: "Thirty plus twenty is fifty. Fifty-seven. Fifty-seven, fifty-eight, fifty-nine, sixty, sixty-one, sixty-two." Then she wrote 62, aligning the digits in the proper columns. Her method showed that she understood that one could partition the numbers and add up the parts in any order. The parts she chose reflected the decimal system used in both counting and writing numbers. For the problem 53 − 27, Amanda produced an incorrect answer, but by a method that further confirmed her understanding of the partition and recomposition principles. She said, "Fifty minus twenty is thirty. Then take away three is twenty-seven and plus seven is thirty-four." Amanda knew that once she had done the subtraction of the tens parts, she needed to add back in one of the units parts and to subtract the other; her error was that she switched the parts, taking away three instead of seven.

Having observed such performances on occasion, we were interested in seeing whether we could document the existence of such partition procedures more systematically. To do so, we conducted a study that extended prior work on children's invented addition algorithms (Groen & Resnick, 1977). That research and other studies of young children's informal arithmetic had established that children use counting procedures of various kinds to do simple addition and subtraction. For example, first and second graders, and even some preschoolers, are known to perform single-digit addition and subtraction as if they have a "counter in the head" that can be set to any number, incremented or decremented by 1 any number of times, and then "read out" to yield an answer. The pattern of reaction times for a set of problems depends on the number of increments or decrements required in the particular counting algorithm the child uses. By studying patterns of reaction times and relating findings to other evidence of children's informal arithmetic strategies, it has been possible to establish that children develop ways of reducing the number of mental counts that are required. For example, when they add two numbers, many children begin by setting the mental counter to the larger of the two addends, even if it was not presented first, and then "counting-in" the smaller addend. This has become known as the *min* procedure because the reaction times it produces are a function of the smaller of the two addends.

It seemed to us reasonable to assume that children might extend such invented counting procedures to the addition of larger numbers, and that they might apply their knowledge of the decimal structure of the number system to invent useful shortcuts that would minimize the amount of mental counting. Consider the case of adding a single-digit number to a two-digit number. Assuming that one is going to use a mental counting procedure for solving these problems, there are four plausible possibilities that call on place value and partition principles to varying degrees:

1. *Min of the Addends.*   Set the mental counter to the two-digit number, then add in the one-digit number in increments of one. This amounts to applying the *min* procedure. Reaction times would be a function of the single-digit number. No understanding of the decade structure of the numbers is required for this procedure. All the child has to know is how to count by ones over the decade barrier (e.g., "29, 30, 31. . .") and up through several decades.
2. *Sum of the Units.*   Set the counter at the beginning of the decade of the two-digit number, then add in the first units digit in increments of one, then add in the second units digit in increments of one. For example, for 23 + 8, the counter starts at 20 and is incremented by 3, then by 8. Reaction time is a function of the sum of the two units digits. Note that this model does not discriminate whether the first or the second units digit is added first. This procedure reflects an understanding of the compositional structure of two-digit numbers, but not full appreciation of the flexibility of recomposition that the number system allows.
3. *Min of the Units.*   Decompose the two-digit number into a tens component and a ones component, then recombine the tens component with whichever of the two units quantities is larger. Set the counter to this reconstituted number and then add in the smaller units digit in increments of one. For example, for 23 + 9, the problem would be recomposed to 29 + 3. The counter would be set at 29 and then incremented 3 times to a sum of 32. Reaction time would be a function of the smaller of the two *units* digits. This procedure is a simple version of the one that Amanda used. It

is based on an understanding of the possibilities for partition and recomposition of numbers within the decimal place value system.

4. *Mental Carry.* A fourth possible procedure for solving these problems is to mimic the carrying procedure for written addition, that is, mentally add the units digits, mentally carry a 1 if necessary, then mentally add the tens digit to the carry digit. In this case, we might assume that the child would use the *min* procedure for adding the units digits. Because the time for adding the units digits would be a function of the smaller of the two units digits, it is difficult to discriminate this procedure from Min of the Units on the basis of reaction time data. A distinction that we can look for, however, is that, when doing mental carry, children are likely to add doubles in the units column particularly quickly as they are known to do when applying the *min* procedure to single-digit problems. A pattern of reaction times that are a function of the smaller of the two units digits, except that doubles are solved as if they took no more time than adding 1, would thus suggest that a child was using the Mental Carry procedure.

The subjects were 12 children (8 boys and 4 girls) in the second and third grades of the same laboratory school used in the pilot interview study. Children were selected by their teachers as average math learners for their age. The average age at the start of the experiment was 7 years 11 months (range: 7 years, 1 month to 8 years, 7 months). The experiment was conducted over a 3-month period during the first third of the school year. Reaction time data on two sets of addition problems were collected. These were the set of 100 single-digit problems with addends 0 through 9, and a set of 100 problems in which a one-digit number was to be added to a two-digit number. The single-digit problems were included to provide a baseline for each individual against which to evaluate data on the upper decade performance. Interviews were also conducted with each child in which the child was presented problems drawn from the reaction time test set and asked to describe how he or she got the answers. Reaction time and interview data were used to establish which of the four mental arithmetic procedures each child was using.

The problems were presented as row-addition problems of the form $m + n = ?$, the child's task being to find the missing number. In the upper decade problems, the tens digit of the double digit number was either 2, 3, or 4; the units digit ranged from 0 to 9. The double-digit number was always presented first. Within each subset of 100 upper digit problems, all possible pairings of units digits were included. Each problem was presented three times. The 600 problems were arranged in 60 blocks of 10 problems each, each block containing an equal number of lower decade (one digit) and upper decade (two digits plus one digit) problems. The order of the presentation of the 60 blocks was randomized across children.

Children were tested individually. They saw each problem centered on a video display terminal and responded on the numeric keypad. Each problem was preceded with a message to press the "next" key on the keyboard. The child pressed "return" when he judged his answer to be complete. The time to the nearest millisecond for each keystroke, as well as the value of the key, were recorded. At the end of each block, the child was informed of the number of correct responses for that block. At the end of a minimum of two blocks, the child was given the option of going on to the next block or terminating the session.

The experiment was performed in a quiet room in the building in which the children attended school. Each child was tested, in sessions lasting about 15 minutes, twice a week for a total of about 10 sessions (depending on the perseverance of the child). Between 2 and 16 blocks of problems were completed in each session. The final session was the interview.

The average number of sessions for all children was 9.9, with a range from 6 to 14 sessions. The average of correct responses across all problems and all children was 94.1%. The results reported are based on the time to the first keystroke for correct problems only. Of the three replicates for each problem, the response with the lowest time was used in the analysis.[5] For the upper decade problems, the three problems with the same units digits in the same order (e.g., 23 + 8, 33 + 8, 43 + 8) were treated as replicates of each other. Data were analyzed individually for each child.

We examined the data for fit to regression models of the four procedures just described (Min of the Addends, Sum of the Units, Min of the Units, and Mental Carry), with and without the doubles assumption. For each model, the pattern of times predicted by the model was regressed on the actual data of each child for the upper decade problems. This yielded F-ratios, slopes, and intercepts for each model. We also regressed each child's data on the lower decade problems on the predicted patterns for each of the models that has been previously studied in research on mental addition.[6]

Table 2.3 summarizes the data from the interview and the reaction time portions of the study for each child. The first column lists the procedures that the child claimed to be using during the interview, in order of frequency of the child's claim. The next column shows the upper decade models that gave significant fit to the child's data, together with the slope parameter for that model. The slope can be interpreted as the amount of time taken for each count. The third column lists the best fitting lower decade model for the child and its slope.

---

[5]This procedure eliminates outliers without the necessity of setting an arbitrary criterion.

[6]The models of interest are: (1) Min, Set counter to the larger number, increment by the smaller; (2) Sum, Count in the first number by ones, count in the second number by ones; and (3) Second Addend, Set counter to the first number, increment by the second number. Each can be fit with and without the assumption that doubles are retrieved from memory.

TABLE 2.3
Models of Children's Mental Arithmetic Strategies

| | | Type of Data | |
| | | Reaction Time for | |
Child	Interview	Upper Decade Problems	Lower Decade Problems
Alex	Min of Units Mental Carry Shortcut Strategies	Min of Units (F = 249.0) Slope = 441	Min Slope = 346
Justin	Min of Addends Min of Units	Min of Units (F = 95.2) Slope = 1002	Min doubles Slope = 992
Karl	Min of Addends	Min of Addends (F = 129.5) Slope = 1164	Min doubles Slope = 960
Paula	Min of Addends	Min of Addends (F = 242.4) Slope = 863	Min doubles Slope = 391
Susan	Mental Carry	Min of Units/Doubles (F = 102.1) Slope = 326	Min doubles Slope = 65
David	Mental Carry	Min of Units/Doubles (F = 102.4) Slope = 582	Min doubles Slope = 203
Lisa	Min of Units Min of Addends	Min of Addends (F = 173.0) Slope = 612 Min of Units (F = 140.8) Slope = 718 Sum of Units (F = 173.7) Slope = 433	Min doubles Slope = 192
Brenda	Min of Addends		
Charles	Mental Carry		
Erica	Mental Carry		

Note: Slopes are measured in milliseconds.

In several cases, the interview and reaction time data converge to allow us to draw a very clear conclusion concerning the child's strategies for upper decade problems. Alex, for example, reported using Min of the Units along with Mental Carry and a variety of shortcut strategies. His reaction time data show a strong fit to Min of the Units, with a slope that makes good sense (i.e., it is somewhat slower) in relation to his slope for the lower decade problems. It is of interest to note that Alex had been one of the children in the laboratory school interview study during the preceding school year. In that study he had shown strong command of the decimal structure and composition principles, a command that is also reflected in the present data. Justin reported using two of the upper decade strategies, but only one gives a significant fit to his reaction time data. The slope is also in good accord with his slope on the lower decade problems. Thus, we can reasonably conclude that Justin was predominantly using the Min of the Units procedure, and that he understood the partition and recomposition principles.

Two other children, by contrast, give rather clear evidence of not using the decimal structure at all in their calculations. Karl and Paula both described themselves as using Min of the Addends exclusively, and their reaction time patterns confirm this. In Karl's case, the slope for upper decade problems is just slightly longer than the slope for lower decade problems; he seems to be a generally slow counter. Paula, on the other hand, takes more than twice as long to count on the upper decade problems.

Finally, two children, Susan and David, reported Mental Carry strategies, and their reaction time patterns seem to confirm their reports. In both cases, the only significant fit was to Min of the Units *with doubles*, which, as we have noted, is the expected pattern for people who are doing a mental analog of carrying. Susan's slope of 65 for the lower decades suggests an adult-like pattern (cf. Ashcraft & Battaglia, 1978; Groen & Parkman, 1972), but David's pattern is more characteristic of children of 7 or 8 years of age.

For four children, our combined interview and reaction time methods were not capable of distinguishing a clear strategy of mental arithmetic. For Brenda, Charles, and Erica, none of the models fit significantly, and we thus have no way of confirming or disconfirming their interview self-reports. For Lisa, all of the upper decade models fit reasonably well, and she also reported using two of the four strategies. Our methods do not allow us to discriminate which routines she was using predominantly.

In summary, of the six children whose performances we have been able to interpret clearly, two gave clear evidence of applying principles of composition and partition to invented mental arithmetic procedures, and two gave clear evidence of not, or not yet, doing so. Two more, because they were using mental analogs of the school-taught procedure, do not allow us to decide what they understand about composition and partition principles. It seems, then, that a minority of primary grade children construct mental calculation procedures that depend on applying knowledge of the composition and partition principles to the decimal structure of the counting numbers. However, although such invented procedures provide strong evidence for understanding of the principles, we cannot conclude from the absence of such procedures that a child does not understand the principles. In particular, the tendency to use school-taught algorithms such as Mental Carry may mask understanding of the principles.

V. INSTRUCTION ON THE PRINCIPLES OF WRITTEN ARITHMETIC

Although the children in the studies just reported do not constitute large or systematic samples of primary school children, the pattern of results is sufficiently clear to suggest the arithmetic knowledge typical for children of this age. Taken together, the results of the three studies presented here suggest that most children develop some command of the principles of decimal coding, composition, and partitioning by the time they encounter subtraction with borrowing in school. However, this understanding seems to have little or no impact on their written arithmetic procedures. If this is so, then many children's difficulty with place value in written arithmetic may result not from a total absence of knowledge of the relevant principles, but from an inadequate linking of the principles with the symbols and syntax of the written algorithm. This suggests that for many children who have difficulty learning or remembering the rules for written arithmetic, it may be useful to provide instruction that explicitly links the principles to the symbols.

To explore this broad hypothesis, we tested a method of instruction called *mapping instruction*, which was designed to help children link their knowledge of the principles to written subtraction (Resnick, 1982). Mapping instruction requires the child to do subtraction problems both with the blocks and in writing, maintaining a step-by-step correspondence between the blocks and written symbols throughout the problem. We thought that this would allow the child to interpret the steps and notations in the written procedure *as if* they were the steps and displays of the blocks procedure. This in turn should allow them to transfer to written arithmetic the understanding that they had developed in the context of concrete materials.

The instructional procedure is schematized in Fig. 2.5. First, the child is shown a subtraction problem written in vertical form and is asked to represent the top number in blocks. He or she is then given a large pile of assorted blocks that serves as the "bank" in making exchanges. The problem is posed as follows to the child: (1) Read the bottom number and try to take away that amount from the display of blocks. In Fig. 2.5, for example, the goal is to take away 9 units, 3 tens, and 1 hundred from the 3 hundreds blocks. (2) Whenever you make a change in the blocks, record that change in the written numbers. This will produce the sequence of exchanges and notations shown in the figure.

In a pilot study, three children who had buggy subtraction algorithms were given approximately 1 hour of mapping instruction in individual sessions. On the posttest several weeks later, all three children had correct subtraction algorithms and were able to explain why their former bugs were incorrect. For example, one of the children, whose former bug was Borrow-Across-Zero, had just performed the problem 3,002 − 9 correctly when she was asked to explain what she had learned. She told the experimenter that she had learned "not to go take it [the 1,000] from here [the 3 in 3,002] and put it all the way over [to the units column] and just leave these [the two zeros] alone." Another child, whose former bug was Don't-Decrement-Zero, was able to explain the meaning of the borrow marks in a way that was not taught directly in the mapping instruction. In the instruction a double exchange procedure was taught for problems with zero tens. The child instead used the idea of directly distributing a borrowed quantity across

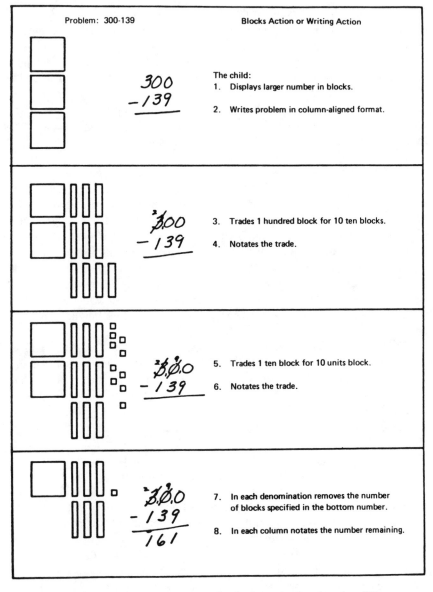

FIG. 2.5. Outline of mapping instruction for borrowing in subtraction. (From Resnick, 1982. ©1982 by Lawrence Erlbaum Associates. Reprinted by permission.)

columns. In the problem 2,003 − 1,467 she said that she had borrowed one thousand. She was then asked to tell where that thousand had been placed. She replied, "Well, 100 is right here (pointing to the 1 of the 13 and to the 9 in the tens column), and 900 is right here (pointing to the 9 in the hundreds column)."

With these encouraging results in hand, we turned next to a more formal instructional experiment (Omanson, 1982), one that would establish the effects of mapping instruction and explore how the instruction works. We expected mapping instruction to induce understanding of the principles of subtraction, and we expected this understanding to prevent the occurrence of bugs in postinstruction performance by providing a basis for accurate planning and checking of steps in the written routine. In the experiment we also considered an alternative explanation of how mapping instruction corrects bugs. This was that the instruction works simply by providing children an opportunity to rehearse the correct routine without making any errors, rather than by helping them transfer knowledge from block arithmetic to written arithmetic. To explore these alternatives we compared mapping instruction in its complete form to another type of instruction, called *prohibition instruction,* which did not use the blocks but consisted only of practicing the written algorithm under conditions in which no incorrect steps were permitted. We expected no improvement in understanding of the principles from prohibition instruction but thought that it might correct certain bugs—those which omit or repair only one or two steps of the correct procedure (e.g., Borrow-From-Zero). We expected prohibition instruction would be ineffective in correcting bugs that omit all or most of the correct borrowing routine (e.g., Smaller-From-Larger). Mapping instruction, however, was expected to correct all types of bugs because of its explicit linking of the correct borrowing procedure to the principles of subtraction. Furthermore, we expected mapping instruction to produce a long-term effect because it was based on understanding that could be used to re-generate correct procedures, whereas we thought that prohibition instruction would not prevent new bugs from arising in later performance.

A. Method

About 80 children from the fourth, fifth, and sixth grades of an urban parochial school were given a written subtraction test designed by Burton (1981) to diagnose buggy algorithms. Twenty children who were diagnosed as having buggy algorithms were chosen for study. These were all children nominated by their teachers as needing help on the special topic of subtraction. Two of the students were dropped from the study after our screening interview because they seemed to lack some prerequisites for our instruction (e.g., the ability to count by hundreds). The 18 students who comprised the final sample included 14 rated as average- to high-ability learners by their teachers, 4 rated as low ability; 8 boys and 10 girls. Seven children were in fourth grade, 8 in fifth, and 3 in sixth.

Fifteen of the 18 children were black and the remainder white. They were divided into two groups that were approximately matched on race, sex, grade, and teachers' rating of ability.

The children were given two preliminary interviews (screening and pretraining) to familiarize them with the blocks and to check some of their basic skills in elementary mathematics, such as counting and naming the values of digits in standard decimal notation. Then they were given a pretest interview that assessed their understanding and performance of subtraction with borrowing. After the pretest, the children received instruction (either mapping or prohibition) followed by an immediate posttest (2 to 7 days after instruction) and a delayed posttest (about 4 weeks after the immediate posttest). The posttests were essentially the same as the pretest, except that different numbers were substituted in the examples.

Each interview was administered individually. The screening, pretraining, and instruction interviews were conducted by one pair of experimenters (one interviewer and one notetaker) and the pretest and posttest interviews were conducted by another pair. Each interview was audiotaped and lasted approximately 40 minutes, except for the screening interview, which lasted about 20 minutes.

Screening. This interview served two functions: to test the children's knowledge of counting and place value, and to introduce them to Dienes blocks, if they were not already familiar with them. The first two sets of questions asked students to read numerals and to count by ones, tens, and hundreds. The remaining questions assessed the children's ability to represent written numbers with the Dienes blocks and to tell what number a display represented. Our purpose here was to ensure that children could learn to use the blocks quickly and that the value of each denomination of blocks was obvious to them. As noted, two children who did not pass the screening were dropped from further participation in the study.

Pretraining. The purpose of this training was to ensure that all the students could represent and solve subtraction problems with the blocks, using the one-for-ten trading procedure. We gave pretraining to children in both the Mapping and Prohibition groups because experience with the blocks during pretraining was necessary in order to answer some of the pretest and posttest questions. We used a quasi-discovery approach to training. In the beginning of each section of training, we gave students an opportunity to work out the problems or to describe how they would work them out. If a child attempted a wrong solution or failed to respond to the question, we tried several prompts; if the prompts failed, we demonstrated the correct procedure for the child. After the child did one problem correctly, she was told that that method was the one we wanted her to use. Then we gave the child several variations of the problem for practice until she could do all types correctly, at least twice consecutively.

The first set of problems included variations of the following: Given a canonical display of blocks (i.e., one with no more than 9 blocks in any denomination), add more blocks to a certain denomination but keep the total value of the display the same. For example, the first problem was to show *34* (initially represented as 3 tens and 4 ones) using more than 4 ones blocks. In these problems we wanted students to develop a procedure for trading that they could apply later within subtraction problems.

The second set of problems were subtraction problems to be worked out in blocks only but presented in written form. The child was told to set up the top number (minuend) in blocks and to try to take away the number of ones, tens, and hundreds shown by the bottom number (subtrahend), starting with the ones. The first problem required no trading, the second required trading a ten for 10 ones, and the third, a hundred for 10 tens. Later problems called for a double trade—i.e., trading a hundred for 10 tens, and then a ten for 10 ones.

The final section of the pretraining focused on what Resnick (1982) has called the "result map." We say that a student has a result map if he or she recognizes that the blocks procedure and the written procedure necessarily produce the same result for any given problem. In the result-map exercise, we asked students to do a simple problem in writing and then predict the answer they would get when they did the same problem with blocks. Then we asked them to do the problem in blocks. If they had not predicted correctly, we gave them a second problem and repeated the question. Once they seemed to understand the idea of result mapping with simple problems, we gave each student a problem chosen to elicit his own bug. The student did the problem in writing first, then in blocks. The purpose of the exercise was to give each student an opportunity to correct his written bug after comparing the written result to the blocks result. The experimenter did not press the student to do so, asking only which answer was right and whether the student could figure out what went wrong. All children in both groups were able to do subtraction problems in blocks without difficulty and all recognized the result map by the end of pretraining.

Pretest and Posttest.   In these tests we first checked students' knowledge of the principles of subtraction as expressed in Dienes blocks. Three aspects of this knowledge that we considered prerequisite to learning from mapping instruction were: (1) knowing the decimal value conventions for blocks and how they correspond to decimal place value in written numbers; (2) knowing the principle of recomposition as it applies to block representations—i.e., knowing that trading one block for ten of the next lower denomination maintains the value of the whole; and (3) knowing how to use the trading procedure in performing subtraction with blocks. Examples of questions assessing this knowledge are given in the first set of entries in Table 2.4. All the students performed well on this part of the test ($x = 90.4\%$).

The second part of the pretest and posttest assessed students' understanding of the value conventions and principles of written subtraction and their performance

TABLE 2.4
Knowledge Assessed by the Pretest and Posttest Interviews

1. Prerequisites for Mapping Instruction
    1.1 Conventions of decimal coding for canonical numerals and blocks
        Sample Item: E: *Puts 4 tens, 8 ones behind barrier.* There is a pile of blocks behind this.
                     The biggest block I have here is this—*shows S a ten.* Guess which of these
                     numbers is the amount that I have. *Shows S: 6 48 350 639.*
    1.2 Principle of recomposition and conservation in blocks
        Sample Item: E: Show me 328 in blocks.
                     S: *Gets out 3 hundreds, 2 tens, 8 ones.*
                     E: *Pushes S's blocks behind a barrier.* I am taking this block out—*shows S a*
                     ten—and now I'm going to add these blocks back in. *Shows S 6 ones*
                     blocks. Will we still have 328 here?
                     S: No.
                     E: Why not?
                     S: You took ten out and only put 6 back in.
    1.3 Subtraction procedure in blocks
        Sample Item: E: Now I want you to do this problem with the blocks (354 − 228).
                     S: *Gets 3 hundreds, 5 tens, 4 ones; trades 1 ten for 10 ones, subtracts 8 ones,*
                     2 tens, 2 hundreds, counts remaining blocks.
2. Conventions of decimal coding for recomposed minuends
        Sample Item: E: *Shows S a subtraction problem already completed.* Let's look at this
                     problem. Can you show me how much this is worth in blocks? *Points to*
                     the 1 next to the 6 in the ones column.
                     S: *Puts out 10 ones blocks.*
                     E: Now show me how much this is worth in blocks? *Points to 4 above 5.*
                     S: *Puts out 4 hundreds blocks.*
                     E: Ok. Now can you show me how much this is worth in blocks? *Points to 12*
                     in tens column.
                     S: *Puts out 12 tens blocks.*
3. Principle of Compensation
    3.1 In adjacent borrowing
        Sample Item: E: *Shows S 423 − 141 already completed.* Here is another problem that
                     someone did. What was she doing when she crossed out this number?
                     Points to the 4 in the hundreds column.
                     S: Borrowing.
                     E: Where did she put what she borrowed?
                     S: In the tens column. *Or points there.*
                     E: How much did she put with this number (2)?
                     S: 10 tens.
                     E: How much did she take from this number (4)?
                     S: 1 hundred.
    3.2 In borrowing over zero—from the hundreds column
        Sample Item: E: *Shows S 503 − 247.* How much did he borrow here? *Points to 5 in*
                     hundreds.
                     S: 100.
                     E: What happened to the hundred that he borrowed? Where did it go?
                     S: It was traded for 10 tens, and 9 of them went to the tens column, and 1 was
                     exchanged for 10 ones, which went to the ones column.

(continued)

TABLE 2.4 (*Continued*)

3.3 In borrowing over 2 zeros—from the thousands column

   Sample Item: E: *Shows S 2005 − 819. How much was borrowed from here? Points to 2 in thousands.*

          S: 1000.

          E: What happened to the thousand that was borrowed? Where did it go?

          S: He traded it for 10 hundreds and put them in the hundreds column, then he took 1 of the hundreds, traded it for 10 tens, and put the tens in the tens column. Then, he took 1 of the tens, traded it for 10 ones, and put them into the ones column.

          E: So could you tell me where the thousand is right now?

          S: 900 is in the hundreds column, and 100 is in the tens and ones columns.

Note: E = Experimenter; S = Student. Student's responses are examples of what we considered correct. Variations of these responses were also considered correct.

of written subtraction. The interview questions were designed to elicit children's "stories" about how borrowing works and focused on the values of the digits in recomposed minuends, such as $\overset{4}{\cancel{5}}\,\overset{9}{\cancel{0}}\,13$ and on an aspect of the principle of recomposition and conservation of minuend quantity. The second and third sets of entries in Table 2.4 present examples of the questions used and the responses we considered indicative of understanding. Inspection of the actual wording of our questions (items 3.1, 3.2, 3.3) makes it clear that we did not actually test whether the children understood that the *total* minuend quantity is conserved across all of the regroupings. Instead, we tested a somewhat weaker version of the principle, which we call the *compensation* principle.[7] Compensation is the constraint that requires that an increment or decrement in one column of the minuend be compensated by an equivalent change in another column. Both the exchange procedure and the redistribution procedure are ways to obey this constraint.

Mapping Instruction.   The mapping instruction consisted of three parts: (1) learning and practicing the full blocks-recording procedure illustrated in Fig. 2.5; (2) "fading," or practicing the recording procedure while the experimenter moved or pretended to move the blocks; and (3) doing the written procedure alone. In part one, the full mapping procedure was taught as a process of recording the block moves. The experimenter asked the child to start doing a subtraction problem with the blocks and to stop after each step and record the changes on the written numbers. As in pretraining, we used a quasi-discovery

---

[7]This is because our analysis of the principles was still evolving at the time the study was designed and we had not yet distinguished between the strong and weak forms of the conservation principle.

approach to teach the procedure, prompting the child when necessary. For example, if a child did not seem to know how to record block changes, we asked him to notice the new number of blocks in a denomination, find the corresponding column in the written number, and change the digit to match the new number in blocks. Each child was given the same initial set of subtraction problems along with a problem chosen to elicit the child's bug. The initial set of problems included four different types of problems requiring (1) one trade from tens to units, (2) one trade from hundreds to tens, (3) two independent trades: one from tens to units and one from hundreds to tens and (4) one double trade: from hundreds to tens in order to trade from tens to units. The child practiced each type of problem until he could solve that type without prompts. Thus we allowed the length of the instructional session to vary from child to child.

In part two (fading) the child was asked to tell the experimenter how to move the blocks. At first, the experimenter moved the blocks as the child directed, and the child recorded the changes on the written problem. Then the experimenter only pretended to move the blocks according to the child's instructions, while the child did the writing. In other words, no actual block display was constructed or modified; the child had to imagine such a display. Finally, the child simply verbalized the block moves and did the writing while the experimenter observed.

In part three the child was given several written subtraction problems and was instructed to think about the blocks while doing them in writing.

Prohibition Instruction.   This instruction consisted of two parts: (1) more training in blocks subtraction, as in pretraining, and (2) prohibition instruction. The blocks training was included to make the prohibition session comparable to the mapping session, by making it longer and giving the children more exposure to the blocks. Prohibition consisted of three phases: (a) learning and practicing the specified procedure with different types of problems, (b) fading, and (c) doing the written procedure alone.

The experimenter (E) began the prohibition instruction by introducing herself as the student's subtraction robot, who would do problems for the student (S) but needed explicit directions about what to write. E and S worked through a set of five problems—the same five that were used in mapping instruction—with S telling E what to do. If S told E to do anything wrong or in the wrong order, E said, "I am not programmed to do it that way. Try again." Otherwise, E wrote what S told her to write. If S could not tell E the correct move after a few guesses, E wrote the correct move and then asked S to continue from there. After doing the first five problems, E and S worked through a list of about 20 more problems, each of which could elicit specific bugs.

In fading, the student took over the writing but still had to tell E what each step would be before actually writing it. Finally, S was asked to work some written problems silently.

B. Results and Discussion

Performance of Written Subtraction.   Neither mapping nor prohibition instruction was very successful in correcting bugs. At the immediate posttest, two of nine Mapping children performed borrowing without bugs. At the delayed posttest, one more student performed without bugs. But meanwhile, one of those who had been correct on the immediate test reverted to her original bug. In the Prohibition group, three children performed without bugs on the immediate posttest and two of these returned to their original bugs at the delayed test. Meanwhile, two other children performed without bugs on the delayed test. In addition, children in both groups (four in Mapping, three in Prohibition) displayed new bugs at the delayed test.

Despite this poor test performance, the performance of the Prohibition group instruction suggested that for most of the children, the correct algorithm was available in memory, along with various buggy routines. Six out of nine children who received prohibition instruction used the correct algorithm throughout instruction, requiring no prohibitions from the experimenter. One other child did every problem correctly except one. In that problem she made two errors but after two prohibitions was able to suggest the correct move herself. For these seven children, the request to proceed carefully that was implicit in the Prohibition instructions was apparently enough to allow them to access an already available correct procedure. The remaining two students had great difficulty from start to finish, receiving about six prohibitions during almost every problem. Neither seemed to learn from the feedback; they made the same type of error repeatedly. Both children showed a basic confusion about when to increment and when to subtract within a column. Thus, their difficulty in choosing correct moves after feedback may have been due to a substantial lack of knowledge of the correct algorithm. If so, it is not surprising that they failed to learn from prohibition instruction.

Understanding Written Subtraction.   We assessed pretest–posttest differences in understanding with two quantitative measures, corresponding to the two categories in sections 2 and 3 of Table 2.4: the value of digits in the recomposed minuend, and the principle of compensation. To measure children's knowledge of the value of digits in recomposed minuends, we looked at each child's responses to all questions that referred to borrowing. We counted the total number of times a child attempted to identify the value of a digit, either verbally or by choosing an appropriate block, and then counted the number of times the child was correct in these attempts. The proportion of correct value assignments to total number of value assignments was our measure of the child's knowledge of values.

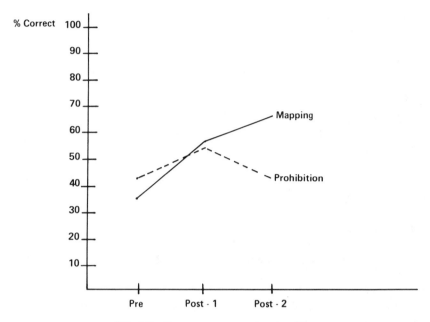

FIG. 2.6.   Percent correct on value questions.

Figure 2.6 shows changes in the mean percent correct on value questions for the two groups. As can be seen, the Mapping group improved from the pretest to the delayed posttest, whereas the Prohibition group did not. An ANOVA was performed on the value scores, comparing Mapping and Prohibition groups on the three tests. There was no main effect for instruction, but the Instruction X Time-of-Test interaction was significant (F $(2,32)$ = 3.66, p < .05). Newman–Keuls comparisons showed a significant difference between pretest and delayed posttest scores for the mapping group (p < .01), but no such difference for the prohibition group.

To measure children's knowledge of the principle of compensation, we looked at each child's responses to the three types of questions listed in section 3 of Table 2.4. A child was given a pass–fail score based on whether she identified correctly both the value of the amount taken from a column and the amount added to a column. Figure 2.7 shows the number of children displaying knowledge of the rule of compensation. The figure suggests that there was an increase in the number of students who used the principle of compensation in the Mapping group, but no increase in the Prohibition group. However, these differences were not reliable in a Chi-square test.

These results indicate that the mapping instruction was more effective than prohibition instruction in teaching understanding, but not to the extent that we had predicted. By the delayed posttest, the children in the Mapping group were identifying correctly only about 65% of the values in borrowing (see Fig. 2.6), and only four of the children were using the rule of compensation (see Fig. 2.7).

Relationship Between Understanding and Written Performance.   Could the failure of mapping instruction to correct bugs be due to the incompleteness of children's understanding after the instruction? To begin to answer this question we need to examine individual patterns of understanding and then look at the relationship between individuals' level of understanding and their performance of the written subtraction procedure.

We can identify five levels of understanding, based on the degree to which the child used place value conventions and the rule of compensation to explain borrowing.

1. At level 1, a child showed no evidence of knowing the value of borrow digits or compensation.

2. At level 2 the child correctly answered at least one of the questions on values of borrow digits—either by stating the value or showing it with blocks.

3. At level 3, the child was able to use the rule of compensation to identify borrowed quantities in the hundreds-to-tens borrow. In other words, he or she

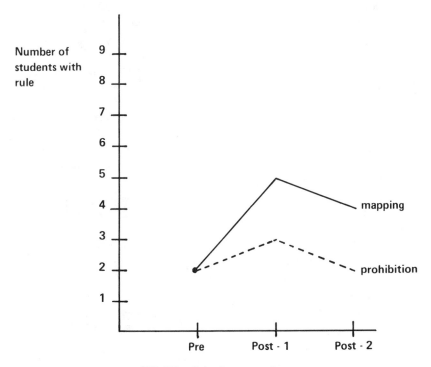

FIG. 2.7.   Rule of compensation.

would say that in $\overset{3}{\cancel{4}}$13 8, 100 was taken from the hundreds column and 100 was put into the tens column. At this level, however, the child failed to apply the idea of compensation to borrowing across zero.

4. At level 4, the child honored the rule of compensation not only in hundreds-to-tens borrows, but in borrowing from the hundreds across zero as well. This involved explaining either how the amount borrowed, 100, was distributed to the other columns, as 90 in the tens column and 10 in the units column, or how 100 became 10 tens, from which 1 ten was subsequently borrowed.

5. Finally, at level 5, the child applied the rule of compensation to all types of borrowing, including borrowing from the thousands across two zeros.

Examining each child's level of understanding, we found that only the two children who reached level 5 in understanding had correct algorithms at the delayed posttest. The three children who advanced to levels 2 and 3 and the four who remained at levels 1 and 2 all displayed buggy algorithms at the delayed posttest. This result raises the possibility that understanding the semantics of subtraction only leads to correct written performance when that understanding reaches a high level. Partial understanding—especially understanding that does not include the compensation principle—may not be adequate to block buggy performance. A second possibility, however, is that the understanding that a child uses to answer questions *about* borrowing is not applied to *performance* of borrowing. This second interpretation would constitute a strong challenge to our initial hypothesis that understanding of the principles, as applied to written arithmetic, would inhibit the performance or development of bugs. We clearly need more cases of successful learning of the principles to decide between these two hypotheses.

C. Expanded Mapping Instruction

To decide between these interpretations and to further establish the effects of mapping instruction, we gave an expanded version of mapping instruction to another sample of children. Eight fourth-grade students with buggy subtraction algorithms were given the expanded mapping instruction and were interviewed according to the same procedure used in the first study.

Some changes were made in the mapping instruction for this expansion. The changes were designed to enhance its effectiveness without changing the essential nature of the instruction. Our analyses of the individuals who learned from mapping in the first sample suggested that the amount of verbalization by the student during instruction was important in transferring understanding of the blocks to written arithmetic. To increase verbalization, the experimenter repeatedly asked the child to explain what the written marks meant and to describe what he or she had done with the blocks. Another modification was designed to help students learn the mapping procedure more easily and was based on the hypothesis that skill in the mapping procedure itself is important in learning. This change consisted of adding at the beginning some practice in recording block trades out of the context of subtraction. For example, we gave the children 3 tens blocks and 4 units blocks and asked them to get more units without changing the whole quantity. We then asked them to show the trade by making appropriate marks on the written number 34. This practice introduced the children to the idea of mapping in a simpler context so that we could alleviate confusion about what was meant by recording the block steps before practice on the full subtraction routine began. It also served to emphasize the principle of conserving the total minuend quantity. We added to the pretest and posttest some questions that would directly assess understanding of minuend conservation.[8]

The results were very similar to those for the initial Mapping group. Following instruction, the students improved in their knowledge of the values of borrowed quantities (75% correct on the delayed posttest) and in their knowledge of the compensation principle (six of eight children correctly expressed this principle on the delayed posttest). However, this new understanding again failed to produce correct written performance. Although there was some temporary improvement at the immediate posttest, all but one of the children had buggy algorithms at the delayed test. Thus, Study II confirmed our basic finding that mapping instruction, in its present form, is not effective in curing subtraction bugs even when it induces understanding of the principles underlying the subtraction procedure.

The practice in recording changes in block displays that we added at the beginning of mapping instruction seemed to have little effect on children's understanding of the principle of conserving the total minuend quantity. To test this we asked the children on the pretest and posttest to compare the minuend before and after borrowing (e.g., after borrowing, 523 would be $\overset{4}{\cancel{5}}{}^{1}23$) and to say whether the recomposed quantity was more than, less than, or equal to the original quantity. On the pretest all eight children said that the quantities were not equal. Most children said that 523 was more because it had 5 hundreds, and $\overset{4}{\cancel{5}}\overset{1}{\cancel{2}}$ 3 only had 4 hundreds. On the delayed posttest all but one of the children (Fred) still said that the quantities were not equal. Although Fred was the only child showing evidence of complete understanding of the principle of recomposition and conservation of the minuend quantity, his buggy algorithm returned at the delayed posttest, indicating that knowledge of this principle was not sufficient to correct buggy performance.

Looking at the data for 16 of the 17 children[9] who received mapping instruction, we can reexamine the relationship between understanding and written per-

---

[8]In the initial study, only the rule of compensation was directly assessed.

[9]One of the children in the expanded mapping sample could not be classified in terms of the five levels of understanding because she used the compensation principle in the more complex problems involving zero, but not in the simpler case of an adjacent borrow.

formance. Figure 2.8 depicts each child's level of understanding and type of written algorithm at the pretest and delayed posttest. We see that there were six students who reached the highest level of understanding as defined by the compensation principle. Three of these students—including Fred, who also showed evidence of understanding the principle of conservation of the minuend quantity—still had buggy algorithms at the posttest. We see, then, that even a high level of understanding, as expressed in answers to questions about borrowing, does not necessarily lead to improved written performance. This result forces us to accept the hypothesis that children can have available all of the principles needed for explaining a procedure without applying the principles to their own performance. Before proceeding to a discussion of the implications of the conclusion for a theory of arithmetic learning and performance, we first want to consider the sources of the great variability observed in the extent to which children learned the principles in the course of mapping instruction.

D. Who Learns from Mapping Instruction

We have seen that mapping instruction does seem to induce learning of the principles of place value arithmetic. However, only about half (9 of 16) of the children in the two studies combined made progress in understanding in the course of this instruction, and only 6 children demonstrated nearly complete understanding of the basic principles of composition, partition, and compensation. We address here the question of what produced these wide individual differences in learning, considering several hypotheses: (1) differences in entering knowledge determine who will learn from instruction; (2) differences in amount of instruction determine who will learn; (3) differences in block manipulation determine who will learn; (4) differences in mastery of the mapping procedure determine who will learn; and (5) differences in verbalization during instruction determine who will learn.

Differences in Entering Knowledge.   A frequent finding in research on children's learning (e.g., Inhelder, Sinclair, & Bovet, 1974; Siegler, 1976) is that learners tend to improve only a level or two in understanding or skill in the course of a single, relatively brief intervention. This tendency toward gradual learning is consonant both with a hierarchical theory of acquisition of new competencies (cf. Gagne, 1962) and with cognitive theories that stress the need for consolidating and reorganizing new knowledge before it is fully appropriated and available for participation in subsequent stages of learning. In light of this, a first question for us is whether the children we observed also progressed only gradually. Inspection of Fig. 2.8 suggests that this is not strictly the case. There is some evidence that beginning at an extremely low level of understanding (i.e., at level 1) made it difficult or impossible to profit fully from mapping instruction. Only two children began at level 1, and neither progressed beyond level 2.

On the other hand, of the children who reached level 5 on the delayed posttest, four had begun at level 2, and two at level 3. These children made very substantial progress and were not limited to moving a single level. Examined another way, of the nine children who began at level 2, four (nearly half) moved to level 5, four made no progress at all, and only one child (Den) moved up a single level. Clearly, a level 2 starting position did not predict the final level of learning. Much the same can be said for a level 3 starting position: Of four children, two moved to level 5 and two stayed at level 3.

Differences in Amount of Instruction.   Because the instruction was adapted to differences in children's responses, there were some variations in the length of sessions and number of problems given to different children. In addition, the children in the second mapping group had considerably longer instructional sessions. It is reasonable to suppose that sheer differences in amount of instructional interaction might account for some of the differences in learning that we observed among the children. Table 2.5 shows the average length of the mapping interviews and the average number of problems worked for children in Groups 1 and 2. The groups are further subdivided into learners—those who reached level 5 on the delayed posttest (six children in all)—and nonlearners—those who did not (ten children). As is shown in this table, children in Group 2 had very much longer instructional sessions, as measured in number of lines in the protocol transcription. This greater amount of instruction is also reflected in differences between the groups in the number of problems worked during instruction.

Four of the seven Group 2 children reached level 5, but only two of the nine Group 1 children did (see Fig. 2.8). There is thus some reason to believe that the greater amount of teaching is at least partly responsible for greater amounts of learning. This interpretation seems to be further supported when we compare learners and nonlearners within Group 2. We see that the learners had longer interviews and worked more problems. On the other hand, time spent and prob-

TABLE 2.5
Length of Interview

	Group		
	1	*2*	*1 and 2*
Total Number of Lines in Protocol			
Learners	259	764	596
Nonlearners	321	550	390
Learners and Nonlearners	307	673	
Total Number of Problems Worked			
Learners	7.0	12.0	10.4
Nonlearners	8.0	9.6	9.4
Learners and Nonlearners	8.7	10.9	

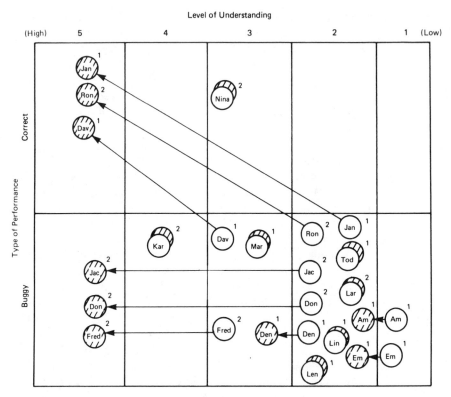

FIG. 2.8.   Students from Mapping groups in Studies I and II at pretest ○ and delayed posttest ⊘.

lems worked did not account for differences in learning in Group 1. There we saw no real differences between learners and nonlearners. We can conclude, therefore, that additional time and more problems are favorable to greater degrees of learning but cannot insure that learning. We need to look more deeply to give a fuller account of differences in learning outcomes.

Manipulation of the Blocks During Instruction.   A component of the mapping instruction that may be related to learning is the amount of time spent manipulating the blocks. It could be argued that a certain amount of handling of the blocks is necessary in order for children to form a mental representation of written subtraction that includes the semantics of the blocks. To assess this, we examined the ratio of block moves by the child to the total number of lines in the protocol. Moving the blocks took only 4 to 10% of the interview time, and nonlearners in both groups manipulated the blocks more than the learners did (9 vs. 5%). Block handling does not in itself account for learning.

Differences in Mastery During Instruction.   It is possible that, despite attempts to adapt the instruction to the individual child, some children were moved too quickly through the successive steps of the mapping instruction plan and were not given enough time to master the elements of mapping that are essential to developing understanding of the written procedure. This might account for their failure to learn the principles.

There are several possible measures of mastery in the course of instruction. One is the extent to which a child smoothly performed the alternation between blocks and writing that is at the heart of mapping instruction. Because the experimenter intervened with prompts or corrections whenever the child failed to alternate smoothly and with the correct moves, we can use the number of interventions by the experimenter on critical problems as a measure of smoothness. One critical problem is the last problem before fading began. This was the last problem on which the children themselves manipulated the blocks, and it was presumed that they could perform the mapping before the experimenter began to fade out the blocks.

In fact, there was no clear relationship between the number of prompts and learning. On the average, the learners were given slightly more prompts than the nonlearners (4.3 vs. 4.0, respectively). In Group 2 this pattern was magnified, with learners receiving almost twice as many prompts as nonlearners (4.8 vs. 2.7). However, in Group 1, the pattern was reversed, with the learners receiving *fewer* prompts than the nonlearners (3.5 vs. 4.6). It appears, then, that mastery of the mapping procedure, as measured by number of prompts given, was neither necessary nor sufficient for learning.

Another way to examine mastery levels is to look at the number of errors made during learning. Errors included incorrect moves in blocks or writing and incorrect statements of what the child planned to do next. One of the most common errors was attempting to do steps in the mapping procedure in the wrong order, such as trying to do all of the borrowing in writing before doing the corresponding block trades. Other types of errors included choosing blocks of the wrong denomination, for example subtracting units blocks instead of tens blocks, and recording a trade by placing the increment mark in the wrong column. On the last problem prior to fading, learners in both groups actually made more errors than nonlearners (2.5 vs. 0.8 in Group 1, 2.0 vs. 0.3 in Group 2). This finding, then, confirms our conclusion that mastery of the mapping *procedure* is a poor indicator of whether or not a child will learn from the instruction.

Verbalization of Quantities During Instruction.   We had hypothesized on the basis of the performance of Group 1 that frequent verbalization of quantities during mapping is important for acquiring understanding of written subtraction. Therefore, in Group 2 we attempted to increase the number of verbalizations of quantities by asking more questions during mapping. For example, if a child finished writing the following marks on the minuend, $\overset{2}{\cancel{3}}\,\overset{9}{\cancel{0}}{}^12$ and did not de-

TABLE 2.6
Verbalizations of Quantity

	Group		
	1	*2*	*1 and 2*
Total Number of Verbalizations			
Learners	76	120	105
Nonlearners	72	111	84
Learners and Nonlearners	73	116	
Number of Correct Verbalizations			
Learners	52.0	86.2	74.8
Nonlearners	48.4	69.7	54.8
Learners and Nonlearners	49.2	79.1	
Ratio Correct to Total Verbalizations			
Learners	.68	.76	.73
Nonlearners	.69	.62	.67
Learners and Nonlearners	.68	.70	

scribe what he or she had written, the experimenter would ask what the 9 above the 0 meant, or how much the 1 next to the 2 was worth. There were three types of responses to these questions, either correct (e.g., answering "9 tens" to the first question), incorrect (e.g., "9 units"), or ambiguous (e.g., if a child said the 12 was worth "12" and not "12 units"). We expected that only a large amount of correct verbalization would facilitate learning.

Table 2.6 shows the total number of verbalizations, the number of correct verbalizations, and the ratio of correct to total verbalizations. We see that Group 2 made about one and one-half times as many verbalizations as Group 1 (116 vs. 73) and that, averaged over both groups, learners made more verbalizations than nonlearners (105 vs. 84). Thus, verbalization is associated with learning. However, is it quantity verbalization in general or only correct verbalization that produces learning? We can see in the second panel of Table 2.6 that Group 2 had more correct verbalizations than Group 1 and learners had more than nonlearners. Furthermore, the third panel shows that learners had a higher ratio than nonlearners of correct verbalizations to total verbalizations (.73 vs. .67). Therefore, it is *correct* verbalization that produces learning, probably because the correct verbalizers were attending more to the quantities involved in borrowing and were rehearsing the correct place value frequently.

The evidence also shows that it is the sheer *amount* of correct verbalization that is associated with learning rather than its density. We found that learners and nonlearners had about the same ratio of correct verbalization to number of lines in the protocol (.14 and .15, respectively). They also had the same ratio of total verbalization to length of interview (.24).

This leads us to the question of whether the learners were mainly responding to the experimenter's questions about the values or whether they were naming the values spontaneously as they worked. In Group 1 the learners frequently stated the correct values spontaneously, that is, their ratio of prompted to total correct verbalizations was low (.37). However, in Group 2 the learners were being prompted more often than the nonlearners in either Group 1 or Group 2 (.66 vs. .46 and .55). One conclusion we can draw from this is that frequent questioning by the instructor is an acceptable means to get the children to verbalize more. Put another way, the instructor does not have to wait for the child to verbalize on her or his own but can intervene positively by asking many questions.

Discussion.   We have attempted in this section to construct an explanation of why some of the children who received mapping instruction improved in their understanding of the principles of subtraction on the posttest and why others did not. We considered several hypotheses and were led to conclude that the child's initial level of understanding manipulation of blocks and mastery of the mapping routine itself did not predict who learned from the instruction. What seemed to characterize the learners was having longer interviews and using this added time specifically to make more *correct verbalizations of the quantities* involved in borrowing. Our results leave open the possibility that better learners evoke more attention from the experimenter, and thus longer instructional sessions. However, the fact that very specific aspects of the exchange, rather than sheer length, seem to be responsible for learning allows us to make relatively strong suggestions for instructional interventions. In particular, the fact that experimenter-prompted verbalizations of quantity produced as much learning as spontaneous ones suggests that teachers can play a very active role in directing children's attention to the quantitative "meaning" of arithmetic notations.

VI.   PROCEDURES AND UNDERSTANDING: CONCLUDING THOUGHTS

The results of our instructional studies raise important questions about the relationship between procedures and understanding in learning. Consider first what we have learned about the processes involved in mapping instruction itself. Our initial idea about how mapping instruction might work evolved from research on learning by analogy (Anderson, Greeno, Kline, & Neves, 1981; Gentner, 1980) and from a computer simulation of one child's learning from mapping instruction (Resnick, Greeno, & Rowland, 1980). The idea was that the child came to mapping instruction with a mental representation of subtraction in blocks that was attached to a rich knowledge base, including the principles of subtraction discussed in this chapter. The child also entered instruction with a mental representation of written subtraction that was purely syntactic in nature. According to this hypothesis, the detailed, step-by-step alternation between the two routines would allow the child to attach to the written symbols the principles he or she already knew with respect to the blocks. This would happen, according to our hypothesis, because the child would come to think of the written symbols as representing the blocks—thus the emphasis in our instruction on using the writing to *record* the results of blocks actions. According to this hypothesis, a smooth integration of the blocks and writing procedures would be necessary, if not sufficient, for understanding of written arithmetic to emerge. One would also expect manipulation of the blocks during instruction to contribute to understanding. Yet we have seen that smooth performance of the blocks-writing alternation is not necessary for understanding to develop and that nonlearners actually manipulated the blocks more than learners.

These findings seem to require that we reject the notion that understanding is transferred directly from blocks to the written arithmetic system as a result of mapping instruction. Instead of attention to the blocks as such, it seems to be attention to the *quantities* that are manipulated in both blocks and writing that produces learning. This seems the most likely interpretation of the fact that verbalization of quantities during instruction shows the strongest relationship to learning. It raises in turn the question of whether blocks—and the mapping procedure—play any important role at all in learning. Perhaps any discussion of the quantities manipulated in written arithmetic, without any reference to the blocks analog, would be just as successful in teaching the principles that underlie written subtraction.

On this point we can only speculate, as our research included no instructional treatment in which quantities were discussed in the absence of blocks. We believe, however, that mapping between blocks and writing may play an important role in learning by helping children to develop an *abstraction*—a higher level representation—that encompasses both blocks and writing. If the analogy between blocks and writing is clear, as it is likely to be when step-by-step mapping is required, then a condition is created in which it is reasonable to construct a new cognitive entity that is neither blocks nor writing, but could be used to characterize both. To do this, one would have to decide exactly what the blocks and the writing have in common, that is, what it is that makes the mapping possible. In the present study, it is the *quantities* represented by blocks and written numerals, together with parallel exchanges among quantities that permits the mapping. On this analysis, the value of mapping instruction would lie in the fact that it sets up conditions in which quantities and exchanges among quantities are likely to be encoded in the context of doing written arithmetic.

Yet even this revised hypothesis about how learners might use the correspondences between two procedures to construct a new mental representation must be treated with caution in light of our finding that even high levels of understanding did not reliably suppress buggy calculation performances. We began our instructional experiments with the assumption that if we could successfully induce higher levels of understanding of an arithmetic procedure, then errors in procedural performance that seemed to derive from the failure to apply certain basic mathematical principles would disappear. The results of our instructional experiments force us to abandon this assumption. Quite obviously, the children did not always call upon all of their relevant knowledge when doing calculation. We need now to consider why this should be and what it implies for a theory of procedural learning and instruction.

Why did some of the children fail to apply their understanding of the mathematical principles that underlie written subtraction to the performance of subtraction calculations? It is not because their knowledge of principles was too abstract or too distant from the particular application. Our children's understanding was invoked in the context of the same procedure they would later perform, and the evidence we used to assess understanding was ability to analyze and justify elements of the procedure. We know that the children in question had the ability to apply the principles to written subtraction calculation. Nevertheless, they failed to do so when they were performing the calculation. To explain this phenomenon, it is useful to combine the distinction made earlier in this chapter between symbolic representations and quantity representations of arithmetic with a commonly made distinction between automated performances and strategic or deliberately controlled ones (e.g., LaBerge & Samuels, 1974; Shiffrin & Schneider, 1977).

Syntactic and Semantic Representations.   As we have noted, the best theory we have for the origin of buggy performances is Brown and VanLehn's (1982) repair theory. The repair theory program produces bugs by generating repairs and checking them against critics. All the critics in the reported program are syntactic in nature, that is, they reflect rules for symbol manipulation but do not embody any knowledge of quantity principles. If we assume that this is also true of children who generate buggy algorithms, then it seems reasonable to say that our instruction represented an effort to insert some "semantic critics" into the repair process, critics that would require that quantities be maintained across exchanges and the like.

What happens if we try to model the effects of instruction by adding to the repair theory program a set of critics that reflect the quantity principles that would reject buggy repairs? Careful consideration of the program suggests that it is not possible to add the new semantic critics without making much more fundamental changes in the program (VanLehn, personal communication). This is because the present program treats subtraction as a system of operations on symbols rather than as a system of operations on quantities. It recognizes which symbolic marks need to be made to do the incrementing and decrementing involved in borrowing, but it does not know that when it puts an increment mark in the units column it is adding 10 or that when it decrements the number in the hundreds column by 1 it is really subtracting 100. This being the case, a critic that checks whether the total quantity has been maintained has nothing to attend to: The program has no representation at all either of the total quantity or of the quantities being transferred in the course of a borrow operation. To incorporate critics that refer to principles of quantity, such as the ones discussed in this chapter, it would be necessary to fundamentally change the entire way that the program represents subtraction to itself.

Representation During Deliberate and Automated Performance.   Our results suggest that the children who learned the principles changed their representation of subtraction from a purely syntactic one in which symbols are manipulated to a more semantic one in which operations are made on quantities. But this new representation was not evoked during automated performance of written subtraction. During both training and testing, subjects were invited to reflect on the subtraction procedure, to perform in a highly controlled, strategic manner. Yet unless the new, semantic representation of subtraction was also evoked in the context of automated performance, the newly acquired semantic critics would not be able to recognize violations of principles during that performance. Bugs, then, would not be suppressed during automated performance. Put another way, if, when they are doing routine calculation, children do not represent the problem as involving quantities but only as digits to be manipulated, then there is no simple way for them to apply their newly learned principles. They must first interrupt their normal performance to *re-represent* the problem for themselves as one involving operations on quantities. But this means giving up all the efficiency of an automated skill and requires paying attention to every step.

A. Instruction for Skill and Understanding

With respect to instruction, this interpretation would lead us to conclude that simply explaining and demonstrating the principles that underlie a procedure to children would not have much of an effect on their calculation performance. Even improving children's understanding to the point where they could construct explanations themselves could not be counted on to eliminate incorrect performance once children had adopted a more or less automatic procedure. For children such as those in our experiment, who have already acquired relatively automatic (albeit buggy) calculation routines, our findings suggest that learning principles alone probably will not be enough to correct calculation errors.

There seems a good possibility that early focus on the principles of a procedural domain and an effort to help children derive procedures from these principles might prevent buggy rules from ever becoming automated. Current work by Champagne and her colleagues (Champagne & Rogalska-Saz, 1984) is exploring this possibility for the domain of place value arithmetic. Champagne's group has developed an extensive computer-based instructional program that teaches children how total quantities and exchanges among the parts of quantities are represented in decimal notation. The program provides up to 15 hours of instruction on these principles prior to introduction of the calculation algorithm itself. Preliminary evidence suggests that the program succeeds well in inducing understanding of the principles as they apply to decimal notation. If it also succeeds in blocking the emergence of buggy calculation procedures, it will imply that more sustained attention to the basic principles of the number system and to how they are incorporated into written numeration would be worthwhile not only for building understanding but also for inducing procedural skill. Most arithmetic textbooks do attempt to explain and demonstrate the rationale for carrying and borrowing, often using pictorial representations resembling Dienes blocks. However, instructional attention passes quickly to efficient calculation, thereby probably encouraging automation of calculation rules that are not well linked to the principles. If Champagne's preliminary results are a guideline, achieving the desired results will require much more extensive attention to the principles than is now common, and much more explicit linkage of principles to written notation.

Another possible approach to the problem of linking understanding to procedural skill is to design instruction that invokes and maintains a generally reflective attitude toward calculation that would include thinking about how the basic principles apply to each step of a calculation procedure. Such instruction would be in the spirit of current research on teaching self-monitoring skills for complex tasks such as reading comprehension (see Palincsar & Brown, 1984). Our mapping instruction did not systematically do this. At the very end of the mapping sequence, children were asked to perform only the written subtraction while thinking about the steps "as if they were writing down what one did with the blocks." The protocols of the instructional sessions suggest that only some children reflected in this way. Furthermore, thinking about writing as a record of work with blocks does not automatically ensure that one is thinking about the *principles* that underlie both block representation and writing. Our instruction thus did not fully test the possibilities for teaching children to reflect on the principles that justify calculation procedures.

In the absence of further tests, our results suggest that if error-free calculation is to be achieved, attention to appropriate forms of automated—that is, *non-reflective*—practice will be needed along with attention to building understanding. Even early and powerful principle-based instruction, or successful cultivation of a reflective attitude toward calculation algorithms, seem unlikely to ensure that a complex, quantity representation of arithmetic will be maintained as a procedure becomes automated. Indeed, continued reflection is contradictory to the very notion of automaticity—which confers power precisely because continued monitoring and attention to a performance is *not* needed. The principles, in other words, may play less of a role in routine skilled performance of arithmetic than is sometimes proposed. On the other hand, our results suggest that analysis of arithmetic procedures may be a powerful way of learning core mathematical principles. If so, it may turn out that acquiring some level of procedural skill is an important step in learning to understand arithmetic.

ACKNOWLEDGMENTS

The research reported herein was funded by the National Science Foundation (NSF) Grant Number SED-8112453, and the National Institute of Education (NIE). The opinions expressed in this chapter do not necessarily reflect the position or policy of the granting agency, and no official endorsement should be inferred.

REFERENCES

Anderson, J. R., Greeno, J. G., Kline, P. J., & Neves, D. M. (1981). Learning to plan in geometry. In J. R. Anderson (Ed.), *Cognitive skills and their acquisition*. Hillsdale, NJ: Lawrence Erlbaum Associates.

Ashcraft, M. H., & Battaglia, J. (1978). Cognitive arithmetic: Evidence for retrieval and decision processes in mental addition. *Journal of Experimental Psychology: Human Learning and Memory, 4*(5), 527–538.

Brown, J. S., & Burton, R. R. (1978). Diagnostic models for procedural bugs in basic mathematical skills. *Cognitive Science, 2,* 155–192.

Brown, J. S., & VanLehn, K. (1980). Repair theory: A generative theory of bugs in procedural skills. *Cognitive Science, 4,* 379–426.

Brown, J. S., & VanLehn, K. (1982). Toward a generative theory of bugs in procedural skills. In T. P. Carpenter, J. M. Moser, & T. A. Romberg (Eds.), *Addition and subtraction: A cognitive perspective*. Hillsdale, NJ: Lawrence Erlbaum Associates.

Brownell, W. A. (1935). Psychological considerations in the learning and the teaching of arithmetic. *The teaching of arithmetic, the tenth yearbook of the National Council of Teachers of Mathematics*. New York: Teachers College, Columbia University.

Brownell, W. A. (1941). The evaluation of learning in arithmetic. In *Arithmetic in general education*. 16th Yearbook of the National Council of Teachers of Mathematics. Washington, DC: N.C.T.M.

Brownell, W. A. (1964). *Arithmetic abstractions: The movement toward conceptual maturity under differing systems of instruction* (Cooperative Research Project No. OE 2-10-103). Berkeley, CA: University of California.

Burton, R. B. (1981). DEBUGGY: Diagnosis of errors in basic mathematical skills. In D. H. Sleeman & J. S. Brown (Eds.), *Intelligent tutoring systems*. London: Academic Press.

Buswell, G. T. (1926). *Diagnostic studies in arithmetic*. Chicago: University of Chicago Press.

Champagne, A. B., & Rogalska-Saz, J. (1984). Computer-based numeration instruction. In V. P. Hansen (Ed.), *Computers in mathematics education*. 1984 Yearbook: National Council of Teachers of Mathematics.

Gagne, R. M. (1962). The acquisition of knowledge. *Psychological Review, 69*(4), 355–365.

Gentner, D. (1980). *The structure of analogical models in science* (Bolt Beranek and Newman Report No. 4451). Cambridge, MA: Bolt Beranek & Newman.

Greeno, J. G., Riley, M. S., & Gelman, R. (1984). Conceptual competence and children's counting. *Cognitive Psychology, 16*(1), 94–143.

Groen, G. J., & Parkman, J. M. (1972). A chronometric analysis of simple addition. *Psychological Review, 79*(4), 329–343.

Groen, G. J., & Resnick, L. B. (1977). Can preschool children invent addition algorithms? *Journal of Educational Psychology, 69,* 645–652.

Inhelder, B., Sinclair, H., & Bovet, M. (1974). *Learning and the development of cognition.* Cambridge, MA: Harvard University Press.

LaBerge, D., & Samuels, S. J. (1974). Toward a theory of automatic information processing in reading. *Cognitive Psychology, 6,* 293–323.

Lankford, F. G. (1972, October). *Some computational strategies of seventh grade pupils* (Final report, Project No. 2-C-013). HEW/OE National Center for Educational Research and Development and the Center for Advanced Studies, University of Virginia.

Omanson, S. F. (1982). *Instruction by mapping: Its effects on understanding and skill in subtraction.* Unpublished master's thesis, University of Pittsburgh, Learning Research and Development Center.

Palincsar, A. S., & Brown, A. L. (1984). Reciprocal teaching of comprehension-fostering and comprehension-monitoring activities. *Cognition and Instruction, 1*(2), 117–175.

Resnick, L. B. (1982). Syntax and semantics in learning to subtract. In T. Carpenter, J. Moser, & T. Romberg (Eds.), *Addition and subtraction: A cognitive perspective.* Hillsdale, NJ: Lawrence Erlbaum Associates.

Resnick, L. B., & Ford, W. W. (1981). *The psychology of mathematics for instruction.* Hillsdale, NJ: Lawrence Erlbaum Associates.

Resnick, L. B., Greeno, J. G., & Rowland, J. (1980). *MOLLY: A model of learning from mapping instruction.* Unpublished manuscript, University of Pittsburgh, Learning Research and Development Center.

Shiffrin, R. M., & Schneider, W. (1977). Controlled and automatic human information processing (Vol. 2). Perceptual learning, automatic attending, and a general theory. *Psychological Review, 84,* 127–190.

Siegler, R. S. (1976). Three aspects of cognitive development. *Cognitive Psychology, 8,* 481–520.

Simon, H. A. (1976). Identifying basic abilities underlying intelligent performance of complex tasks. In L. B. Resnick (Ed.), *The nature of intelligence.* Hillsdale, NJ: Lawrence Erlbaum Associates.

Young, R. M., & O'Shea, T. (1981). Errors in children's subtraction. *Cognitive Science, 5*(2), 153–177.

3 The Psychology of Verbal Comprehension

Robert J. Sternberg
Yale University

I. INTRODUCTION

Verbal comprehension refers to a person's ability to understand linguistic materials, such as newspapers, magazines, textbooks, lectures, and the like. Verbal comprehension has been recognized as an integral part of intelligence in both psychometric theories (e.g., Guilford, 1967; Thurstone, 1938; Vernon, 1971) and information-processing theories (e.g., Carroll, 1976; Hunt, 1978; Sternberg, 1980) and has, under a variety of aliases, been an important topic of research in both differential and experimental psychology.

The theoretical construct of verbal comprehension can be and has been operationalized in various ways. Most often, it is directly measured by tests of vocabulary, reading comprehension, and general information. Indeed, vocabulary has been recognized not only as an excellent measure of verbal comprehension, but also as one of the best single indicators of a person's overall level of intelligence (e.g., Jensen, 1980; Matarazzo, 1972). The importance of verbal comprehension in general, and of vocabulary in particular, to the measurement of verbal intelligence is shown by the fact that both of the two major individual scales of intelligence—the Stanford–Binet and the Wechsler—contain vocabulary items, and by the fact that many group tests also contain vocabulary items (which may be presented in any of a number of forms, e.g., synonyms, antonyms, verbal analogies with very low-frequency terms, and so on). Because of its centrality both to the theory and measurement of intelligence and to everyday interactions with the environment, it seems important to understand the antecedents of observable individual differences in vocabulary levels.

The theory of verbal comprehension proposed in this chapter comprises two parts. The first is a subtheory of *decontextualization,* which accounts for how an aspect of verbal comprehension—learning from context—develops. Issues of inferring meaning from the larger passage and from word structure, as well as those of knowledge acquisition, are treated. The second is a subtheory of information processing in verbal comprehension, that is, of the skills one uses in one's current verbal functioning, including metacognitive or executive skills. Thus, the first accounts for how ability becomes "crystallized"; the second accounts for how crystallized ability is utilized in information processing. Each of these two subtheories is considered in turn. In order for my presentation of the theory of the acquisition of verbal comprehension skills to be fully meaningful, it must first be placed in the context of other efforts toward the same or similar goals. There have been three major approaches to understanding the origins and development of verbal comprehension. These three major approaches are now considered briefly.

II. ALTERNATIVE COGNITIVE APPROACHES TO THE ACQUISITION OF VERBAL COMPREHENSION SKILLS

The three major approaches to the acquisition of verbal comprehension skills are a "knowledge-based" approach, a "bottom-up" approach, and a "top-down" approach. The knowledge-based approach deals with the role of prior information in the acquisition of new information. The bottom-up approach deals with speed of execution of certain very basic mechanistic cognitive processes. The top-down approach deals with higher order utilization of cues in complex verbal materials.

A. The Knowledge-based Approach

The knowledge-based approach assigns a central role to old knowledge in the acquisition of new knowledge. Although "knowledge" is often referred to in the sense of domain-specific information, the knowledge-based approach can also encompass research focusing on general world knowledge, knowledge of structures or classes of text (as in story grammars), and knowledge about strategies for knowledge acquisition and application (see, e.g., Bisanz & Voss, 1981). Proponents of this approach differ in the respective roles they assign to knowledge and process in the acquisition of new knowledge. A fairly strong version of the approach is taken by Keil (1984), who argues for the primacy of knowledge over process in cognitive development.

Proponents of the knowledge-based approach usually cite instances of differences between expert and novice performance—in verbal and other domains—that seem to derive principally from knowledge differences rather than from processing differences. For example, Keil (1984) suggests that development of ability to use metaphor and morphemes seems to be due more to differential knowledge states than to differential use of processes or speed of process execution. Chi (1978) has shown that whether children's recall performance is better than that of adults depends on knowledge of a domain and, particularly, upon the relative expertise of the children and adults in a domain. Chiesi, Spilich, and Voss (1979) and Spilich, Vesonder, Chiesi, and Voss (1979) have shown the importance of prior knowledge about baseball in the acquisition of new information about this topic. In related research, Chase and Simon (1973) found that differences between expert and novice performance in chess seemed largely to be due to differential knowledge structures rather than processes (but see Charness, 1981).

A rather extensive study of the relations between verbal comprehension ability and word knowledge was conducted by Curtis (1981). Curtis assessed levels of word knowledge for each of 37 college students for each of 24 stem words and 72 answer options. She did her analysis in terms of three levels of word knowledge: (1) decoding, measured by the percentage of words that each subject was able to read aloud correctly, (2) semantic familiarity, which was defined as the percentage of words for which a subject, in addition to correct decoding, could produce any accurate semantic information at all, regardless of the nature of that information, and (3) semantic precision, which was the percentage of responses for which the subject provided a correct decoding and a synonym or correct explanation of the word's meaning. Scores from a 115-item multiple-choice vocabulary test (which drew from several standardized tests) were regressed on each of the three components of word knowledge plus speed of lexical access. Curtis found that, overall, the vocabulary test seemed most to measure word familiarity. In a related analysis, Curtis regressed Verbal Scholastic Aptitude Test scores on measures of familiarity, precision, and speed. Overall, precision had the highest weight and speed the lowest (and nonsignificant) weight. Interestingly, however, there was an apparent interaction between skill level of the subjects and the obtained regression weights. For high verbal subjects, precision had a slightly higher standardized regression weight than did familiarity, whereas for lower verbal subjects, familiarity had a much higher regression weight than did precision. Speed had a trivial weight in each case. These results suggest that for a difficult verbal ability test such as the SAT, different skills may be measured at different points along the ability continuum.

I have no argument with the position that the knowledge base figures largely in differences in performance between experts and novices in both verbal and nonverbal domains. But accounts that slight the role of information processing in the development of expertise seem to beg the question of how the differences in knowledge states came about in the first place. For example, why did some people acquire better vocabularies than others? Or in the well-studied domain of chess, why is it that of two individuals given equally intensive and extensive exposure to the game, one will acquire the knowledge structures needed for expertise, and the other will not? In sum, I accept the importance of old knowledge in the acquisition of new knowledge. But I do not believe the overemphasis on process that characterized some previous research should be replaced by an overemphasis on knowledge in present research. Rather, it should be recognized that knowledge and process work interactively in complex ways. What is needed to understand what these ways are?

B. The Bottom-up Approach

Bottom-up research has emerged from the tradition of investigation initiated by Earl Hunt (e.g., Hunt, 1978, 1980; Hunt, Lunneborg, & Lewis, 1975) and has been elaborated by a number of other investigators (e.g., Jackson & McClelland, 1979; Keating & Bobbitt, 1978; see also Perfetti & Lesgold, 1977, for a related approach). According to Hunt (1978), two types of processes underlie verbal comprehension ability—knowledge-based processes and mechanistic (information-free) processes; Hunt's approach has emphasized the latter. Hunt et al. (1975) studied three aspects of what they called "current information processing" that they believed to be key determinants of individual differences in developed verbal ability. These were: "(a) sensitivity of overlearned codes to arousal by incoming stimulus information, (b) the accuracy with which temporal tags can be assigned, and hence order information can be processed, and (c) the speed with which the internal representations in STM and intermediate term memory (ITM, memory for events occurring over minutes) can be created, integrated, and altered" (p. 197). The basic hypothesis motivating this work is that individuals varying in verbal ability differ even in these low-level mechanistic skills—skills that are free from any contribution of disparate knowledge or experience. Intelligence tests are hypothesized to measure these basic information-processing skills indirectly by measuring their products directly, both in terms of their past contribution to the acquisition and storage of knowledge (such as vocabulary), and their present contribution in the current processing of information.

Perfetti (1983) has suggested that four basic, bottom-up verbal processes underlie some, but not all, individual differences in reading ability. These processes are (1) word decoding (i.e., the transformation of a printed input into one or more of its corresponding linguistic forms), (2) letter recognition (i.e., recognizing the constituent letters of a word), (3) name retrieval (i.e., accessing the location in memory and producing the name of a verbal string), and (4) semantic access (i.e., activation of the meaning components of a word stored in memory). In a series of experiments, Perfetti has demonstrated that each of these skills is related to measures of verbal ability and reading skill (e.g., Perfetti & Hogaboam, 1975).

In a typical experiment employing the bottom-up approach to verbal comprehension, subjects are presented with the Posner and Mitchell (1967) letter-matching task. The task comprises two experimental conditions, a physical-match condition and a name-match condition. In the physical-match condition, subjects are presented with pairs of letters that either are or are not physical matches (e.g., "AA" or "bb" versus "Aa" or "Ba"). In the name-match condition, subjects are presented with pairs of letters that either are or are not name matches (e.g., "Aa," "BB," or "bB" versus "Ab," "ba," or "bA"). Subjects must identify the letter pair either as a physical match (or mismatch) or as a name match (or mismatch) as rapidly as possible. The typical finding in these experiments is that the difference between mean name match and physical match times within a group of subjects correlates about −.3 with scores on a test of verbal ability.

The finding described earlier seems to be widely replicable, but its interpretation is a matter of dispute (Carroll, 1981; Hogaboam & Pellegrino, 1978; Sternberg, 1981). I have been and remain concerned that .3-level correlations are abundant in both the abilities and personality literatures (indeed, they are rather low as ability correlations go) and provide a relatively weak basis for causal inference. A further concern is that most of the studies that have been done on the name minus physical match difference have not used adequate discriminant validation procedures. When such procedures are used, and perceptual speed is considered as well as verbal ability, this difference seems to be much more strongly related to perceptual speed than it is to verbal ability (Cornelius, Willis, Blow, & Baltes, 1983; Lansman, Donaldson, Hunt, & Yantis, 1982), although these findings are subject to alternative interpretations. Thus, the obtained correlation with verbal ability may reflect, at least in part, variance shared with perceptual abilities of the kind that the letter-matching task would seem more likely to measure. But whatever may be the case here, it seems likely that speed of lexical access plays some as yet undetermined role in verbal comprehension.

The role of speed of lexical access seems to increase as the complexity of the decision motivating the access increases. Goldberg, Schwartz, and Stewart (1977) had subjects perform a comparison task at three levels of complexity. The first level was simply physical comparison (e.g., are "A" and "A" a physical match?). The second level was homophone comparison (e.g., are "here" and "hear" a sound match?). The third level was taxonomic-category comparison (e.g., are "cat" and "dog" a match with respect to belonging in the category of animals?). These authors found a greater difference between the performance of preidentified high- and low-verbal subjects on the homophone and taxonomic comparison tasks than on the physical comparison task. The results suggest that the more "top-down" the level of comparison, the greater the difference between high and low verbals.

A similar effect of "level of processing" can be seen in the studies that have been done relating performance on a sentence-picture comparison task to verbal ability (Baddeley, 1968; Hunt, Lunneborg, & Lewis, 1975; Lansman, Donaldson, Hunt, & Yantis, 1982). In this paradigm, initiated by Clark and Chase (1972), subjects are shown a sentence, such as "Plus is above Star," and a picture. They are required to indicate as quickly as possible whether the sentence and picture do or do not correspond. Correlations between latencies on this task and scores on verbal ability tests are typically in the −.4 to −.6 range. These correlations are higher than those obtained for the Posner and Mitchell (1967) task (see Hunt, 1984; Hunt et al., 1975), presumably because the complexity of processing required is greater. These results lead quite naturally to a consideration of the last, "top-down," approach to understanding verbal comprehension skills.

C. Top-down Approach

Top-down processing refers to expectation–or inference-driven processing, or to "knowledge-based" processing, to use Hunt's (1978) terminology. Top-down processing has been an extremely popular focus for research in the past decade, with many researchers attempting to identify and predict the sorts of inferences a person is likely to draw from a text and how these inferences (or lack thereof) will affect text comprehension (see, e.g., Kintsch & van Dijk, 1978; Rieger, 1975; Rumelhart, 1980; Schank & Abelson, 1977). Usually, top-down researchers look at how people combine information actually present in the text with their own store of world knowledge to create a new whole representing the meaning of the text (e.g., Bransford, Barclay, & Franks, 1972).

The first of a small handful of investigators who looked at the use of inference in the acquisition of word meanings from context were Werner and Kaplan (1952), who proposed that learning from context provides a major source of vocabulary development. They devised a task in which subjects were presented with an imaginary word followed by six sentences using that word. The subjects' task was to guess the meaning of the word on the basis of the contextual cues they were given. They found that performance improves gradually with age, although the various processes underlying performance did not necessarily change gradually. They did not, however, provide an explicit model of these processes.

Daalen-Kapteijns and Elshout-Mohr (1981) pursued the Werner-Kaplan approach by having subjects think aloud while solving Werner-Kaplan type problems. They found, among other things, that high- and low-verbal subjects learn word meanings differently, with high verbals performing a deeper analysis of the possibilities for a new word's meaning than low verbals. In particular, the high-verbal subjects used a well-formulated strategy for figuring out word meaning, whereas the low-verbal subjects seemed not to.

Keil (1981) presented children in grades kindergarten, 2, and 4 with simple passages in which an invented word was the topic of discussion, for example: "THROSTLES are great, except when they have to be fixed. And they have to be fixed very often. But it's usually very easy to fix throstles." Subjects were asked what else they knew about the new word (here, "throstle"), and what sorts of things the new word might refer to. Keil found that even the youngest children could make sensible inferences about the general categories the new terms denoted and about their properties (see also Keil, 1979, 1981, 1984).

Jensen (1980) has suggested that vocabulary is an excellent measure of intelligence "because the acquisition of word meanings is highly dependent on the deduction of meaning from the contexts in which the words are encountered" (p. 146). Marshalek (1981) has tested this hypothesis using a faceted vocabulary test, although he did not directly measure learning from context. He found that subjects with low-reasoning ability did, in fact, have major difficulties inferring meanings of words. Moreover, reasoning was related to vocabulary measures at the lower end of the vocabulary difficulty distribution, but not at the higher end. Together, these findings suggest that a certain level of reasoning ability may be prerequisite for extraction of word meaning. Above this level, the benefits of reasoning begin to decrease rapidly.

Quite a different top-down approach to the understanding of verbal comprehension has been taken by Daneman (1984; Daneman & Carpenter, 1980). The theory motivating this research is that functional working-memory capacity—involving complex processing in the working-memory store—is critically involved in individual differences in reading skill. Daneman's study required subjects to read a successive string of unrelated sentences and to memorize the last word in each sentence. For example, one set of three sentences was: (1) He had patronized her when she was a schoolgirl and teased her when she was a student; (2) he had an odd elongated skull, which sat on his shoulders like a pear on a dish; (3) the products of digital electronics will play an important role in your future.

Scores on this span measure are surprisingly low, usually in the range of 3–5 words. More interesting, however, is the fact that scores on the span measure typically correlate in the .4 to .6 range with scores on tests of verbal ability. Even higher correlations have been obtained with scores on measures of ability to integrate linguistic information. It thus appears that Daneman's span measure provides a promising route to understanding the role of working memory in reading.

These three basic approaches to understanding the cognitive bases of verbal comprehension—a knowledge-based one, a bottom-up one, and a top-down one—are complementary, and ultimately each would be necessary to understanding fully the nature and development of verbal comprehension. In the next section, I present our own approach, which is largely top-down in character, to understanding the antecedents and development of verbal comprehension skills.

III. SUBTHEORY OF DECONTEXTUALIZATION: LEARNING FROM CONTEXT AND WORD STRUCTURE

Our first subtheory in the theory of the development of verbal skills emphasizes learning from context and examines the role of word structure in comprehension (see Sternberg & Powell, 1983; Sternberg, Powell, & Kaye, 1983). We believe that the ability to infer the meanings of unfamiliar words from context deserves a prominent place within a discussion of verbal comprehension for three reasons. First, a theory describing how people use context to infer the meanings of words could tell us much about vocabulary building skills. Identifying what types of information people of different ability levels use to construct a tentative definition of a word and how additional information influences a working definition of a word could also tell us about how to train vocabulary acquisition skills. Second, a theory of learning from context can help explain why vocabulary is the single best predictor of verbal intelligence. Our hypothesis is that learning from context reflects important vocabulary acquisition skills, the net products of which could, in theory, be measured by the full extent of one's vocabulary. Thus, according to our view, vocabulary tests are such good predictors of one's overall verbal intelligence because they measure one's ability to acquire new information. Third, a theory of learning from context is useful in illuminating the relationship between the more fluid, inferential aspects of verbal intelligence, usually measured by tests of verbal analogies, and the more crystallized, knowledge-based aspects of verbal intelligence, usually measured by vocabulary tests (see Horn & Cattell, 1966). Learning from context thus provides a way of integrating the two aspects of verbal ability—comprehension and vocabulary—and of placing vocabulary acquisition within the framework of general cognitive theories of language comprehension.

Two basic ideas underlie our theory of learning from context. The first idea pertains to why some verbal concepts are easier to learn than others: The difficulty of learning a new verbal concept is in large part a function of the degree of facilitation (or inhibition) provided by the context in which the new verbal concept is embedded; the same or very similar contextual elements that facilitate (or inhibit) learning are hypothesized also to facilitate (or inhibit) later retrieval of the concept and also its transfer to new situations. The second accounts for why some individuals are better at learning verbal concepts than others: Individual differences in verbal comprehension can be traced in large part to differences in ability to use context, and to be wary of contextual cues that inhibit learning; the same or very similar sources of individual differences are hypothesized for differential ability later to retrieve verbal concepts and to transfer them appropriately to new situations.

The theory distinguishes between two intrinsic characteristics of a passage—contextual cues that convey various types of information about an unknown word, and mediating variables that affect the perceived usefulness of the contextual cues. The contextual cues determine the quality of a definition that theoretically can be inferred for a word from a given context. The mediating variables determine constraints imposed by the relationship between the previously unknown word and the context in which the word occurs that affect how well a given set of cues will be actually utilized. In addition, the theory examines the role of internal cues—information available in the structure of a word via prefixes, suffixes, Latinate stems, etc.—and variables that mediate their use. Moreover, the theory specifies the processes by which the cues and mediating variables are utilized. These various aspects of the theory are now explained in turn.

IV. CONTEXTUAL AND INTERNAL CUES AND THEIR MEDIATING VARIABLES

The first of the subtheories that comprise our theory specifies contextual cues, mediating variables, and processes as the basic categories of influences on the likelihood that meanings of unknown words will be correctly inferred.

A. Contextual Cues

We propose that contextual cues can be classified into eight categories, depending on the information they provide. We make no claim that the eight categories are mutually exclusive, exhaustive, or independent in their functioning. Nor do we claim that they in any sense represent a "true" categorization scheme of context cues. However, this classification scheme is useful in understanding subjects' strategies in deriving meanings of words from context. Not every type of cue will be present in a given context, and even when a cue is present, our theory proposes that the usefulness of the cue will be mediated by the variables described in the next section. The eight categories follow.

1. Temporal Cues. Cues regarding the duration or frequency of X (the unknown word), or regarding when X can occur; alternatively, cues describing X as a temporal property (such as duration or frequency) of some Y (usually a known word in the passage). (Example: I saw the WEX *last night.*)

2. Spatial Cues. Cues regarding the general or specific location of X, or possible locations in which X can sometimes be found; alternatively, cues describing X as a spatial property (such as general or specific location) of some Y. (Example: I saw the WEX *in the forest.*)

3. Value Cues. Cues regarding the worth or desirability of X, or regarding the kinds of affects X arouses; alternatively, cues describing X as a value (such as worth or desirability) of some Y. (Example: I was *afraid of* the WEX.)

4. Stative Descriptive Cues.   Cues regarding properties of X (such as size, shape, color, odor, feel, etc.); alternatively, cues describing X as a stative descriptive property (e.g., shape or color) of some Y. (Example: The WEX was *gray.*)

5. Functional Descriptive Cues.   Cues regarding possible purposes of X, actions X can perform, or potential uses of X; alternatively, cues describing X as a possible purpose, action, or use of Y. (Example: The WEX *snarled* at me.)

6. Causal/Enablement Cues.   Cues regarding possible causes of or enabling conditions for X; alternatively, cues describing X as a possible cause or enabling condition for Y. (Example: The WEX *made me run for my life!*)

7. Class Membership Cues.   Cues regarding one or more classes to which X belongs, or other members of one or more classes of which X is a member; alternatively, cues describing X as a class of which Y is a member. (Example: The WEX is a *canine.*)

8. Equivalence Cues.   Cues regarding the meaning of X, or contrasts (such as antonymy) to the meaning of X; alternatively, cues describing X as the meaning (or a contrast in meaning) of some Y. (Example: The WEX I saw, like most other *wolves,* was fierce.)

Consider a sentence that contains several such cues, "At dawn, the BLEN arose on the horizon and shone brightly." "At dawn" provides a temporal cue; "arose" provides a functional descriptive cue; "on the horizon" provides a spatial cue; "shone" provides another functional descriptive cue; finally, "brightly" provides a stative descriptive cue. With all these different cues, most people would find it very easy to figure out that the neologism BLEN is a synonym for SUN.

B. Mediating Variables

Whereas the contextual cues provide information that might be used to infer the meaning of a word from a given verbal context, problems remain, for instance, of recognition of the applicability of a description to a given concept, weeding out irrelevant information, and integrating the information into a coherent model of the word's meaning. For this reason, a set of seven mediating variables is also proposed that specifies relations between a previously unknown word and the passage in which it occurs, each of which influences the usefulness of the contextual cues either positively or negatively.

1. Number of Occurrences of the Unknown Word.   The usefulness of a given kind of cue is highly variable and depends largely on the associated constellations of cues for the word. For example, the meaning of a given temporal cue may be enhanced by a spatial cue associated with a subsequent appearance of the unknown word, or the temporal cue may gain in usefulness if it appears more than once in conjunction with the unknown word. On the other hand, multiple occurrences of an unfamiliar word can also be detrimental if the reader has difficulty integrating the information gained from cues surrounding separate appearances of the word, or if only peripheral features of the word are reinforced and are therefore incorrectly interpreted as being of central importance to the meaning of the unfamiliar word.

2. Variability of Contexts in Which Multiple Occurrences of the Unknown Word Appear.   Varied contexts, for example, different kinds of subject matter or different writing styles, and even two distinct illustrations within a text of word usage are likely to supply added information about the unknown word. Variability of contexts increases the likelihood that a wide range of cues will be supplied, and thus increases the probability that a reader will get a full picture of the scope of a given word's meaning. In contrast, mere repetition of a given unknown word in essentially the same context is unlikely to be as helpful as a variable-context repetition, because few or no really new cues are provided regarding the word's meaning. However, variability can also present a problem in some situations and for some individuals: If cues are difficult to integrate across appearances of the word, or if an individual has difficulties in making such integrations, then the variable repetitions may actually obfuscate the word's meaning.

3. Importance of the Unknown Word to Understanding the Context In Which It Is Embedded.   If determining a given unknown word's meaning is judged to be necessary for understanding the surrounding material, the reader's incentive for figuring it out is increased. If the word is judged to be unimportant to understanding what one is reading (or hearing), one is unlikely to invest any great effort in figuring out what the word means. Whereas in explicit vocabulary-training situations, the individual may always be motivated to infer a word's meanings, in real-world situations, this will not be the case. Thus, we need to know the extent to which an individual reader can recognize which words are important to a passage, and which are not. In some cases, it really may not be worth the individual's time to figure out a given word's meaning. Importance varies at particular levels of text organization, so we distinguish between the sentence and paragraph levels. The ability to recognize the significance of a word to a larger passage may be seen as one form of comprehension monitoring of the type studied by Markman (1977, 1979), Flavell (1981), Collins and Smith (1982), and others.

4. Helpfulness of Surrounding Context in Understanding the Meaning of the Unknown Word.   A given cue's helpfulness depends on the nature of the unknown word and upon the location of the cue in the text relative to that word. A temporal cue describing when a *diurnal* event occurs would probably be more helpful than a spatial cue describing where the event occurs in aiding an individual to figure out that "diurnal" means *daily*. In contrast, a spatial cue would probably be more helpful than a temporal cue in figuring out that *ing* is a low-lying pasture. Consider also how the location of the cue relative to the unknown word can affect cue helpfulness. If a given cue occurs in close proximity to the word, then there is probably a relatively high likelihood that the cue's relevance will be recognized. If the cue is separated from the known word by a substantial portion of text, its relevance may never be recognized; indeed, the cue may be misinterpreted as relevant to a more proximal unknown word. Helpfulness may also be mediated by the cue's coming before as opposed to after the unknown word. Rubin (1976), for example, found that context occurring before the placement of a blank in a cloze test was more helpful to figuring out what word should go in the blank than was context occurring after the placement of the blank.

5. Density of Unknown Words. If a reader is confronted with a high density of previously unknown words, he or she may be overwhelmed and be unwilling or unable to use available cues to best advantage. When the density of unknown words is high, it can be difficult to discern which of the cues apply to each of the unknown words. Utilization of a given cue may depend on figuring out the meaning of some other unknown word, in which case the usefulness of that cue (and very likely of other cues as well) is decreased.

6. Concreteness of the Unknown Word and the Surrounding Context. Concrete concepts are generally easier to apprehend, in part because they have a simpler meaning structure. Familiar concrete concepts such as *tree, chair,* and *pencil* are relatively easy to define in ways that would satisfy most people; familiar abstract concepts such as *truth, love,* and *justice,* however, are extremely difficult to define in ways that would satisfy large numbers of people. A concrete concept such as *ing* might appear more opaque embedded in a passage about the nature of reality than it would embedded in a passage about the nature of food sources; similarly, an abstract concept such as *pulchritude* (beauty) might be more easily apprehended in a passage about fashion models than in one about eternal versus ephemeral qualities.

7. Usefulness of Previously Known Information in Cue Utilization. Inevitably, the usefulness of a cue will depend on the extent to which past knowledge can be brought to bear upon the cue and its relation to the unknown word. The usefulness of prior information will depend in large part on a given individual's ability to retrieve the information, to recognize its relevance, and then to apply it appropriately.

C. Knowledge-acquisition Components and Representation of Information

The theory of external decontextualization also relies upon three knowledge-acquisition components, or processes. These processes operate on the contextual cues and their efficacy is determined by the mediating variables.

1. Selective Encoding.   When new words are presented in actual contexts, cues relevant to inferring their meanings, to decontextualization, are embedded within large amounts of irrelevant information. A critical task facing the individual is that of sifting out the "wheat from the chaff": recognizing just what information in the passage is relevant for word decontextualization.

2. Selective Combination.   Selective combination involves combining selectively encoded information to form an integrated, plausible definition of the unknown word. Simply sifting out the relevant cues is often not enough to arrive at a tentative definition of the word: One must know how to combine the cues into an integrated knowledge representation.

3. Selective Comparison.   Selective comparison involves relating newly acquired information to information acquired in the past. Decisions about information to encode and how to combine it are guided by retrieval of old information. A cue will be all but useless if it cannot somehow be related to past knowledge.

Verbal information is theorized to be represented in terms of a network model that is similar in some respects to the node models found in Rumelhart and Norman's (1975) and Collins and Loftus's (1975) models of semantic memory. A given concept is represented as the "center" of a network describing the concept. Nodes describing its properties emanate from the concept. Nodes for different concepts are connected via the concept names, which serve as the origin for nodes with descriptive attributes. Unlike other network models, the kinds of nodes extending from the concept, and from other nodes, correspond to the properties of cues used to understand word meanings, as specified by the proposed theory of cue utilization. For example, spatial cues are fed into (where?) nodes, functional-descriptive cues are fed into (do?) nodes, stative descriptive cues are fed into (look like?) nodes, class membership cues are fed into (what?) nodes, equality cues are fed into (equals?) nodes, and so on. Each node has an associated attribute, e.g., an attribute for (look like?) might be "gray" and an identification of the attribute as being necessary, sufficient, or characteristic of the concept. An example of this form of representation for "kangaroo" is shown in Fig. 3.1.

How is the proposed representation developed during the course of acquisition of a verbal concept? This question is addressable in terms of the cues, mediating variables, and processes in the proposed theory. A general description of the development of representations is presented first, followed by a specific example of how this development occurs. It is assumed that initial processing is done sentence-by-sentence, although further processing may follow if a subject reviews a passage and uses higher order units (e.g., pairs of sentences) as a basis for further understanding. A person begins building up a representation of text as soon as he or she starts reading the text.

The subject begins selective encoding of information about the to-be-defined (target) word from the first sentence in which the word appears. The target word at this point becomes the center point of a new network; characteristic and defining attributes can "grow" into appropriate nodes in working memory. The information also activates matching information stored in long-term-memory networks. The activated knowledge then influences which further facts will be selectively encoded and fed into the nodes in the newly forming network. As more information about the new word is selectively encoded and incorporated, the subject's activated knowledge base in long-term memory is reduced: Concepts that might have helped define the word are excluded by the additional information, and hence can be dropped from active consideration.

When the subject has finished processing all of the information in the passage, he or she will select concepts from the long-term-memory knowledge base whose nodes are still activated. The full network structures for these concepts is then compared to the newly formed network structure. If no such concepts exist (e.g., all concepts in long-term memory have been excluded as possible meanings of the word), the subject will either reprocess the passage, or else view the new network structure as corresponding to a new concept unrelated to any already in long-term memory. If one or more such concepts exist, the subject will compare defining attributes of the unknown word's network to defining attributes of the networks for each of the possible meanings. The subject will then select the activated concept that has the most defining attributes in common with the target concept, create a new concept, or else seek further information. A new concept will be based upon an extension of that concept in long-term memory that most resembles the new one, appropriately modified to take into account nodes in the new representation that do not match the nodes of the old representation. So, for example, if *ing* is found to be closest in its representation to *pasture*, but to differ from *pasture* in having nodes describing the *ing* as low-lying, then *ing* will be defined as a "pasture that is low-lying." In some instances, the given information may allow the individual to propose a definition that he or she knows is more general than the precise one because there was simply insufficient information to restrict the meaning of the new concept.

Errors in understanding the meaning of a new word can occur in at least three ways. First, information about the new word's meaning as provided in the text will inevitably be incomplete. Thus, one may not have sufficient basis for choosing among alternative possible meanings stored in long-term memory, or one may provide a new but incomplete definition. Second, information about the new word's meaning may be misencoded. A cue in the passage may be misconstrued, so that the representation one builds up is simply wrong. Third, information in the passage may be properly encoded but lead to an incorrect representation of the new word because the information is misleading. In such a case, cues may actually serve to lead a subject astray.

The ideas expressed earlier can be illustrated by tracing the development of a representation of a word, as in Fig. 3.2. The buildup shown is for a hypothetical individual: Differences, and probably major ones, appear in the representational buildups of various people as a function of their decontextualization skills (application of knowledge-acquisition components to contextual cues as mediated by the mediating variables) and prior knowledge. The subject is shown the following brief story about a BLUMEN and is asked what a BLUMEN is.

He first saw a BLUMEN during a trip to Australia. He had just arrived from a business trip to India, and felt very tired. Looking out at the plain, he saw a BLUMEN hop across it. It was a typical marsupial, getting its food by chewing on the surrounding plants. Squinting because of the bright sunlight and an impending headache, he noticed a young BLUMEN securely fastened in an opening on its mother's belly.

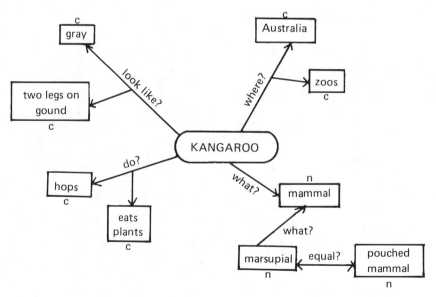

FIG. 3.1.   A hypothetical individual's mental representation of information according to the proposed theory. Attributes with the letter "n" adjacent to them are specified as necessary; attributes with the letter "c" are specified as characteristic (nonnecessary). *Note.* From "A Theory of Knowledge Acquisition in the Development of Verbal Concepts" by R. J. Sternberg, 1984, *Developmental Review, 4,* p. 123. Copyright 1984 by Academic Press. Reprinted by permission.

1. He first saw a BLUMEN during his trip to Australia.
   a. Selectively encode

   BLUMEN   (saw,   Australia)
                ↑   ↑
              stative   spatial
       descriptive   locative
               ↓   ↓
           visible   in Australia
             n   c

   b. Selectively combine

   c. Selectively compare
        visible objects first seen in Australia

Aborigines	Animals		Plants
	Kangaroo	Rabbit	Eucalyptus
	Koala	Sheep	

2. He had just arrived from a business trip to India and felt very tired.
   a. Selectively encode
       ∅
   b. Selectively combine
       (same as 1b)
   c. Selectively compare
       (same as 1c)

3. Looking out at the plain, he saw the BLUMEN hop across it.
   a. Selectively encode

   BLUMEN   (at the plain,   hop)
                    ↑   ↑
                spatial   functional
                 ↓   descriptive
           on plains   ↓
              c   hops
                            c

   b. Selectively combine

   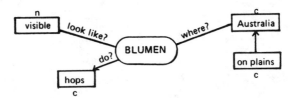

   c. Selectively compare
        visible objects first seen in Australia, that hop across plains

~~Aborigines~~	Animals		~~Plants~~
	Kangaroo	~~Koala~~	~~Eucalyptus~~
	Rabbit	~~Sheep~~	

112

4. It was a typical marsupial, getting its food by chewing on the surrounding plants.
   a. Selectivley encode

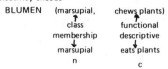

```
BLUMEN    (marsupial,      chews plants)
              ↑                 ↑
             class          functional
          membership       descriptive
              ↓                 ↓
          marsupial         eats plants
              n                 c
```

   b. Selectively combine

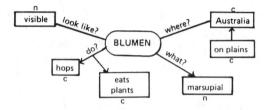

   c. Selectively compare
       visible objects first seen in Australia, that hop across plains, are marsupials, and chew plants
       Animals
       Kangaroo   ~~Rabbit~~

5. Squinting because of the bright sunlight and an impending headache, he noticed a young BLUMEN securely fastened in an opening in front of its mother.
   a. Selective encode
      ∅
   b. Selectively combine
      (same as 4b)
   c. Selectively compare

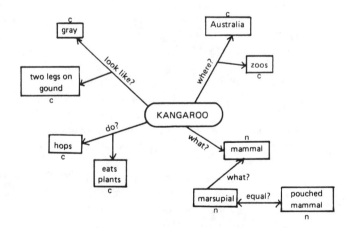

FIG. 3.2. A hypothetical individual's build-up of a mental representation for a story about a BLUMEN (kangaroo). Attributes with the letter "n" adjacent to them are specified as necessary; attributes with the letter "c" are specified as characteristic. *Note.* From "A Theory of Knowledge Acquisition in the Development of Verbal Concepts" by R. J. Sternberg, 1984, *Developmental Review, 4,* p. 125–127. Copyright 1984 by Academic Press. Reprinted by permission.

In Step 1 (see Fig. 3.2), the subject considers the first sentence and *selectively encodes* two facts, that the individual saw a BLUMEN and that he first saw it on a trip to Australia. The first cue, a stative-descriptive cue, indicates that the BLUMEN is visible; the second cue, a spatial-locative cue, indicates that BLUMENS can be found in Australia. In *selective combination,* the representation of BLUMEN grows two nodes, a (look-like?) node for the stative-descriptive cue and a (where?) node for the spatial cue. In *selective comparison,* the subject's knowledge about things that can be seen in Australia is activated in long-term memory. The names (network central entries) of these concepts are placed into working memory and the subject constructs a list corresponding to possible meanings of BLUMEN. This list will be reduced in successive steps as entries in long-term memory and even classes of entries are found to be irrelevant to the new word's meaning. As each entry is deleted from the list of possible meanings in working memory, the nodes in long-term memory corresponding to that entry are deactivated.

In Step 2, the subject considers the second sentence. Because the subject is now using his or her activated knowledge to guide what should be selectively encoded, none of the information in this sentence is perceived as relevant because the new information is uninformative (again, for *this* individual) with respect to BLUMENS, and their visibility in Australia. No further encoding, combination, or comparison is done.

In Step 3, the subject considers the third sentence, *selectively encoding* that BLUMENS can be found on plains (a spatial cue related to the subject's knowledge that plains exist in Australia) and that BLUMENS hop (a functional-descriptive cue related to the subject's knowledge about how some animals in Australia move). The subject now *selectively combines* the new information with the information already in the BLUMEN network, adding two new nodes. The subject grows "on plains" out of "Australia," so that, according to the modified network, BLUMENS are now found on plains in Australia. "Hops" is fed into the (do?) node. In particular, by *selectively comparing* the new information with the activated information in long-term memory corresponding to the names of concepts being considered as possible word meanings in working memory, the subject can eliminate all names that do not represent objects that hop or that are found on plains.

In Step 4, the subject *selectively encodes* the facts that a BLUMEN is a marsupial and that it chews plants. (Someone who does not know what a marsupial is might ignore the information, or attempt to infer its meaning from context.) In *selective combination,* two further nodes are grown, a further (do?) node and a (what?) node. The two new attributes that have been added to the network can be used to eliminate names of objects whose network representations in long-term memory (which are still activated) do not represent marsupials that chew plants. Thus, *selective comparison* continues to reduce the relevant prior knowledge base at the same time that selective encoding and combination are increasing the relevant new knowledge base.

In Step 5, the subject fails selectively to encode any of the information in the sentence as relevant to the meaning of BLUMEN. This failure may derive either from his or her not realizing that there is relevant information, or from his or her not knowing how to use it. This failure illustrates how some of the mediating variables specified by the proposed theory can affect the buildup of a word representation. With successive presentations of the word, the chances improve that the representation will be more nearly complete.

The subject now checks whether there are any concept names left in working memory that meet all of the constraints of the representation. If there is only one such concept, the subject compares defining attributes of the network representation corresponding to the already stored word. If the attributes match or pass a criterion for being close enough, the subject defines the new word in terms of the old, in this case, "kangaroo." If the attributes do not match or are not close enough to accept the old name as a definition, the subject either offers a definition that represents a new concept different from any already stored in long-term memory, or else goes back to the passage and tries to obtain further information. If multiple old concept names are left in working memory, the subject compares the defining attributes of the new concept to the defining attributes of all of the remaining old concepts and selects the best of the options if it is good enough (over criterion); if it is not good enough (i.e., it is under criterion), the subject either defines a wholly new concept or else goes back to the passage for further information. Again, this new concept will be a modification of the best old-fitting concept, with the modification reflecting the mismatch between the new concept and the old one.

In conclusion, definitions of new words are constructed by adding defining and characteristic attributes onto new network representations at the same time that one reduces in size a list of possible meanings for the new word. The reduction is accomplished by comparing attributes of the new word to attributes of the listed words (as stored in long-term memory) and removing from the list words whose attributes do not match the attributes of the new word. Eventually, one is left with a built-up representation of the new word, and, usually, a reduced list of possible meanings. One then compares in working memory attributes of the new word to attributes of each of the words on the reduced list, and either (1) chooses one as the correct meaning, if the match is close enough, (2) comes to view the new word as a new concept because it does not match any old concepts in memory, or (3) returns to the passage for more information. Should one see the word again in another context, one can return to the building-up process, and use the new information to refine and elaborate the network representation of the new word. This refinement and elaboration is likely to lead to a more correct definition in the final comparison process.

D. Data Testing the Theory
of External Decontextualization

We have some preliminary data regarding the validity of the proposed theory. In particular, we have tested only the cue-utilization and mediating-variable sub-theories (Sternberg & Neuse, 1983; Sternberg & Powell, 1983).

Experiment 1. The theory was first tested (Sternberg & Powell, 1983) by asking 123 high school students to read 32 passages of roughly 125 words that contained from 1 to 4 of 37 targeted nouns that are extremely low-frequency words. Each target word could appear from 1 to 4 times, resulting in 71 presentations altogether. Literary, newspaper, scientific, and historical writing styles were used equally often. This literary-style sample is representative.

> Two ill-dressed people—the one a tired woman of middle years and the other a tense young man—sat around a fire where the common meal was almost ready. The mother, Tanith, peered at her son through the *oam* of the bubbling stew. It had been a long time since his last *ceilidh* and Tobar had changed greatly; where once he had seemed all legs and clumsy joints, he now was well formed and in control of his hard, young body. As they ate, Tobar told of his past year, recreating for Tanith how he had wandered long and far in his quest to gain the skills he would need to be permitted to rejoin the company. Then all too soon, their brief *ceilidh* over, Tobar walked over to touch his mother's arm and quickly left.

The students' task was to define, as best they could, each of the low-frequency words within each passage (except for multiple occurrences of a single word within a given passage, which required only a single definition). They were not permitted to look back to earlier passages and definitions in making their current responses.

Qualities of definitions were rated independently by three trained raters. Because mean interrater reliability was .92, an average of the three ratings was used as a definition-goodness score for each word for each subject. These averages were then averaged over subjects to obtain a mean goodness-of-definition rating for each word. The main independent variables were ratings of the number or strength of the occurrences of our contextual cues and mediating variables (with the exact nature of the rating depending on the independent variable) with respect to their roles in helping in the deciphering of the meaning of each low-frequency word.

Theory testing was done via multiple regression. We used a stepwise multiple-regression procedure in which we allowed only three variables plus a regression intercept to enter into our final models. The decision to limit the number of variables was made on the basis of our judgment of the degree of refinement of our data, and in the hope of minimizing the risks of capitalization upon chance that inhere in stepwise regression. Because of multicollinearity (correlation among) independent variables, it was not possible to make strong inferences regarding the "true" subsets of variables that were differentially relevant from one passage style to the next. Variables that entered into at least one of four regressions were enablement, stative-descriptive, functional-descriptive, and equivalence cues, plus mediating variables of helpfulness and importance. The correlations between predicted and observed goodness ratings were .92 for literary passages, .74 for newspaper passages, .85 for science passages, and .77 for history passages. All these values were statistically significant.

We concluded on the basis of these data that the contextual cues and mediating variables proposed by our subtheories provided good prediction of the goodness-of-definition data, although we certainly do not believe that our model accounted for all the reliable variance. Indeed, the square roots of the internal-consistency reliability coefficients (based on all possible split halves of subjects) for our four data sets, which place upper limits on the values of R, were all .98 or above, showing that there was a considerable amount of reliable variance not accounted for by the fitted model. Nevertheless, the fits of the model subsets seemed sufficiently high to merit some optimism regarding our initial attempts to understand differential word difficulty in learning from context. Moreover, performance on the task was successful in distinguishing high from low-verbal subjects: Definition goodness ratings for individual subjects correlated .62 with IQ, .56 with vocabulary, and .65 with reading comprehension scores. The data, although extremely limited, are consistent with the notion that the proposed theory of cognitive competence is on the right track, at least in the domain of verbal declarative knowledge.

This first study had some clear limitations. Independent variables were nonorthogonal (multicollinear), resulting in difficulties isolating the effects of each variable; the possibility of interactions among model variables was not examined; and the population was limited to upper middle-class high school students. A second study was designed to expand upon the first by removing these limitations.

Experiment 2. A second study, also done in collaboration with Janet Powell, was designed to circumvent certain of the limitations of the first study. Subjects were 190 students in the 9th through 12th grades of a suburban high school. Each subject received 13 short passages, each containing one extremely low-frequency noun. In one condition, the words were defined for the subjects. In another condition, the words were not defined. The subjects' task was to rate the helpfulness of each of a series of segments for defining the unknown word. Ratings were made on a 1 (low) to 7 (high) scale. The following passage fragments show two segmentation conditions: one with longer segments, and one with shorter segments:

    . . . and when he removed his hat, // she, who preferred "ageless" men, // eyed
his increasing *phalacrosis* // and grimaced.
    . . . and when he removed // his hat // she, // who preferred // "ageless" men,
// eyed // his increasing // *phalacrosis* // and grimaced.

Subjects were to rate the helpfulness of each segement—long or short—to
defining *phalacrosis* (baldness). A set of raters independently rated each segment
for the contextual cues, if any, it contained. For example, "and grimaced," a
short segment, provides a value cue, and "when he removed his hat" provides a
temporal and a spatial cue. It should be noted that for the most part, even
segments containing cues contained only weak cues. Only a few segments contained strong cues. The mean helpfulness ratings were then averaged across
segments for each cue type, in order to compute the cue's mean helpfulness. This
averaging procedure yielded helpfulness weights for the various contextual cues,
without introducing the multicollinearity problems that emerge from multiple
regression.

The mean importances were 1.81 for setting (temporal and spatial) cues, 2.37
for value cues, 2.72 for stative-descriptive cues, 2.42 for functional cues, 2.51
for causal cues, 2.71 for class membership cues, and 3.20 for equivalence cues
(including antonyms). The mean rating when there was no cue at all was 1.61.
Because each of these means is based upon roughly 1,000 observations, on the
average, the differences are highly reliable. As would be expected, equivalence
cues were the most helpful. These were followed by stative-descriptive and class
membership cues (both of which deal with static properties) and then by functional and causal cues (both of which deal with active properties). Value cues
were less helpful, and setting cues were the least helpful of all. It thus appears
that all of the cues help somewhat, relative to the no-cue control segments, but
they help differentially.

In this experiment, the cues were very weak, and no attempt was made to
balance them precisely. The follow-up experiment used more salient and closely
controlled cues. This experiment also tested aspects of the theory other than the
context cues and incorporated elements of training in the design.

Experiment 3.   In a third experiment (Sternberg & Neuse, 1983), we tested
81 sophomores and juniors in an inner-city high school. The subjects were
divided into two basic groups, a training group (59 subjects) and a control (no-
training) group (22 subjects). The mean IQ of the subjects was 97, with a
standard deviation of 11.

The experimental design in the third experiment involved seven independent
variables: (1) training group (experimental, control), (2) testing time (pretest,
posttest), (3) test format (blank, nonword), (4) clue type (stative descriptive,
functional descriptive, class membership), (5) unknown word type (abstract,
concrete), (6) restrictiveness of context with respect to the meaning of the un-

known word (low, high), and (7) sentence function of the unknown word (subject, predicate). These variables were completely crossed. Treatment group was a between-subject variable; all other variables were within subject and were manipulated via a faceted testing arrangement. Two different test forms were used, and half the subjects received the first form as a pretest and the second form as a posttest; the other half received them in reverse order. Test items, involving either neologisms or blanks (cloze procedure), were each presented in the context of a single sentence. Subjects were asked either to define the neologism or to fill in the blank, as appropriate. There were 48 items on each test. Scores on the pretest were correlated .74 with an IQ test (Henmon–Nelson) given before training, and .71 with an alternative form of the test given after training. Scores on the posttest were correlated .65 and .64, respectively, with the two administrations of the IQ test.

The training sequence was spread out over six sessions. The topics covered were (1) What is context? (2) Using sentence context; (3) 20 questions (spotting clue types); (4) Cues I (temporal, spatial, stative-descriptive, equivalence); (5) Using paraphrase to figure out word meanings; (6) Cues II (functional-descriptive, causal); and (7) Mystery words (neologisms presented in sentences or paragraphs). The six class periods proved ample to cover this range of theory-based material.

In the experimental group, significant main effects were obtained for testing time (posttest higher than pretest), clue type (stative-descriptive hardest, functional-descriptive in-between, category membership easiest), context restrictiveness (higher restrictive more difficult than lower restrictive), and sentence function (predicates harder than subjects). In the control group, significant main effects were obtained for clue type (same ordering of means as aforementioned) and restrictiveness of context (same ordering of means as aforementioned). Thus, there was a significant pre to posttest gain in the trained group, but not the untrained group. However, the interaction between group and training effect was not statistically significant. In addition, there were a number of statistically significant interactions between independent variables, suggesting that model effects were not wholly independent and additive, but rather were interactive.

Taken as a whole, these results suggest (1) that subsets of the cues and moderating variables do have additive effects that can be quantified and isolated, (2) that the additive effects are supplemented by interactive ones, and (3) that at least some training of decontextualization skills is possible. The set of results is thus supportive of the ideas in the theory of verbal decontextualization but emphasizes the need to consider interactions as well as main effects in analyses of model fits.

The greatest disappointment in this experiment was the weakness of the training effects. However, we learned enough from this experiment to design an experiment that aimed at achieving training effects, without the "distraction" of testing other things; the next experiment was therefore directed specifically at obtaining improvements in decontextualization ability through theoretically based training.

Experiment 4.   In this experiment, 150 New Haven area adults (nonstudents) of roughly average intelligence participated in a study involving one of five conditions. There were three training conditions and two control conditions. Subjects in all three training conditions and one of the control conditions received exactly the same practice words and passages, but different instruction (if any) regarding the passages. Passages were similar to those in Experiment 1.

The 30 subjects in each of these conditions were given a 25-item pretest as well as other tests, and a 25-item posttest measuring skill in figuring out word meanings. The pretest and posttest were *transfer* tests; they measured skill in figuring out word meanings: They did not merely test recall of words. Our goal was not to train specific vocabulary but rather to train vocabulary-learning skills. All words in the experiment were extremely rare English-language words. The same pretest and posttest words were used in each condition, and training words were the same across conditions. Items were scored on a 0–2 point scale, for a maximum score of 50 points per test. Each training session lasted 45 minutes, exclusive of the various kinds of testing, which brought session length to 2½ hours. The conditions, which were between subjects, were as follows:

1. *Process training*: Subjects were taught and given practice using the mental processes (selective encoding, selective combination, selective comparison) alleged by the theory to be involved in figuring out meanings of new words from context.

2. *Contextual-Cue training*: Subjects were taught and given practice using the contextual cues upon which the mental processes operate (e.g., class membership, stative-descriptive).

3. *Mediating-Variable training*: Subjects were taught and given practice using the mediating variables that affect how well the processes can be applied to the cues (e.g., the location of a cue in the passage relative to the unknown word).

4. *Vocabulary-Memorization control*: Subjects were asked to memorize definitions of 75 extremely rare words (that otherwise did not appear in the experiment), and were tested on their memory for these words.

5. *Context-Practice control*: Subjects were given exactly the same practice that was given to subjects in the three training conditions, except that the practice occurred in the absence of training.

The mean pretest–posttest gain scores (out of 50 points possible on each test) were 7.2 for the process condition, 5.2 for the contextual-cue condition, 7.6 for the mediating-variables condition, 1.1 for the word-memorization control condition, and 2.6 for the context-practice condition. The results are clear: The training groups showed significantly greater gains than did the control groups. Two additional features of the means are worthy of note: First, as would be expected, the controls receiving relevant practice showed greater gain than did the controls receiving irrelevant memorization. The practice control condition is actually similar to many contextual training programs, which consist of little more than practice. Yet, to the extent that other programs involve any training at all, it is in contextual cues, which provide the least facilitation of all three training conditions.

In conclusion, theoretically motivated instruction in learning words from context can make a significant and substantial difference in people's ability to learn word meanings, on their own, from context. In just 45 minutes of training, substantial gains in decontextualization ability were obtained. Of course, the durability of this training has yet to be shown.

Experiment 5.   In all the experiments reported up to this point, presentation of words was written, and subjects had as much time as they needed to read the passages and define the words. In everyday life, however, new words may be encountered in oral as well as in written presentations, and one may not always have as much time as one would desire to figure out the meanings. A further experiment addressed the question of what effects, if any, mode of presentation (oral, written) and rate of presentation (fast, slow) would have on quality of decontextualization. In particular, the experiment would allow a determination of whether subjects' decontextualization skills are in part a function of the medium and rate at which information is presented.

Subjects were 62 Yale undergraduate and graduate students, equally divided between the sexes. Each subject received 15 passages of roughly 135 words per passage. Each passage contained either two or four neologisms. Of the 15 passages, 5 dealt with literary or artistic topics, 5 with scientific topics, and 5 with history and current events. Subjects also received the Nelson–Denny Reading Test.

The main independent variables were type and rate of presentation. In the written-fast condition, subjects were allotted 45 seconds to read each passage. In the written-slow condition, subjects were allotted 65 seconds per passage. In the oral-fast condition, passages were read aloud at a rate of 145 words per minute. In the oral-slow condition, passages were read aloud at a rate of 95 words per minute. Subjects were not allowed to look back after they finished reading; similarly, replay of the tapes of the oral presentations was not allowed.

Quality of definitions was rated on a 0 (low) to 2 (high) scale. Consider first the effect of mode of presentation. Mean quality ratings were 1.56 for the written conditions and 1.59 for the oral conditions—the difference between means was not significant. Consider next the effect of rate of presentation. Mean quality ratings were 1.67 for the slow-presentation condition and 1.48 for the fast-presentation condition—this difference was significant. The interaction between mode and rate was not significant. Hence, rate, but not mode of presentation, affected quality of decontextualization.

The correlations across items of each of the four conditions with each other were generally in the range from .6 to .8. Thus, the various conditions were similar, but not identical, in what they measured. Correlations with the Nelson–Denny Reading Comprehension score were .61 for the written-slow condition, .77 for the written-fast condition, .64 for the oral-slow condition, and .45 for the oral-fast condition. Thus, the condition most resembling that of a standardized reading test—the written-fast condition—showed the highest correlation with such a test. As would be expected, the written conditions combined correlated more highly with the Nelson–Denny scores (.63) than did the oral conditions combined (.45).

Experiment 6.   In the previous experiment, the written and oral conditions did not differ in the quality of decontextualization they afforded, but this lack of difference may have stemmed from subjects in the written conditions not being allowed to look back at the passages after they finished reading them. Although such a manipulation increases the comparability of the written and oral conditions, it is perhaps less representative of most everyday reading than is a condition in which subjects are allowed to look back. A further experiment was thus conducted in order to determine the effects of looking back.

Sixty Yale students participated in an experiment that was parallel to the preceding one, except that there were two main manipulations: rate of presentation (fast versus slow) and lookback (allowed or not allowed). Presentation of passages was written only. As before, slow passage presentation resulted in better performance (mean quality score = 1.38) than did fast passage presentation (mean quality score = 1.34). The effect of lookback was clearcut: Subjects allowed to look back at passages in defining the new words had a mean definitional quality score of 1.53. Subjects not allowed to look back had a mean quality score of just 1.19. There was no interaction between rate and look-back conditions. Thus, lookback does facilitate decontextualization.

Correlations across item types between condition were in the range from .7 to .9. Thus, the various conditions were measuring similar skills. Correlations with the Nelson–Denny Reading Comprehension score were moderate, but the pattern was perplexing: .50 for slow look-back, .35 for fast look-back, .68 for slow no-look-back, and .48 for fast no-look-back. The correlations showed, if anything, the opposite to the pattern one might have predicted on the basis of surface similarities and dissimilarities of the experimental tasks to the Nelson–Denny test.

E. Decontextualization of Internal Context

Subjects use more than external context to figure out meanings of previously unknown words. They use internal context as well. By internal context, I refer to the morphemes within a word constituted of multiple morphemes that combine to give the word its meaning. People attempting to figure out meanings of words will often use not only external context of the kinds discussed earlier, but internal context deriving from their prior knowledge of a new word's constituent morphemes. Together, the two kinds of context provide a potentially powerful set of clues for figuring out meanings of new words.

Research on the use of internal context has proceeded along somewhat different lines from research on the use of external context: The major theoretical issue seems to have been whether affixed words (such as *predisposed*) are stored in memory in unitary form (i.e., as *predisposed*), in a set of lexically decomposed forms (i.e., as *pre-dis-pose-d*), or in both of these kinds of forms, with the form that is accessed in a given instance depending on the task and task context. Research on internal context is less advanced than research on external context (but see Freyd & Baron, 1982). Nevertheless, recent research on how affixed words are stored in memory is relevant to the concerns of this chapter: If such words are stored only as single lexical entries, then one might expect comprehenders to have considerable difficulty in the use of internal context for inferring word meanings; if, on the other hand, affixed words are stored as sets of separate morphemes, either instead of or in addition to lexical entries for the complete words, then one might expect comprehenders to be able to use internal context fairly freely in inferring word meanings.

Evidence for the view that affixed words are stored as sets of separate lexical entries corresponding to their individual morphemes can be traced back at least to Taft and Forster (1975). These investigators performed three experiments employing a lexical-decision task. In this task, subjects are presented with a string of letters and have to decide as quickly and as accurately as possible whether the letter string does or does not constitute a real English-language word. Three major results of interest emerged. First, nonwords that were stems of prefixed words (e.g., *juvenate*, which is the stem for *rejuvenate*) took longer to recognize as nonwords than did nonwords that were not stems of prefixed words (e.g., *pertoire*, for which the *re-* in *repertoire* does not function as a prefix). This result suggested that the nonword stem was directly represented in the lexicon and that one or more extra steps were needed to identify the stem as a *non*word. Second, words that could occur both as free morphemes—which can stand by themselves as words (e.g., *vent* as a word)—and as bound morphemes—which cannot stand by themselves as words (e.g., *vent* when serving as the stem of the word *invent*)—took longer to identify as words when the bound form was more frequent in the English language than was the free form. This result suggested that the existence of *vent* (or any other comparable letter string) as a bound morpheme and possibly as a salient and separate nonword lexical entry in memory may interfere with or in some other way lengthen the latency for recognition of *vent* (or any other comparable letter string) as a free morpheme that can stand as a word in its own right. Third, prefixed nonwords took longer to identify as nonwords when they contained a real stem (e.g., *dejuvenate*, in which *juvenate* is a real stem) than did control nonwords that did not contain a real stem (e.g., *depertoire,* in which *pertoire* is not a real, i.e., separable, stem). This result again suggested that the stem may have been stored separately and hence interfered with recognition of the total letter string as a nonword. Taft and Forster presented a model of word recognition that incorporated the notion that morphemes are each represented as separate lexical entries. Further support for a notion of separate storage of individual morphemes can be inferred from a study of Murrell and Morton (1974), although the purpose of this study and the theoretical framework in which it was placed were different from those that are of concern here.

The Taft and Forster view of storage of affixed words by their individual morphemes was challenged by Manelis and Tharp (1977), who interpreted data from two of their own experiments as supporting the view that words are stored only as single units. These investigators also employed a lexical-decision task. Certain controls were introduced in stimulus selection that had not been implemented in the Taft and Forster (1975) studies. Two main results emerged. First, in a crucial comparison of latencies for words that were affixed with latencies for words that were not affixed, no significant difference emerged. Although this result supported the notion that affixed and nonaffixed words are stored in the same way, other results strongly suggested that the two kinds of words are not identically processed, so that there was at least some ambiguity in the results. Second, a test condition designed to encourage subjects to use lexical decomposition failed to show the significant difference that would have supported the conclusion that decomposition was used. On the basis of these results, the investigators accepted a simple model in which affixed words are stored unitarily in the same form as nonaffixed words.

Subsequent research (Stanners, Neiser, & Painton, 1979; Taft, 1979) has attempted to reconcile the two views presented earlier by suggesting that both forms of representation may be used and accessed at different points in information processing or in different tasks or task contexts. Of particular interest in this latter regard is a study by Rubin, Becker, and Freeman (1979), which was interpreted by its authors as suggesting that decomposition is used only if special strategies are evoked as a result of a stimulus list that is heavily biased in favor of affixed words. At this point, the issue of just what differences, if any, exist between the representation and processing of affixed words remains unresolved.

The studies described earlier have all used a lexical decision task, or some variant of it, to test the form in which affixed words are represented in memory. Obviously, any one paradigm can provide only limited information regarding a given psychological issue. Holyoak, Glass, and Mah (1976) and Kintsch (1974) have done related experiments that address the issue of lexical decomposition from a more semantic point of view. These investigators used semantic-decision and memory experiments to investigate lexical decomposition. Because the hypotheses they investigated, and hence the experimental paradigms, did not bear primarily on the representation and processing of affixed words, the research is not described in detail. It is worth noting, however, that the results of these experiments generally suggest that the representation of complex words is unitary, and that lexical decomposition is not routinely done. But some of the experiments suggest that lexical decomposition is possible under at least some circumstances.

The findings just discussed have not been directly embodied in tests of verbal comprehension. Such tests do not separately measure people's knowledge of prefixes, stems, and suffixes, or their ability to integrate these kinds of knowledge. But in standard vocabulary tests, in which unknown words are presented for definition in the absence of any external context, the use of internal cues provides the only viable means of figuring out meanings. Introspective reports of vocabulary-test takers suggest that they use their knowledge of prefixes, stems, and suffixes to figure out meanings of at least some words. Internal context, like external context, can on occasion impede attempts to infer word meanings. For example, *meliorate* and *ameliorate* have essentially the same meaning, despite the addition of the prefix *a-* in the latter form.

Psychologists and educators interested in vocabulary training have recognized the importance of internal context in vocabulary-skills training programs. Both Johnson and Pearson (1978) and O'Rourke (1974), for example, have incorporated training on intraword cues into their vocabulary development programs. Indeed, the phonics approach to reading instruction can be viewed as preparatory to a program of training students on the use of internal contextual cues.

To summarize, evidence regarding the representation and processing of affixed words is mixed. My own reading of the evidence is similar to that of Miller and Johnson-Laird (1976), who have suggested that the subjective lexicon of each individual is organized in terms of the critical morphemes of derived words, even though each word has its own entry. Such an organization would allow people to use lexical decomposition in inferring the meanings of new words, at the same time that such use would require a distinct extra effort on the individual's part. In terms of our present interest in the use of internal context in inferring word meanings, the result of previous investigations leave open the question of whether or under what circumstances individuals actually do use their knowledge of word stems and affixes to figure out the meanings of affixed or other complex words.

F. Context Cues

Because internal context is much more impoverished than is external context, the diversity of kinds of cues is much more restricted (see, e.g., Johnson & Pearson, 1978; O'Rourke, 1974). The four kinds of cues constituting our scheme (Sternberg, Powell, & Kaye, 1983) are:

1. *Prefix cues:* Prefix cues generally facilitate decoding of a word's meaning. Occasionally, the prefix has a special meaning (e.g., *pre* usually means "be-

fore") or what appears to be a prefix really is not (e.g., *pre* in "predation"); in these cases, the perceived cue may be deceptive.

2. *Stem cues*: Stem cues are present in every word but such cues may be deceptive if a given stem has multiple meanings and the wrong one is assigned.

3. *Suffix cues*: Suffix cues, too, generally facilitate decoding of a word's meaning; in unusual cases where the suffix takes on an atypical meaning, or in cases where what appears to be a suffix really isn't, the perceived cue may be deceptive.

4. *Interactive cues*: Interactive cues are formed when two or even three of the word parts just described convey information in combination that is not conveyed by a single cue.

The usefulness of these kinds of cues in decoding meanings can be shown by an example. Suppose one's task is to infer the meaning of the word *thermoluminescence* (see Just & Carpenter, 1980). Many people know that the prefix *thermo-* refers to heat, that the root *luminesce* is a verb meaning "to give off light," and that the suffix *-ence* is often used to form abstract nouns. Moreover, a reasonable interpretation of a possible relation between *thermo-* and *luminesce* would draw on the knowledge that heat typically produces light. Note that the correct inference derives from an interaction between the prefix and stem: Neither cue in itself would suggest that the light emitted from heat would be a relevant property for inferring word meaning. These cues might be combined to infer (correctly) that *thermoluminescence* refers to the property of light emission from heated objects.

Again, we make no claims that this simple (and unoriginal) parsing of internal cues represents the only possible classification scheme, although we think it probably represents one, but not the only, plausible parsing. Collectively, these kinds of cues provide a basis for a person to exercise his or her competence in inferring word meanings.

G. Mediating Variables

Again, there exists a set of variables that mediate the usefulness of cues. Our model includes five variables that affect cue usefulness. These variables are similar but not identical to those considered for external context:

1. *Number of occurrences of the unknown word*: Internal cues are the same on every presentation of a given unknown word; however, one's incentive to try to figure out the word's meaning is likely to be increased for a word that keeps reappearing.

2. *Importance of the unknown word to understanding the context in which it is embedded*: Again, a word that is important for understanding the context in which it occurs is more likely to receive attention. One can skip unimportant

words, and often does. As before, the unknown word's importance to a sentence will be less compelling than its importance to a paragraph.

3. *Density of unknown words*: If unknown words occur at high density, one may be overwhelmed at the magnitude of the task of figuring out the meanings of the words and give up this task. Yet, it is possible that the greater the density of unfamiliar words in a passage, the more difficulty the reader will have in applying the external context cues, and hence the more important will be the internal context cues. A high density of unfamiliar words may encourage word-by-word processing and a greater focus on internal cues. This mediating variable interacts with the next one to be considered.

4. *Density of decomposable unknown words*: Because internal decontextualization may not be a regularly used skill in many individuals' repertoires, individuals may need to be primed for its use. The presence of multiple decomposable unknown words can serve this function, helping the individual become aware that internal decontextualization is possible and feasible. In this case, the strategy is primed by repeated cues regarding its applicability.

5. *Usefulness of previously known information in cue utilization*: Again, one's knowledge of words, word cognates, and word parts will play an important part in internal decontextualization. The sparsity of information provided by such cues (in contrast to external cues) almost guarantees an important role for prior information.

H. Knowledge-acquisition Components

The knowledge-acquisition components relevant to decontextualization of internal context are the same as those for decontextualization of external context and hence are not be repeated here, other than by name: selective encoding, selective combination, and selective comparison.

I. Data Testing the Theory of Internal Decontextualization

We have sought to study use of internal context in two experiments.

Experiment 7. Our goal in our first study of internal decontextualization (Kaye & Sternberg, 1983) was to determine the extent to which secondary school and college students could derive the correct definitions of very low-frequency words on the basis of their knowledge of frequently used prefixes and stems. We sought to determine whether these students were attending to either of the words' constituents (prefix or stem) while attempting to define the words. We also examined relationships between students' metacognitive knowledge of such words and their actual performance in defining them. Given the present state of research in this area, we felt there is a need to know *whether* individuals use internal context before examining in detail *how* individuals use such context. Thus, our study tested a prerequisite for our theory, rather than the theory itself, which we plan to test in subsequent research.

We tested 108 students, of whom 58 were in secondary school (approximately equally balanced among grades 8, 10, and 11) and of whom 50 were undergraduates at a state university. Each subject was exposed to 58 prefixed words that were selected each to contain 1 of 15 commonly used Latin prefixes and 1 of 15 commonly used Latin stems. Because there were 15 different prefixes and 15 different stems, there were a total of 30 different individual word parts. Each prefix and each stem appeared in from two to six different words. All words were of very low frequency and of 2–3 syllables in length. Each subject received half of the words in a multiple-choice word-definitions task and the other half of the words in a word-rating task. Words presented in each of the two tasks were counterbalanced across subjects.

In the word-definitions task, each word was paired with four possible definitions, one of which was correct. One of the incorrect definitions retained the meaning of the prefix only, one retained the meaning of the stem only, and one retained the meaning of neither the prefix nor the stem. An example of such a problem is

> EXSECT
> (a) to cut out   (totally correct)
> (b) to throw out   (prefix only correct)
> (c) to cut against   (stem only correct)
> (d) to throw against   (totally incorrect)

In the (metacognitive) word-rating task, each word was paired with four questions querying subjects' assessments of the state of their knowledge and its relation to each of the words: (1) How familiar is the word? (2) How easily can you define the word? (3) How similar is the word to another word you have seen or heard? (4) How similar is the word to another word you can define? Subjects responded by circling numbers arrayed on a 7-point scale, with more positive responses to the questions answered in terms of higher numbered values on the scale.

All subjects were also asked to rate the 30 word parts for their meaningfulness (i.e., familiarity of meaning). This task, which occurred at the end of the experiment, also involved a 7-point rating scale.

A hierarchical multiple regression procedure was used to predict scores both on the learning-from-context cognitive task and on the metacognitive ratings of words and word parts. In such a procedure, sets of independent variables are entered into the regression in a fixed order and in successive steps. The variables entered at the first level of the hierarchy were always "dummy variables" for age, test form (i.e., which set of test words was received in which task), and age

× test form. This level was used to control for the effects of those variables that might be expected to affect test performance but that were not directly relevant to the question of how subjects answered the test items or made their ratings. The particular independent variables entered at the second level of the hierarchy were the theoretically relevant ones and varied from one regression to the next. Consider, for example, the question of whether subjects are using prefixes in order to figure out word meanings. If they are, then performance on a word with a given prefix, such as the *ex* in the earlier example, should be better predicted by performance on other words with this prefix than by performance on words not sharing this prefix. If subjects are not using prefixes, then performance on words sharing the same prefix should be no better a predictor of performance on the given word than should performance on words not sharing the same prefix. The same logic applies for word stems. Thus, a typical independent variable at the second level of analysis would be performance on other words sharing the same prefix (for determining whether subjects use prefixes in figuring out word meanings) or sharing the same stem (for determining whether subjects use stems in figuring out word meanings). The variable entered at the third level of the hierarchical regression was an interaction term between the variables at the first and second levels of analysis.

The results suggested that college students, but not high school students, were able to use internal context to help infer word meanings. Values of R (the correlation between predicted and observed scores on each of the test items) were generally statistically significant for college students but not for high school students. However, both high school and college students had accurate metacognitive knowledge, that is, their metacognitive knowledge was predictive of their cognitive performance (and vice versa). Significant values of R for the various regressions ranged from .53 to .78 with a median of .63. The pattern of results suggested that the word stem was the central focus for determining what each of the various words meant, with the prefix modifying this stem meaning. Interestingly, knowledge of prefixes was better than knowledge of stems, at least for our word sample. This result may be attributable to the much larger number of stems than of prefixes in the language.

Experiment 8.   A follow-up experiment, done in collaboration with Daniel Kaye, involved 80 college students. The students were divided into four groups, which were presented with varied tests of decontextualization skill. Every test contained decomposable words, decomposable pseudowords, nondecomposable words, and nondecomposable pseudowords. The decomposable items had meaningful prefixes and stems; the nondecomposable items did not. The words were genuine, although of low frequency; the pseudowords, of course, were not genuine. As in the previous experiment, each test item had associated with it four answer options, one of which was correct, and the others of which were incorrect. For the decomposable words, one distractor was correct in stem only, one in prefix only, and one in neither stem nor prefix. Although there were a total of 240 items, each subject received only 180 of these. In each of the four conditions, one of the four types of test items was omitted. Hence, subjects received only three of the four item types—decomposable words, decomposable pseudowords, nondecomposable words, and nondecomposable pseudowords.

We found that we could obtain significant prediction of success on words with a given prefix from other words containing that prefix, but a different stem (median $R = .48$), and that we could obtain significant prediction of success on words with a given stem from other words containing that stem, but a different prefix (median $R = .45$). Thus, in this experiment with college students, it appears that internal context was consistently used to figure out word meanings.

In conclusion, the data collected to date indicate the usefulness of the theory of verbal decontextualization for understanding something of how individuals acquire their vocabularies. The theory can explain, at some level, both differences in difficulty of learning individual words (stimulus variance) and differences in individuals' abilities to learn words (subject variance). Differences in word difficulty are understood in terms of differences in cue availability, applicability of mediating variables, and interactions between different cues and mediating variables. Differences between subjects are understood in terms of their differential ability to use selective encoding, selective combination, and selective comparison upon the cues, and in terms of differences in susceptibility to the mediating variables.

IV. SUBTHEORY OF INFORMATION PROCESSING IN REAL-TIME VERBAL COMPREHENSION

Consider now how verbal comprehension skills are executed in real time. I first describe two general alternative approaches to this issue and then consider in more detail our own approach.

A. Alternative Approaches to Understanding Real-Time Verbal Comprehension

Approaches emphasizing current functioning seem divisible into two subapproaches—those that are essentially molar, dealing with information processing at the level of the word, and those that are essentially molecular, dealing with information processing at the level of word attributes. I consider each subapproach in turn.

A Molar Subapproach. The molar subapproach examines comprehension and understanding of individual words or groupings of words. A proponent of this approach, Marshalek (1981), administered a faceted vocabulary test along with a battery of standard reasoning and other tests. The facets of the vocabulary test were word abstractness (concrete, medium, abstract); word frequency (low, medium, high); item type (vague recognition—easy distractors in a multiple-choice recognition task; accurate recognition—difficult distractors in a multiple-choice recognition task; definition—subjects have to provide word definition rather than being given multiple-choice); and blocks (two parallel blocks of words). Marshalek found that vocabulary item difficulty increased with word abstractness, with word infrequency, with item formats requiring more precise discrimination of word meaning, and with task requirement (such that word definition was harder than word recognition). He also found that partial concepts are prevalent in young adults and that word acquisition is a gradual process. Vocabulary level seemed to be related to reasoning performance at the lower but not the higher end of the vocabulary difficulty distribution. These results led Marshalek to conclude that a certain level of reasoning ability may be prerequisite for extraction of word meaning (see also Anderson & Freebody, 1979). Above this level, the importance of reasoning begins rapidly to decrease.

Marshalek's approach to understanding verbal comprehension is of particular interest because it breaks down global task performance into more specific facets. It is possible, in his research, to score each subject for the various facets of performance as well as for the overall level of performance. I believe this to be a valuable step toward understanding current verbal functioning. One concern I have, though, is with whether the experimenter-defined facets correspond to significant psychological (subject-defined) aspects of performance. Although these facets may differentiate more and less difficult items, and better and poorer performers, it is not clear how understanding these facets of performance gives us what could in any sense be construed as a causal-explanatory account of verbal comprehension and individual differences in it. The causal inferences that can be made are, at best, highly indirect.

A Molecular Subapproach.   The molecular subapproach is the kind that we have taken in our work on the real-time representation and processing of information during verbal comprehension. The aim is to understand verbal comprehension in terms of how attributes of words are encoded and compared and also to understand decision making in real-time reading through the specific decisions that are made about allocating time. For example, one would seek to understand performance on a synonyms test in terms of actual comparisons between the attributes of a given target word and the attributes of the potential synonyms given in a multiple-choice list. At minimum, one would have to know what kinds of attributes are stored, as well as how these attributes are stored, how they are accessed during verbal comprehension performance, and how they are used to examine the target and the options. Our theory of these phenomena (McNamara & Sternberg, 1983; Sternberg & McNamara, 1985), and some data testing the theory, are presented next.

V. PERFORMANCE COMPONENTS

In work investigating the performance components of real-time information processing, Timothy McNamara and I have sought to understand the mental representations and processes people use in understanding and comparing word meanings.

A. Alternative Models of Word Representation

Several alternative models have been proposed for how word meaning is represented mentally. I now consider some of the major models that have been proposed.

Defining Attribute (Nonadditive) Models. Traditional models of word meaning make use of necessary and sufficient—i.e., defining—attributes of words (Frege, 1952; Russell, 1956). The meaning of a word is decomposed into a set of attributes such that the possession of these attributes is necessary and sufficient for a word to refer to a given object or concept. For example, a bachelor might be represented in terms of the attributes: *unmarried, male,* and *adult.* Being an unmarried male adult is then viewed as necessary and sufficient for being labeled as a bachelor. (Some might add *never-before-married* as an additional required attribute.) Traditional models can be viewed as "nonadditive" in the sense that either a given word has the attributes necessary and sufficient to refer to a given object or concept, or it does not; there are no gradations built into this model of representation.

Characteristic Attribute (Additive) Models. A second class of models, one that has been more in favor in recent times, might be referred to as "characteristic attribute" models. In these models, word meaning is conceptualized in terms of attributes that tend to be characteristic of a given object or concept but neither necessary nor sufficient for reference to that concept. A well-known example of the usefulness of this kind of model stems from Wittgenstein's (1953) analysis of the concept of *game.* It is extremely difficult to speak of necessary attributes of a game. Similarly, it is difficult to speak of any attributes that guarantee something's being a game: Hence, it is difficult to find any sufficient attributes of a game. Yet, games bear a "family resemblance" to each other. In today's parlance, various games cluster around a "prototype" for the concept of a game (Rosch, 1978). Games are either close to or remote from this prototype, depending on the number of characteristic attributes they have. Chess might be viewed as quite close to the hypothetical prototype, whereas solitaire might be viewed as further away.

The class of additive models can be divided into at least three submodels according to how the attributes are used to refer to a concept: First, the reference of a word might be determined by the *number of attributes* possessed by an object that match attributes in the word's definition (Hampton, 1979; Wittgenstein, 1953). If the number of matching attributes exceeds some criterion, then the object is identified as an example of the word; otherwise, the object is not so identified. Second, the referent of a word might be determined by a *weighted sum of attributes.* This model is like the first one, except that some attributes are viewed as more critical than are others and hence are weighted more heavily (Hampton, 1979). For purposes of our analyses, the first model is viewed as a special case of the second (the weighted case) and is not treated as qualitatively distinct. Third, the referent of a word might be determined by a *weighted average of attributes,* in which case the sum of the attributes is divided by the number of attributes. The second and third models are distinguished by whether or not a given sum of weights counts equally without respect to the number of weights entered into the sum. To our knowledge, the difference between summing and averaging models has not been addressed in the literature on word meaning and reference, although it has certainly been considered in other contexts, such as information integration in people's formation of impressions about each other (e.g., Anderson, 1979).

Mixture Models.   A third class of models specifies words as being decomposable into both defining and characteristic attributes. An example of such a model would be that of Smith, Shoben, and Rips (1974), who proposed that words can be viewed as comprising both defining and characteristic attributes. Consider, for example, the concept of a *mammal.* Being warm blooded would be a defining attribute, whereas being a land animal would be a characteristic attribute, in that most, but not all, mammals are land animals.

In the mixture model (or at least the proposed variant of it), not all words need refer to concepts having both defining and characteristic attributes (Clark & Clark, 1977; Schwartz, 1977). For example, one might view a word, such as *game,* as having only characteristic attributes. Intuitively, it seems much easier to find defining attributes for some kinds of concepts than for others, and this class of models capitalizes upon this intuition. It seems less likely that any words have only defining attributes. Indeed, we are unable to think of any words that do not have at least some characteristic attributes that are neither necessary nor sufficient for referring to a concept.

B. Tests of Alternative Models of Representation

We conducted four initial experiments to test the alternative models of word-meaning representation (McNamara & Sternberg, 1983). Our concern in these experiments was with how word meaning is represented psychologically. The issues of interest to us are not, of course, necessarily the same as those issues of concern to philosophers of meaning and linguists.

The first experiment was intended to (1) determine whether people identify necessary and/or sufficient attributes of concepts and objects and (2) collect rating data needed for a second experiment that tested the various models of representation. Ten Yale students participated in the study. The study involved three kinds of nouns: (1) natural-kind terms (e.g., eagle, banana, potato), (2) defined-kind terms (e.g., scientist, wisdom), and (3) proper names (e.g., Queen Elizabeth II, Aristotle, Paul Newman). Proper names were included because, in the philosophical literature, they have been heavily used as the basis for generalization to all nouns. The main independent variables in the experiment were the type of term about which a rating was to be made (natural kind, defined kind, proper name) and the type of rating to be made (necessary attributes, sufficient attributes, importance of attributes—see following). The main dependent variable was the value of the assigned ratings. Subjects were first asked to list as many properties as they could think of for the various objects of the three kinds noted earlier. Then they were asked to provide three kinds of ratings (with the order of the kinds of ratings counterbalanced across subjects). The first rating was necessity: Subjects were asked to check off those attributes, if any, that they believed to be necessary attributes for each given word. The second was sufficiency: Subjects were asked to check off those attributes, if any, that were sufficient attributes for each given word. They were also asked to indicate minimally sufficient subsets of attributes (such that the subset in combination was sufficient to define a word). In both of these ratings, it was emphasized that there might well be *no* necessary or sufficient properties (or subsets of properties) at all. The third rating was importance: Subjects were asked to rate how important each attribute was to defining each of the given words. These ratings were used to determine how characteristic each attribute is of the concept it helps describe. There were four major results.

First, all subjects found at least one necessary attribute for each of the eight natural kind and proper name terms. All but one subject found at least one necessary attribute for each of the defined kinds. One could therefore conclude that individuals conceive of words of these three kinds as having at least some necessary attributes. Examples of some of these attributes are, for a diamond, that it scratches glass, is the hardest substance known, and is made of carbon; and for Albert Einstein, that he is dead, was a scientist, was male, and that he invented the equation $E = MC^2$.

Second, all subjects found at least one sufficient attribute or subset of attributes for all natural kind terms. Almost all subjects found at least one sufficient attribute or subset of attributes for defined kinds and proper names. One could therefore conclude that most individuals conceive of most words as having at least some sufficient attributes or subsets of attributes. Examples are, for an eagle, that it is a bird that appears on quarters, and for lamp, that it is a light source that has a shade.

Third, roughly half of the natural kind and defined kind terms were conceived as having attributes that were both necessary and sufficient. More than three-fourths of the proper names were conceived as having such attributes. Examples are, for sandals, that they are shoes that are held on with straps and that do not cover the whole foot, and for a diamond, that it is the hardest substance known.

Fourth, internal-consistency analyses revealed that subjects agreed to a great extent which attributes were important, necessary, sufficient, and necessary and sufficient (with internal-consistency reliabilities generally in the mid .80s; for necessity ratings and sufficiency ratings, reliabilities were generally a bit lower, usually in the mid .70s).

The second experiment was intended to (1) determine the extent to which people use defining (necessary and sufficient) and characteristic (neither necessary nor sufficient) attributes when deciding whether or not an object is an exemplar of a word, (2) to test four simple models and three mixture models of word meaning, and (3) to determine how generalizable the results were across word domains. Nine of the ten subjects from the first experiment participated in this experiment. A within-subjects design was used in order to control for possible individual differences in the representation of meaning of specific words. The subjects received booklets with a given word at the top of the page, followed by a list of attributes. The subject's task was to give a confidence rating that the attributes actually described an exemplar of the word at the top of the page. Attribute descriptions were compiled for each subject in order to provide discrimination among alternative models of word representation. The main independent variables were ratings of necessity, sufficiency, necessity and sufficiency, and importance, as taken from Experiment 1. The main dependent variable was the confidence rating that the description referred to an exemplar of the target word. Subjects rated their confidence that a given word was, in fact, exemplified by the description appearing below it. For example, they might see the word TIGER at the top of the page, followed by four attributes: "member of the cat family," "four legged," "carnivorous," and "an animal." They would rate on a 1–8 scale how likely that list of attributes was to describe a particular tiger.

The alternative representational models tested were a model positing (1) use only of defining (necessary and sufficient) attributes, (2) use of an unweighted sum of attributes, (3) use of a weighted sum of attributes, (4) use of a weighted mean of attributes, (5) use of defining attributes as well as a weighted sum of all attributes, and (6) use of defining attributes as well as a weighted mean of all attributes. Models were fit by linear regression with individual data sets concatenated; that is, there was no averaging across either subjects or items, and thus there was just one observation per data point for a total of 863 data points. Proportions of variance accounted for by each of the six respective models in the confidence-rating data were .36 for (1), .01 for (2), .02 for (3), .11 for (4), .45 for (5), and .38 for (6), concatenated over word types. Data for individual subjects reflected the pattern for the group. It was concluded that in making decisions about whether sets of attributes represent exemplars of specific words, individuals appear to use both defining and characteristic attributes via the weighted sum model.

The third experiment paralleled the first, in that it replicated it as well as also provided needed ratings data for the subsequent experiment. Because the results were almost identical to the first experiment's, they are not presented separately here.

The fourth experiment was designed to verify the results of the second experiment by using converging operations. Response latency and response choice were used as dependent variables, and the subjects' task was to choose which of two attribute lists better described a referent of a given word. For example, subjects might see "SOFA," followed by two lists of attributes: (1) "used for sitting, found in living rooms, slept on, furniture," and (2) "slept on, rectangular in shape, found in bedrooms." The 32 subjects would have to decide whether (1) or (2) was a better exemplar of sofa. Models were fit to group-average data. In this experiment, as in the previous two, natural kinds, defined kinds, and proper names appeared in equal numbers as stimulus terms.

The results again supported the mixture model combining defining attributes with summed characteristic attributes. For response choices, fits of five of the models described earlier were .48 for (1), .57 for (3), .46 for (4), .65 for (5), and .57 for (6). Model (2), the unweighted variant of model (3), was not separately tested.

VI. MODEL OF INFORMATION PROCESSING

The data for the four experiments taken as a whole seemed to support the mixture model in which defining attributes and characteristic attributes are considered, with the former attributes considered both nonadditively and as a weighted sum combined with the latter attributes. This model was then taken as the representational model for testing a process model.

We have proposed a model that assumes that, in Experiment 4, (1) subjects tested both answer options in order to make sure that they picked the better of the two options and (2) subjects compared answer options on the basis of both defining attributes (when present) and weighted sums of attributes. A flow chart for the model can be found in Fig. 3.3.

A. Quantification of the Model

Quantification of the processing model, which serves as a basis for testing it, is explained by referring to the following stimulus item: "TENT" followed by (1) "Made of canvas, supported by poles, portable, waterproof" and (2) "A shelter,

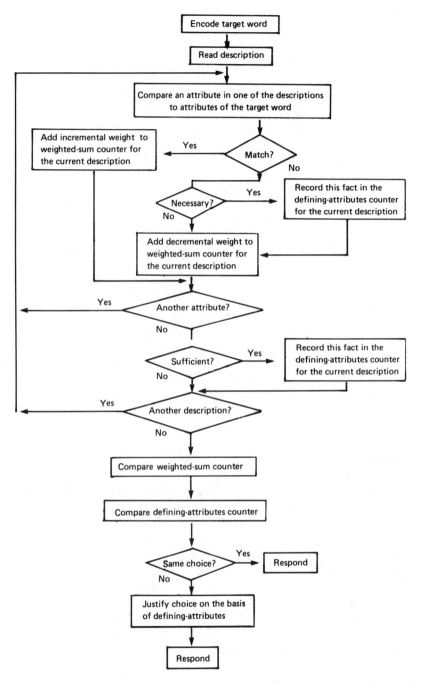

FIG. 3.3. Flow chart for real-time model of information processing during attribute comparison. *Note.* From "Mental Models of Word Meaning" by T. P. McNamara and R. J. Sternberg, 1983, *Journal of Verbal Learning and Verbal Behavior, 22,* p. 465. Copyright 1983 by Academic Press. Reprinted by permission.

used for camping, made of canvas." The six parameters of the model and the variables used to estimate them were as follows:

1. *Reading time* was estimated by the total number of words in the two descriptions, excluding the target word. In the example, the total number of words is 16. The value of this variable ranged from 4 to 34 across items (mean = 14.0).
2. *Processing time for negations* was estimated by the number of negated attributes in the descriptions, which is 0 for the example. The value of this variable ranged from 0 to 2 across items (mean = 0.6).
3. *Time for comparison of attributes in the descriptions to attributes of the target word* was estimated by the total number of attributes in the two descriptions. According to the model, each attribute in each description is compared to the attributes of the encoded target word. The weights of matching and mismatching attributes are added to a weighted-sum counter for the description currently being processed. (There is a weighted-sum counter for each description.) Mismatching attributes are also checked for necessity and, if they are necessary, this information is recorded in a defining-attributes counter for the description currently being processed. (There is a defining-attributes counter for each description.) When all attributes in a description have been compared to the attributes of the target word, the description is checked for sufficiency. If the description is sufficient, this fact is recorded in the defining-attributes counter for that description. In the example, the comparison variable would take the value 7, the number of attributes in the two descriptions. The comparison variable ranged from 3 to 8 across items (mean = 5.7).
4. *Comparison of options on the basis of defining attributes* was estimated by the absolute difference between the number of subjects for whom the second description was sufficient and the number of subjects for whom the first description was sufficient, or by the absolute difference between the number of subjects for whom a negated attribute in the first description was necessary and the number of subjects for whom a negated attribute in the second description was necessary. According to the model, comparison time decreases as the difference between the defining-attributes counter for the first description and the defining-attributes counter for the second description increases; i.e., subjects are faster the more dissimilar the options are. We needed to use a continuous variable to estimate a dichotomous construct (the necessity or sufficiency of a set of attributes) because we were modeling group-average data and a given description was not equally good or bad for all subjects. The difference between the two descriptions capitalized on this inherent variability in our stimuli. This comparison variable was linearly scaled so that small values on the variable corresponded to large differences between the two descriptions, and hence to fast comparison times. In the example, the first description was sufficient for none of the subjects and the second was sufficient for 11 subjects. Thus, the comparison variable was a linear function of the number 11 (precisely 26 − 11, or 15).

5. *Comparison of options on the basis of weighted sums of attributes* was estimated by the absolute difference in summed weights between the two descriptions. It was assumed that comparison time decreases as the difference between the weighted-sum counter for the first description and the weighted-sum counter for the second description increases. This variable, like the preceding, was linearly scaled so that small values on the variable corresponded to large differences between the two descriptions. In the previous example, the first description had a weighted sum of 11.32 and the second description had a weighted sum of 11.44. Hence, the comparison variable was a linear function of 0.12 (precisely 17.76 − 0.12, or 17.64).

6. *Justification* was relevant when the difference in summed weights and the difference in defining attributes predicted opposite choices. In such cases, the choice of an answer option on the basis of definingness alone had to be justified. The stimulus items were constructed so that for 60 of the 156 pairs of descriptions, there were no differences in definingness between the descriptions. For these items, the justification variable always took the value 0, because there could be no discrepancy between choices. The difference in weighted sums and the difference in definingness predicted opposite choices for 10 of the remaining 96 items. For these items, the justification variable took the value 1. In the example, both the difference in definingness and the difference in weighted sums predict that the second options should be chosen. Thus, the value of the justification variable is 0.

Tests of the Model of Information Processing.   The model described earlier was tested in terms of its ability to account for mean response latencies on the 156 items. Responses were included in the mean latencies even if they were errors according to the model. Fits changed trivially when errors were excluded. Fit of the model (R^2) was .79, with an RMSD of .66 second. Standardized parameter estimates were .42 for reading time, .37 for processing negations, .33 for comparison to target word, .23 for definingness comparison, .33 for weighted-sum comparison, and .07 for justification. All estimates were statistically significant. The proposed model thus provided a good account of the processing of attribute information, accounting for nearly 80% of the total variance in response latencies (and with only six independent variables on 156 data points). The standardized regression coefficients for the model seemed generally reasonable. They indicated that weighted sums of attributes were somewhat more important than defining attributes in deciding which option was the better exemplar of the target word.

B. Correlations with Ability Tests

Correlations were computed between overall mean latencies on the decision task and scores from the Nelson–Denny Reading Test and the Differential Aptitudes Test (DAT). In particular, we used vocabulary, reading comprehension, and reading rate scores from the former test, and the verbal reasoning score from the latter test. The only significant correlation involving latency was that between overall mean latency and reading rate ($-.37$). However, the multiple correlation between mean latency, on the one hand, and both reading rate and comprehension, when taken together, was a significant .47. (The correlation between comprehension and reading rate was .07, and the correlation between comprehension and mean latency was .27; neither correlation was significant.) Both reading rate and comprehension made statistically significant contributions to the multiple correlation, with respective weights of .38 and .30. Thus, reading rate and comprehension, when considered together, were moderately strongly related to latency in our task.

To conclude, the results from the four experiments taken together provide a reasonably coherent picture of both the representation of meaning and the processes used to make reference to a concept. In particular, individuals seem to use an additively based mixture model in their representation of word information and to be able to combine the represented information in a way that enables them to choose synonyms. Obviously, our work on real-time processing is incomplete. It has yet to be extended beyond the level of individual words and is in need of further interface with the theory of learning from context. Nevertheless, the two aspects of the theory of verbal comprehension, taken in combination, seem to provide a relatively comprehensive view of how crystallized intelligence develops and functions.

VII. METACOMPONENTS

Virtually everyone is confronted with much more material to read than they can possibly handle in the time available for reading. College freshmen, for example, are often bewildered by a reading load that would seemingly take all their time if they were to attempt to read with care all their course material. Professionals in psychology and other fields often find it impossible to keep up with the literature simply because there is so much. Clearly, individuals have to husband their reading time and attention.

A number of investigators have recognized the importance of metacomponents, or executive processes, in reading. For example, Brown (1978, 1980) has proposed that metacognitive skills operate in conjunction with an "automatic" mode of reading. Taking a developmental approach, Brown has reported that young children are deficient at, among other things, (1) predicting the difficulty of a task and recognizing when task difficulty has changed (see, e.g., Salatas & Flavell, 1976); (2) monitoring comprehension—being aware of whether one does or does not understand (see, e.g., Markman, 1977, 1979, 1981); (3) apportioning study-time—studying in anticipation of a future test—which includes determining what is important to remember and what is not, choosing a strategy to maximize learning, assessing one's success with the chosen strategy, and determining whether a different strategy should be tried (see, e.g., Masur, McIntyre, & Flavell, 1973); and (4) predicting test performance—knowing when a task has been mastered.

A strength of this approach is that executive processes provide a means for accounting for many of the complexities of skilled reading. To date, most of the evidence for the importance of executive control in cognitive performance resides largely in comparisons of performance across groups differing substantially in developmental level. Deficiencies in executive skills have been shown to be responsible for at least some limitations in cognitive performance that are characteristic of young children. The importance of efficient executive functioning to adult skilled performance remains largely an open question (Brown, 1980).

Richard Wagner and I have conducted two experiments in order to investigate executive processes in reading of expository texts by adults (Wagner & Sternberg, in press). This research addresses issues raised previously.

A. Isolating a Time-Allocation Metacomponent

In a first experiment, 40 Yale undergraduates were each presented with 44 untitled passages of about 150 words apiece. One-fourth of the passages were from novels, one-fourth from newspapers, one-fourth from humanities textbooks, and one-fourth from science (natural and social) textbooks. Although there were eight different questions per passage, a given subject saw only two of them. These two questions dealt with the gist of the passage (i.e., general points), or its main idea, or specific details in the passage, or analysis and application of specific points (i.e., inferences and evaluations from the text). Which subjects received which questions for which passages was counterbalanced across subjects. Subjects also received the Nelson–Denny Reading Test and the Differential Aptitude Test Verbal Reasoning (verbal analogies) subtest.

Subjects received 11 trials of 150 seconds each. Each trial involved 4 reading passages, for a total of 44 passages. For each passage subjects were informed whether they would be tested for gist, main ideas, details, or analysis and application. By pressing an appropriately designated key on a computer console the subjects could determine the order of presentation of passages within trial, and the duration of viewing. Note, then, that subjects were basically free to allocate their time to the four types of questions as they wished.

Mean latencies for passages read for each of the question types were 38.0 for gist, 37.6 for main idea, 39.8 for details, and 40.4 for analysis and application. The times differed significantly, with the times for gist and main idea comprehension significantly shorter than the times for detail comprehension and for analysis and application comprehension. Thus, subjects did allocate time systematically to spend more time reading passages for which they would receive more demanding questions. Patterns of accuracy in responding to the question types also were systematic: Mean numbers of questions answered correctly (out of 16) for each type of question were 13.3 for gist, 12.6 for main idea, 10.5 for details, and 8.2 for analysis and application. These means, too, differed significantly from one another. The means for gist and main idea comprehension were significantly higher than those for details, which in turn was significantly higher than for analysis and application.

Overall number of questions correctly answered by each subject for all types of questions was significantly correlated with vocabulary (.57), comprehension (.48), and DAT verbal reasoning (.78). Most of the subscores were also significantly correlated with Nelson–Denny and DAT scores, and all correlations were in the predicted (positive) direction. Thus, our reading questions did seem to measure skills related to those measured by standard tests of reading comprehension.

The central question, from our point of view, was whether time allocation was systematically related to task performance. A time-allocation score was computed for each subject by subtracting the amount of time spent on reading passages for gist and main idea from the amount of time spent on reading passages for details and for analysis and application. Presumably, a higher difference score would reflect greater sensitivity in time allocation: The higher the score, the relatively greater the time spent on reading the more difficult questions and the relatively lesser the time spent on reading for the less difficult questions. Time allocation score correlated .30 with total number of passage comprehension questions answered correctly. But one might well ask whether this correlation merely reflects some skill already measured by standard reading comprehension tests, which seem to measure primarily performance components rather than metacomponents. We therefore predicted accuracy in answering questions on the reading task from DAT Verbal Reasoning score, Nelson–Denny total score (reading comprehension + vocabulary), Nelson–Denny reading rate, and time allocation. The question addressed was whether time allocation would make a significant contribution to the regression after the other, standard test variables were added to the equation. In fact, it did. The semipartial regression weight for the time allocation parameter was .30, which was statistically significant. The overall multiple correlation was .85. Thus, our metacomponential measure of reading time allocation makes a significant contribution in predicting task performance over and above that made by standardized test scores (including vocabulary, comprehension, verbal reasoning, and reading rate). Again, metacomponential processing seems to be important in real-time verbal comprehension.

B. Strategies in Using Adjunct Information

In a second experiment, 90 Yale undergraduates were divided into three groups. In a control group, subjects received eight passages and 44 questions taken from the reading comprehension sections of two editions of the Graduate Record Examination of the Educational Testing Service. Four of the passages were approximately 175 words in length. There were three questions on each. The other four passages were approximately 500 words in length with eight questions on each.

In a difficulty-information group, subjects received passages and questions identical to those used in the control group, but with two indications of difficulty. General difficulty information informed subjects of the average difficulty of the set of questions associated with each passage. This information was conveyed through a table containing the average difficulty of the questions associated with each passage and the number of questions per passage (either three or eight questions per passage). Specific difficulty information informed subjects of the difficulty level of each question. This information was conveyed by labeling each question on a scale of relative difficulty. Both general and specific difficulty information was presented through use of the phrases "very difficult," "moderately difficult," "moderately easy," and "very easy." Difficulty level was determined by the proportions of the examinees who passed the question when it was administered nationwide as part of the Graduate Record Examinations.

In an importance-information group, subjects received passages and questions identical to those received in the other two groups (but without any difficulty information). However, the most important sentences in the passages (as determined by the judgment of the experimenters) were highlighted with a yellow marker pen. Approximately 45% of the text was highlighted.

Subjects in the difficulty-information condition were instructed to use the difficulty information to maximize their performance. They were not told how to do so, however. Examples of questions labeled as to their difficulty were provided. Subjects in the importance information condition were instructed to use the importance information to maximize their performance. Again, they were not told how to do so. An example of a highlighted text was provided.

In all conditions, subjects reported the time (from an easily visible clock) when they started work on each reading passage. At the conclusion of the task, subjects in all groups provided written descriptions of their task strategies. Subjects in the two experimental conditions also described whether they made use of the adjunct difficulty or importance information, and if so, how. Reference ability measures of reading and reasoning abilities were the same as those employed in the previously described experiment.

Task performances in terms of total number of questions answered correctly (out of 44 total) for the control, difficulty information, and importance information conditions were 25.7, 23.6, and 21.6. These means did not differ significantly. Written reports of task strategies provided by subjects were scored for explicit mention of revising strategy during task performance. Twenty-eight percent of subject reported strategy revision during task performance. This percentage remained essentially constant across conditions: 30, 30, and 23% for the control, difficulty-information, and importance-information conditions, respectively. Two reasons were given for strategy revision: A strategy chosen before beginning the task was not working out, or a strategy was changed when time began to run out so that the subject would have a chance of answering the remaining questions. Subjects who reported strategy revision performed significantly better on the task than subjects who did not, achieving a mean total score of 26.1, as opposed to 22.7. Subjects who reported strategy revision also attained significantly higher scores on the DAT Verbal Reasoning Test than did subjects who did not (45.7 vs. 44.1); scores on the Nelson–Denny Reading Test did not differ significantly between groups, however.

The record of the times when subjects began work on each passage and order in which passages were read enabled us to score the presence or absence of the strategy of reading passages in their order of difficulty. No attempt was made to distinguish between subjects who followed this strategy exclusively and subjects who followed this strategy for only part of the reading task. Fifty-three percent of subjects in the difficulty condition used this strategy. These subjects obtained higher average task scores than subjects who did not, 26.3 versus 20.6. Subjects using this strategy also obtained marginally significantly higher scores on the Nelson–Denny Reading Test (136.3 vs. 123.9) and had a higher reading rate as measured by the Nelson–Denny (348.8 versus 286.8). Performance on the DAT Verbal Reasoning Test did not differ between the two types of subjects (43.9 vs. 44.1). More able subjects, then, used general difficulty information in planning their order of passage reading. It was possible to determine the validity of subjects' written reports of task strategies by comparing actual strategy as determined from the record of passage order with written reports of strategy. All subjects who used the strategy of reading passages in order of their difficulty reported doing so; conversely, no subjects who did not use this strategy reported doing so.

Subjects' written reports of task strategy were scored for (1) the presence of a strategy of using the specific difficulty information and for (2) indications that the specific information was distracting. Twenty-seven percent of subjects reported using the specific difficulty information. These subjects described using a strategy of matching how much effort they spent searching for and evaluating possible answers to the difficulty level of the questions. Subjects who reported using the specific difficulty information actually performed less well on the task than did subjects who did not report use of specific difficulty information (18.8 vs. 25.4). These subjects also obtained lower Nelson–Denny Reading Test scores (111.0 vs. 136.5), but performance on the DAT Verbal Reasoning Test did not differ significantly across groups (41.6 vs. 44.8). Twenty percent of subjects reported that the specific difficulty information was distracting, often because the difficulty rating of a particular question did not correspond to the subjects' own perceptions of difficulty. Subjects also reported that they disliked being told how difficult a question was; in some cases, knowing that a question was very difficult made them anxious. Subjects who reported the specific difficulty information as distracting performed better on the task than did subjects who did not (31.2 vs. 21.8). No reliable differences were found on the reference ability tests, however, for this comparison. Overall, then, more able subjects were (1) more likely to use *general* difficulty information for planning order of passage selection, were (2) less likely to use *specific* difficulty information, and were (3) more likely to find the *specific* difficulty information distracting.

Three strategies for using importance information were identified. Twenty-seven percent of subjects reported using a strategy of reading highlighted sections exclusively. Task performance for subjects using this strategy was comparable to that of subjects who did not use the strategy (21.8 vs. 21.6), as was performance on the Nelson–Denny Reading Test (125.0 vs. 130.1). Subjects who used this strategy did perform better on the DAT Verbal Reasoning Test, however (46.9 vs. 44.3). A related strategy was reading the highlighted sections more carefully than the nonhighlighted sections, but not exclusively. Forty-three percent of subjects reported using this strategy, but performance on the task and reference ability measures was comparable for subjects who reported using this strategy and those who did not. A final identifiable strategy was one of searching for answers in the highlighted portions. This was an understandable strategy because a majority of the answers were to be found in the highlighted sections and subjects were informed of this fact. Thirty-three percent of subjects reported using this strategy. Task performance was comparable for subjects who reported using this strategy and those who did not (23.8 vs. 20.6). Subjects who reported using this strategy performed better on the Nelson–Denny Reading Test, however (139.8 vs. 123.7). Their performance on the DAT Verbal Reasoning Test was comparable to that of subjects who did not use this strategy (46.1 vs. 44.4).

To conclude, the proposed theory of real-time verbal comprehension appears to give a good account of processing at the word level and of time allocation at the passage level. The theory is by no means a complete theory of real-time processing but may at least provide a step in that direction. In combination, the theory of how verbal comprehension develops and the theory of how verbal comprehension functions in real time seem to provide a reasonable start toward understanding the psychology of verbal comprehension.

VIII.   CONCLUSIONS

A theory of the psychology of verbal comprehension has been presented that deals with two major aspects of comprehension: the acquisition of verbal concepts and the real-time processing of verbal concepts. The theory of real-time processing deals both with the performance components, or nonexecutive processes of comprehension, and with the metacomponents, or executive processes of comprehension. Thus, the theory as a whole deals with all three aspects of verbal information processing in my more general theory of intelligence (Sternberg, 1985): knowledge-acquisition components, performance components, and metacomponents.

The subtheory of knowledge-acquisition components specifies three processes—selective encoding, selective combination, and selective comparison—that are applied to context cues. The efficacy of their application is affected by mediating variables that make it differentially difficult to apply the processes to the cues. Multiple experiments were conducted in order both to test the subtheory and to examine its implications for training verbal-comprehension skills. The experiments provide support for the subtheory and also show its efficacy as a basis for training decontextualization skills. Indeed, the results suggest that learning from context is a good method for training vocabulary-acquisition skills only when the training is theoretically based.

The subtheory of performance components in real-time verbal comprehension attempts to deal with how individuals process the meanings of words as they are encountered, for example, when an individual is taking a vocabulary test. In this subtheory, words are understood as comprising sets of defining and characteristic attributes, which are interrogated when one is making a decision about the meaning of a given word, and about how this meaning compares to that of another word. A set of experiments showed that the subtheory of verbal comprehension provides a good account of people's real-time processing of word meanings.

The subtheory of metacomponents deals with how executive processes are used in reading. In particular, how do subjects allocate their limited time and mental resources to maximize their reading comprehension? The results suggest that better and poorer readers allocate their time and resources differently, and in particular, that better readers are more planful in their time and resource allocation. Better readers, for example, do more global planning for reading than do poorer readers.

The theory of verbal comprehension presented here is obviously incomplete in the scope of questions with which it can deal: For example, it says nothing about use of phonics, grammar, and syntax in verbal comprehension. At the same time, the theory probably covers more ground than many other extant theories of verbal comprehension. Most importantly, the proposed theory carries us some way beyond psychometric notions, such as those of Thurstone (1938), or even more recent notions of multiple intelligences, such as those of Gardner (1983), which specify "verbal ability" or "verbal intelligence" without providing a clear and coherent anatomy of the domain. Indeed, the advantage of information-processing theories is that they can go beyond naming a domain and actually help theorists specify just what kinds of mental processing occur within the domain.

Although alternative approaches to understanding verbal comprehension have been compared in this chapter, the comparison is in no way intended to suggest that certain approaches are useful and others not so. To the contrary, multiple approaches must be used in conjunction to elucidate as many aspects of verbal comprehension as possible. Thus, for example, although my own research has tended to be top-down rather than bottom-up or knowledge-based with respect to the investigation of knowledge-acquisition processes, it should be self-evident that bottom-up as well as top-down processes are involved in knowledge acquisition, and that such processes are interactive with knowledge: They are knowledge-driven processes in search of further knowledge. Thus, further development of theories of verbal comprehension will almost certainly have to utilize a knitting of current theories and approaches in order more fully to understand the phenomena that constitute the psychology of verbal comprehension.

ACKNOWLEDGMENTS

Preparation of this chapter was supported by Contract N0001483K0013 from the Office of Naval Research and Army Research Institute. I am grateful to Daniel Kaye, Timothy McNamara, Elizabeth Neuse, Janet Powell, and Richard Wagner for the collaborations in research on verbal comprehension that helped make this chapter possible.

REFERENCES

Anderson, N. H. (1979). Algebraic rules in psychological measurement. *American Scientist, 67,* 555–563.
Anderson, R. C., & Freebody, P. (1979). *Vocabulary knowledge.* (Tech. Rep. No. 136). Champaign, IL: University of Illinois, Center for the Study of Reading.
Baddeley, A. D. (1968). A 3-minute reasoning test based on grammatical transformation. *Psychonomic Science, 10,* 341–342.
Bisanz, G. L., & Voss, J. F. (1981). Sources of knowledge in reading comprehension. In A. Lesgold & C. A. Perfetti (Eds.), *Interactive processes in reading.* Hillsdale, NJ: Lawrence Erlbaum Associates.
Bransford, J. D., Barclay, J. R., & Franks, J. J. (1972). Sentence memory: A constructive versus interpretive approach. *Cognitive Psychology, 3,* 193–209.
Brown, A. L. (1978). Knowing when, where, and how to remember: A problem of metacognition. In R. Glaser (Ed.), *Advances in instructional psychology* (Vol. 1). Hillsdale, NJ: Lawrence Erlbaum Associates.
Brown, A. L. (1980). Metacognitive development and reading. In R. Spiro, B. Bruce, & W. Brewer (Eds.), *Theoretical issues in reading comprehension.* Hillsdale, NJ: Lawrence Erlbaum Associates.
Carroll, J. B. (1976). Psychometric tests as cognitive tasks: A new "structure of intellect." In L. B. Resnick (Ed.), *The nature of intelligence.* Hillsdale, NJ: Lawrence Erlbaum Associates.
Carroll, J. B. (1981). Ability and task difficulty in cognitive psychology. *Educational Researcher, 10,* 11–21.
Charness, N. (1981). Aging and skilled problem solving. *Journal of Experimental Psychology: General, 110,* 21–38.
Chase, W. G., & Simon, H. A. (1973). The mind's eye in chess. In W. G. Chase (Ed.), *Visual information processing.* New York: Academic Press.

Chi, M. T. H. (1978). Knowledge structures and memory development. In R. S. Siegler (Ed.), *Children's thinking: What develops?* Hillsdale, NJ: Lawrence Erlbaum Associates.

Chiesi, H. L., Spilich, G. J., & Voss, J. F. (1979). Acquisition of domain-related information in relation to high and low domain knowledge. *Journal of Verbal Learning and Verbal Behavior, 18*, 257–274.

Clark, H. H., & Chase, W. G. (1972). On the process of comparing sentences against pictures. *Cognitive Psychology, 3*, 472–517.

Clark, H. H., & Clark, E. V. (1977). *Psychology and language.* New York: Harcourt Brace Jovanovich.

Collins, A. M., & Loftus, E. F. (1975). A spreading-activation theory of semantic processing. *Psychological Review, 82*, 407–28.

Collins, A., & Smith, E. E. (1982). Teaching the process of reading comprehension. In D. K. Detterman & R. J. Sternberg (Eds.), *How and how much can intelligence be increased?* Norwood, NJ: Ablex.

Cornelius, S. W., Willis, S. L., Blow, S., & Baltes, P. B. (1983). Training research in aging: Attention processes. *Journal of Educational Psychology, 75*, 257–270.

Curtis, M. E. (1981). *Word knowledge and verbal aptitude.* Unpublished manuscript, University of Pittsburgh.

Daalen-Kapteijns, Van, M. M., & Elshout-Mohr, M. (1981). The acquisition of word meanings as a cognitive learning process. *Journal of Verbal Learning and Verbal Behavior, 20*, 386–399.

Daneman, M. (1984). Why some people are better readers than others: A process and storage account. In R. J. Sternberg (Ed.), *Advances in the psychology of human intelligence* (Vol. 2). Hillsdale, NJ: Lawrence Erlbaum Associates.

Daneman, M., & Carpenter, P. A. (1980). Individual differences in working memory and reading. *Journal of Verbal Learning and Verbal Behavior. 19*, 450–466.

Flavell, J. H. (1981). Cognitive monitoring. In W. P. Dickson (Ed.), *Children's oral communication skills.* New York: Academic Press.

Frege, G. (1952). On sense and reference. In P. Geach & M. Black (Eds.), *Translations from the philosophical writings of Gottolb Frege.* Oxford: Basil, Blackwell, & Mott.

Freyd, P., & Baron, J. (1982). Individual differences in acquisition of derivational morphology. *Journal of Verbal Learning and Verbal Behavior, 21*, 282–295.

Gardner, H. (1983). *Frames of mind: The theory of multiple intelligences.* New York: Basic Books.

Goldberg, R. A., Schwartz, S., & Stewart, M. (1977). Individual differences in cognitive processes. *Journal of Educational Psychology, 69*, 9–14.

Guilford, J. P. (1967). *The nature of human intelligence.* New York: McGraw–Hill.

Hampton, J. A. (1979). Polymorphous concepts in semantic memory. *Journal of Verbal Learning and Verbal Behavior, 18*, 441–461.

Hogaboam, T. W., & Pellegrino, J. W. (1978). Hunting for individual differences: Verbal ability and semantic processing of pictures and words. *Memory and Cognition, 6*, 189–193.

Holyoak, K. J., Glass, A. L., & Mah, W. A. (1976). Morphological structure and semantic retrieval. *Journal of Verbal Learning and Verbal Behavior, 15*, 235–247.

Horn, J. L., & Cattell, R. B. (1966). Refinement and test of the theory of fluid and crystallized ability intelligences. *Journal of Educational Psychology, 57*, 253–270.

Hunt, E. B. (1978). Mechanics of verbal ability. *Psychological Review, 85*, 109–130.

Hunt, E. B. (1980). Intelligence as an information processing concept. *British Journal of Psychology, 71*, 449–474.

Hunt, E. B. (1984). Verbal ability. In R. J. Sternberg (Ed.), *Human abilities: An information processing approach.* San Francisco: Freeman.

Hunt, E., Lunneborg, C., & Lewis, J. (1975). What does it mean to be high verbal? *Cognitive Psychology, 7*, 194–227.

Jackson, M. D., & McClelland, J. L. (1979). Processing determinants of reading speed. *Journal of Experimental Psychology: General, 108,* 151–181.

Jensen, A. R. (1980). *Bias in mental testing.* New York: Free Press.

Johnson, D. D., & Pearson, P. D. (1978). *Teaching and reading vocabulary.* New York: Holt.

Just, M. A., & Carpenter, P. A. (1980). A theory of reading: From eye fixations to comprehension. *Psychological Review, 87,* 329–354.

Kaye, D. B., & Sternberg, R. J. (1983). *Development of lexical decomposition ability.* Unpublished manuscript.

Keating, D. P., & Bobbitt, B. L. (1978). Individual and developmental differences in cognitive-processing components of mental ability. *Child Development, 49,* 155–167.

Keil, F. C. (1979). *Semantic and conceptual development.* Cambridge, MA: Harvard University Press.

Keil, F. C. (1981). Constraints on knowledge and cognitive development. *Psychological Review, 88,* 197–227.

Keil, F. C. (1984). Mechanisms of cognitive development and the structure of knowledge. In R. J. Sternberg (Ed.), *Mechanisms of cognitive development.* San Francisco: Freeman.

Kintsch, W. (1974). *The representation of meaning in memory.* Hillsdale, NJ: Lawrence Erlbaum Associates.

Kintsch, W., & van Dijk, T. A. (1978). Toward a model of text comprehension and production. *Psychological Review, 85,* 363–394.

Lansman, M., Donaldson, G., Hunt, E., & Yantis, S. (1982). Ability factors and cognitive processes. *Intelligence, 6,* 347–386.

Manelis, L., & Tharp, D. A. (1977). The processing of affixed words. *Memory and Cognition, 5,* 690–695.

Markman, E. M. (1977). Realizing that you don't understand: A preliminary investigation. *Child Development, 48,* 986–992.

Markman, E. M. (1979). Realizing that you don't understand: Elementary school children's awareness of inconsistencies. *Child Development, 50,* 643–655.

Markman, E. M. (1981). Comprehension monitoring. In W. P. Dickson (Ed.), *Children's oral communication skills.* New York: Academic Press.

Marshalek, B. (1981). *Trait and process aspects of vocabulary knowledge and verbal ability* (NR154–376 ONR Technical Report No. 15). Stanford, CA: School of Education, Stanford University.

Masur, E. F., McIntyre, C. W., & Flavell, J. H. (1973). Developmental changes in apportionment of study time among items in a multitrial free recall task. *Journal of Experimental Child Psychology, 15,* 237–246.

Matarazzo, J. D. (1972). *Wechsler's measurement and appraisal of adult intelligence* (5th ed.). Baltimore: Williams & Wilkins.

McNamara, T. P., & Sternberg, R. J. (1983). Mental models of word meaning. *Journal of Verbal Learning and Verbal Behavior, 22,* 449–474.

Miller, G. A., & Johnson-Laird, P. N. (1976). *Language and perception.* Cambridge, MA: Harvard University Press.

Murrell, G. A., & Morton, J. (1974). Word recognition and morphemic structure. *Journal of Experimental Psychology, 102,* 963–968.

O'Rourke, J. P. (1974). *Toward a science of vocabulary development.* The Hague: Mouton.

Perfetti, C. A. (1983). Individual differences in verbal processes. In R. F. Dillon & R. R. Schmeck (Eds.), *Individual differences in cognition* (Vol. 1). New York: Academic Press.

Perfetti, C. A., & Hogaboam, T. (1975). Relationship between single word decoding and reading comprehension skill. *Journal of Educational Psychology, 67,* 461–469.

Perfetti, C. A., & Lesgold, A. M. (1977). Discourse comprehension and individual differences. In P. Carpenter & M. Just (Eds.), *Cognitive processes in comprehension: The 12th annual Carnegie symposium on cognition*. Hillsdale, NJ: Lawrence Erlbaum Associates.

Posner, M. I., & Mitchell, R. F. (1967). Chronometric analysis of classification. *Psychological Review, 74*, 392–409.

Rieger, C. (1975). Conceptual memory. In R. C. Schank (Ed.), *Conceptual information processing*. Amsterdam: North–Holland.

Rosch, E. (1978). Principles of categorization. In E. Rosch & B. B. Lloyd (Eds.), *Cognition and categorization*. Hillsdale, NJ: Lawrence Erlbaum Associates.

Rubin, D. C. (1976). The effectiveness of context before, after, and around a missing word. *Perception and Psychophysics 19*, 214–216.

Rubin, G. S., Becker, C. A., & Freeman, R. H. (1979). Morphological structure and its effect on visual word recognition. *Journal of Verbal Learning and Verbal Behavior, 18*, 757–767.

Rumelhart, D. E. (1980). Schemata: The building blocks of cognition. In R. J. Spiro, B. C. Bruce, & W. F. Brewer (Eds.), *Theoretical issues in reading comprehension: Perspectives from cognitive psychology, linguistics, artificial intelligence, and education*. Hillsdale, NJ: Lawrence Erlbaum Associates.

Rumelhart, D. E., & Norman, D. A. (1975). The active structural network. In D. A. Norman & D. E. Rumelhart (Eds.), *Explorations in cognition*. San Francisco: Freeman.

Russell, B. (1956). On denoting. In R. C. Marsh (Ed.), *Logic and knowledge*. London: George Allen & Unwin.

Salatas, H., & Flavell, J. H. (1976). Behavioral and metamnemonic indicators of strategic behaviors under remember instruction in first grade. *Child Development, 47*, 80–89.

Schank, R. C., & Abelson, R. P. (1977). *Scripts, plans, goals, and understanding*. Hillsdale, NJ: Lawrence Erlbaum Associates.

Schwartz, S. P. (1977). *Naming, necessity, and natural kinds*. London: Cornell University Press.

Smith, E. E., Shoben, E. J., & Rips, L. J. (1974). Structure and process in semantic memory: A featural model for semantic decisions. *Psychological Review, 81*, 214–241.

Spilich, G. J., Vesonder, G. T., Chiesi, H. L., & Voss, J. F. (1979). Text processing of domain-related information for individuals with high and low domain knowledge. *Journal of Verbal Learning and Verbal Behavior, 18*, 275–290.

Stanners, R. F., Neiser, J. J., & Painton, S. (1979). Memory representation for prefixed words. *Journal of Verbal Learning and Verbal Behavior, 18*, 733–743.

Sternberg, R. J. (1980). Sketch of a componential subtheory of human intelligence. *Behavioral and Brain Sciences, 3*, 573–584.

Sternberg, R. J. (1981). Intelligence and nonentrenchment. *Journal of Educational Psychology, 73*, 1–16.

Sternberg, R. J. (1985). *Beyond IQ: A triarchic theory of human intelligence*. New York: Cambridge University Press.

Sternberg, R. J., & McNamara, T. P. (1985). The representation and processing of information in real-time verbal comprehension. In S. E. Embretson (Ed.), *Test design: Contributions from psychology, education, and psychometrics*. New York: Academic Press.

Sternberg, R. J., & Neuse, E. (1983). *Utilization of context in verbal comprehension*. Unpublished manuscript.

Sternberg, R. J., & Powell, J. S. (1983). Comprehending verbal comprehension. *American Psychologist, 38*, 878–893.

Sternberg, R. J., Powell, J. S., & Kaye, D. B. (1983). Teaching vocabulary-building skills: A contextual approach. In A. C. Wilkson (Ed.), *Classroom computers and cognitive science*. New York: Academic Press.

Taft, M. (1979). Recognition of affixed words and the word frequency effect. *Memory and Cognition, 7*, 263–272.

Taft, M., & Forster, K. I. (1975). Lexical storage and retrieval of prefixed words. *Journal of Verbal Learning and Verbal Behavior, 14*, 638–647.

Thurstone, L. L. (1938). *Primary mental abilities.* Chicago: University of Chicago.

Vernon, P. E. (1971). *The structure of human abilities.* London: Methuen.

Wagner, R. K., & Sternberg, R. J. (in press). Executive control of reading. In B. Britton (Ed.), *Executive control processes in reading.* Hillsdale, NJ: Lawrence Erlbaum Associates.

Werner, H., & Kaplan, E. (1952). The acquisition of word meanings: A developmental study. *Monographs of the Society for Research in Child Development* (No. 51).

Wittgenstein, L. (1953). *Philosophical investigations.* Oxford: Basil, Blackwell, & Mott.

4

Classroom Behavior and Achievement of Japanese, Chinese, and American Children

Harold W. Stevenson
University of Michigan

James W. Stigler
University of Chicago

G. William Lucker
University of Texas, El Paso

Shinyin Lee
University of Michigan

C. C. Hsu
National Taiwan University

S. Kitamura
Tohoku Fukushi College

I. INTRODUCTION

Asian children's superior achievement in mathematics and science is well known. Japanese students consistently have been among the top performers in international studies of achievement in mathematics and science (e.g., Comber & Keeves, 1973; Husén, 1967), whereas American children typically lag behind. In fact, rarely in such comparative studies do the average scores of American children even fall within the range of scores of children in the top countries. Nor is there any indication that the scores of American children are improving. For example, in a study of achievement in mathmatics and science commissioned in 1983 by the *Dallas Times Herald*, American 12-year-olds received the lowest average scores in mathematics in eight countries. The American children were able to answer only 25.3% of the questions correctly, whereas their Japanese peers were able to answer 50.2%. These scores placed the Japanese children at the top and the American children at the bottom of a list of countries that also included children from Sweden, Australia, England, Canada, France, and Switzerland. Preliminary results from the Second International Mathematics Study offer a similar picture (Crosswhite, Dossey, Swafford, McKnight, & Cooney, 1985). For example, among eighth graders from 20 countries, Japanese children received the highest scores in arithmetic, algebra, geometry, statistics, and measurement. The average scores of the American children on these tests ranged from the 8th to the 18th position.

A. Rationale for the Study

Most of the previous studies have involved students at the sixth-grade level or beyond. In a recent study of first and fifth graders in Japan, Taiwan, and the United States, we found large cross-cultural differences in mathematics achievement as early as the first grade (Stigler, Lee, Lucker, & Stevenson, 1982). Chinese and Japanese children received significantly higher scores than did their American counterparts at both first and fifth grades. The differences were significant for items involving skill in mathematical operations and problem solving.

Differences in achievement were not limited to mathematics. The children's reading skills also differed, but to a smaller degree than their skills in mathematics. The average scores of the American first graders were below those of the Chinese children on a reading test involving three types of items: oral reading of single words and of meaningful text, and reading comprehension. Japanese children tended to obtain scores that fell between those of the American and Chinese children. These patterns of difference were repeated at the fifth grade.

Several hypotheses have been proposed to account for the superiority of children from Chinese and Japanese families, such as differences in IQ (e.g., Lynn, 1982), socialization processes (e.g., Azuma, Kashiwagi, & Hess, 1981; DeVos, 1973), and educational practices (e.g., Cummings, 1980; Rohlen, 1983; Wilson, 1970). The first hypothesis has received little support from research. Differences in level of intellectual functioning do not appear to offer a satisfactory interpretation of the cross-national differences in achievement. Stevenson and Azuma (1983) have recently shown that, primarily because of sampling problems, there is little basis for accepting the hypothesis proposed by Lynn that Japanese children have higher IQs than American children. Moreover, in a study of the relation of cognitive ability to children's achievement in reading and mathematics, both the level of cognitive function and relations between cognitive ability and achievement were similar among Chinese, Japanese, and American children (Stevenson, Stigler, Lee, Lucker, Kitamura, & Hsu, 1985).

The present study is concerned with the third of the three factors, children's educational experiences. (Differences in socialization practices are discussed in a later report.) Until now, the information that has been available about Chinese and Japanese classrooms comes primarily from the conclusions reached by skilled observers such as Cummings, Rohlen, and Wilson. But in each case these conclusions are those of a single individual who spent many hours visiting classrooms in one of the cultures. There were no comparative studies in which observers collected observations systematically by means of an objectively defined observational system. We sought to conduct such a study. Our primary purpose in this chapter is to describe characteristics of Chinese, Japanese, and

American classrooms that provide clues concerning possible bases of differences in children's levels of achievement.

B. Schooling in Japan, Taiwan, and the United States

Before discussing the details of the study, it is important to have a general picture of schooling in the three countries. Elementary education is universal in all three countries. Over 99% of school-age children attend elementary school in all three countries, and the majority go on to middle school. Entrance to high school in both Japan and Taiwan is determined by scores on nationwide entrance examinations. Consequently, educational practices in elementary and middle school often are influenced by the impending examinations.

Educational policy in Taiwan is highly centralized. The curriculum is specified by the Ministry of Education, and all schools, including private schools, follow it. Textbooks are published by the Ministry and every school uses the same set. In Japan, the Ministry of Education publishes a detailed curriculum for all schools. Although the Ministry does not publish the textbooks, private publishers must conform to their guidelines. These practices contrast sharply with those of the United States, where local school boards, principals, and even individual teachers make choices about the curriculum and textbooks.

Children in Taiwan and Japan spend more time in school than do their American peers. Chinese and Japanese children spend 5½ days a week in school. American children attend school 5 days a week. The school year in Taiwan and Japan ranges between 230 and 240 days, whereas in the United States it ranges between 170 and 180 days. First graders in each country spend roughly 30 hours a week in school. By the later grades of elementary school, Japanese children are in school approximately an hour a day longer, and Chinese children, 2 hours a day longer than American children.

The physical arrangement of classrooms also is different. In Taiwan and Japan, desks typically are arranged in rows facing the teacher's desk at the front of the class. Desks in American schools often are arranged in groups, permitting the teacher to work more easily with small groups of children. Many more children are enrolled in each classroom in Taiwan and Japan than in the United States.

C. Overview of the Study

Many observational studies of American classrooms have been conducted, and recommendations about effective practices have been made (e.g., Brophy, 1983). Nevertheless, by looking at what happens in the classrooms of other cultures, especially those in which the level of achievement is high, we may gain new perspectives on possible determinants of children's achievement.

Before we could begin our study, it was necessary to develop a method of classroom observation applicable to Chinese, Japanese, and American classrooms. We reviewed many observational schemes used in studies of American classrooms, and we visited many elementary school classrooms in the three countries. With this information, we devised a comprehensive time-sampling observational scheme that we believed would give us a reliable picture.

The times of classroom observations and the children to be observed were selected randomly across a period of several weeks. The observers' attention was focused on the children for some of the observations and on the teacher for others. The observers, guided by tape-recorded cues, watched a particular child (or the teacher) for a brief interval and then recorded what was observed on a standard coding sheet. Variables coded included classroom organization, classroom leader, subject being studied, children's responsiveness to the teacher, type of feedback provided by the teacher, and appropriate and inappropriate behavior displayed by the children. We hoped these variables would provide clues about important ways in which American classrooms differed from those in the other two countries.

The subjects for our study were the Chinese, Japanese, and American first- and fifth-grade children whose achievement scores were referred to earlier. These scores, based on carefully constructed, individually administered achievement tests, provide reliable measures of the children's achievement in reading and in mathematics. A great deal of additional information was obtained from their teachers and parents and from the children themselves. The data discussed in the present report are primarily those obtained from the classroom observations.

II. THE SAMPLES: 3 CITIES, 33 SCHOOLS, 120 CLASSROOMS, 1440 TARGET CHILDREN

The study was conducted with children from 20 first-grade and 20 fifth-grade classrooms in the Minneapolis metropolitan area, Sendai (Japan), and Taipei (Taiwan). The Minneapolis metropolitan area was chosen primarily because we did not want to include ethnic status of the American children as a factor in our study. There are few minority children in Minneapolis; most are from white, English-speaking, native-born families. In addition, the metropolitan area of Minneapolis is large enough to provide schools that differ in size and neighborhoods that differ in socioeconomic status. After discussions with colleagues in Japan and the United States, it was agreed that the Japanese city most similar in size and other characteristics to Minneapolis was Sendai, located 240 miles northeast of Tokyo in the Tohoku region. Only two large Chinese cities, Taipei and Hong Kong, were possible sites when the study was initiated. Taipei was chosen because it is a modern city comparable in size to the Minneapolis–St.

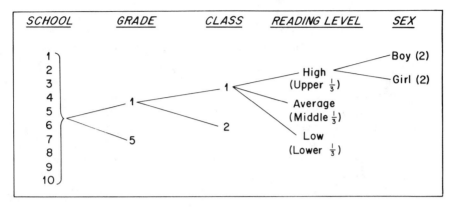

	U.S.	Taiwan	Japan
Grade 1 (N)	240	240	240
Grade 5 (N)	240	240	240

	U.S.	Taiwan	Japan
School (N)	13	10	10
Class (N)	40	40	40

FIG. 4.1. Outline of the procedure for selecting subjects.

Paul metropolitan area, and because Chinese is the dominant language. In Hong Kong both Chinese and English are used daily.

Great care was taken in developing a procedure that would ensure selection of representative samples of children within each city. It was crucial that the samples be obtained in the same manner. Our goal was to select 10 schools in each city that would be representative in terms of location, socioeconomic status of the families whose children attended the school, and source of funding (public or private). We discussed our goals with educational authorities in each city and obtained a list of schools by region and families' socioeconomic status. Schools were then selected at random so that the 10 schools would constitute a representative sample. Two classrooms from each school were randomly chosen at both first and fifth grades, yielding a total of 20 first-grade and 20 fifth-grade classrooms in each city. The only exception was Minneapolis. Because there was not a sufficient number of first- and fifth-grade classrooms in the 10 schools initially selected, 13 schools were required to obtain the desired 40 classrooms. In Taipei and in Minneapolis, one private school was chosen. The remaining schools chosen in these cities, and all the schools chosen in Sendai were public schools.

For observations of individual children, 2 boys and 2 girls were chosen randomly from the upper, middle, and lower thirds of each classroom as indicated by their scores on an individually administered test of reading achievement. (We sampled children according to reading ability because the observational study was part of a larger project that focused on reading achievement.) There were, therefore, 240 target children, 120 boys and 120 girls, in each country at each grade level. This procedure is summarized in Fig. 4.1.

In some cells, the actual number of children departed slightly from 240; the N for individual cells varied from 237 to 246. At the time the children were first seen—approximately 4 months after the opening of the school year—the mean ages of the first graders in Minneapolis, Taipei, and Sendai were, respectively, 6.8, 6.7, and 6.8 years; and of the fifth graders, 10.9, 10.8, and 10.9 years.

A. Teachers

There were more women than men serving as teachers in the 40 classrooms in all three cities. The proportion of male teachers was 20% in the U.S., 22% in Taiwan, and 43% in Japan. The American teachers in our sample had an average of 15.4 years of teaching experience. In Japan the average was 17.4 years, and in Taiwan 16.6 years.

The teachers' training differed greatly in the three countries. The American teachers had many more years of formal education than did teachers in Japan or Taiwan. All the American teachers were college graduates, and 11 had advanced degrees. Training in Taiwan followed a different pattern. Most teachers (85%) were graduates of a 5-year teacher training program, which they entered after completing middle school. The remaining teachers were graduates of regular universities. In Japan, 68% of the teachers had received a B.A. degree, but none had graduate training. Most of the American and Japanese teachers with college degrees had majored in elementary education: 76% in the United States and 70% in Japan.

B. Schools

The schools we visited in Taipei and Sendai are much older than those in Minneapolis. The 13 Minneapolis schools were built an average of 23 years ago. The schools in Taipei were established an average of 34 years ago, and in Sendai, 47 years ago. Elementary schools in the three cities differ greatly in size. The schools in the Minneapolis metropolitan area in our study had an average of 498 pupils, with a range from 250 to 800. The average number of students in the classes was 22 in first grade and 24 in fifth grade. Taipei schools are large and crowded. The average number of students attending the schools in our sample was 2,790, with a range from 390 to 4,500. The average number of students in each classroom was 45 at Grade 1 and 48 at Grade 5—about twice the size of

Minneapolis classrooms. Japanese schools were of intermediate size compared to those in the United States and Taiwan, with an average of 1,020 pupils, and a range from 735 to 1,257. There was an average of 39 pupils in each first- and fifth-grade classroom.

Each week, first graders spent an average of 29.9 hours in school in Minneapolis, 27.5 in Taipei, and 30.7 in Sendai. By fifth grade, the average increased markedly in Taipei to 44.1 hours and in Sendai to 37.3 hours. In Minneapolis the time spent in school at fifth grade (30.4 hours) remained very similar to that found in the first grade. The teachers reported they were at school an average of 43 hours a week in Minneapolis, 47 in Taipei, and 51 in Sendai. The actual time spent teaching was very similar, 28 hours a week in Minneapolis and Sendai and 30 hours a week in Taipei. Thus, of the time spent at school, the American teachers estimated that they spent 66% of the time teaching, the Chinese teachers, 64%, and the Japanese teachers, 54%. The remaining time was spent in preparation, correcting papers, working with individual children, meetings and other activities related to school.

III. OBSERVATIONAL PROCEDURE AND CODING SYSTEM

We faced the problem of deciding between an observational procedure that relied on an objective coding system and one that used a descriptive approach. Our decision was to adopt an objective coding system. Because our observations would be conducted by residents of each city, we believed it would be very difficult to train observers to record descriptive observations in a comparable manner when they were from three cultures and spoke three different languages.

A time-sampling method was developed. Each of the 20 first-grade classrooms and each of the 20 fifth-grade classrooms in the three cities were to be visited 40 times over a period of 2 to 4 weeks. Thus, 1,600 hours of observation were to be conducted in the classrooms in each city—800 hours at each grade level.

We wanted to be able to describe each classroom as well as individual children within each classroom. Therefore, some of the observations were focused on the children and others on the teachers. If all observations had been of individual children, many events that occur with low frequency for an individual child but with a moderate frequency within each classroom would have been missed.

Our goal was to sample each child's behavior for 200 10-second intervals spaced over randomly chosen times in a 2-week period. This would yield approximately 33 minutes of observation of each child. Behavior was observed for a 10-second interval followed by a 10-second period for coding. The observations of each teacher were made during 480 15-second intervals totaling 120 minutes. A

15-second coding interval followed each 15-second observation. This procedure yielded 8.5 hours of observational data for each classroom (33 minutes of observation of each of 12 children and 120 minutes of observation of the teacher). Including the time observers spent in recording, in transition from one type of observation to another, and in rest periods, it was necessary for observers to be present in each classroom for approximately 40 hours.

Six children were observed during each observational period. The 12 target children were divided into two subgroups composed of equal numbers of boys and girls. Each observational period contained five blocks of observations of children and three blocks of observations of the teacher. Each child was observed for two successive 10-second intervals during each block. The maximum number of successive blocks of either children or teacher was two (e.g., children, children, teacher, children, teacher, teacher, children, children). If all members of a subgroup left the room, the observer followed the children.

It turned out to be impossible to schedule more than 30 hours of observation in each of the 20 Sendai classrooms. Thus, statements pertaining to a grade in Sendai are based on 600 observational periods. In Minneapolis there were holidays, illnesses, and, because the observations in all three cultures were scheduled during the last several months of the school year, we sometimes found it was over before all the observations could be completed. (Absences during the time an observation was scheduled for a particular child occurred 2.7% of the time in Minneapolis, an amazingly low .1% in Taipei, and 3.8% in Sendai.) All the scheduled observations were completed in Taipei. Thus, the actual number of observational periods is 1,200 in Sendai, 1,353 in Minneapolis, and 1,600 in Taipei.

Of the 247 hours in which observations were not conducted in Minneapolis, 107 were in first grade and 140 were in fifth grade. The median number of observational hours omitted for each classroom was 2. Many classrooms had no omissions and the maximum number of omissions for a classroom was 10. A careful inspection of the times during the school day in which the missing observations had been scheduled indicated that they were randomly distributed.

The process of organizing the observational schedules obviously was complex. To eliminate confusion on the part of the observers, all relevant information concerning the school, grade, children, and time for a particular observation were coded on the outside of envelopes. Within the envelope were recording sheets organized in the order the children and the teacher were to be observed. The combinations of variables for each classroom were generated by means of a computer program. Thus, the observers simply had to select an envelope and follow the directions it contained.

A. Overview of the Observational Method

Two principles guided the design of our observational method. First, we sought to include variables that were relevant to classrooms in all three cultures. For

TABLE 4.1
Major Observational Categories

Subject matter
    Language arts, mathematics, social studies, music, art, moral education,
    study period, other
Classroom organization
    Class, group, individual
Leader of the activity
    Teacher, other adult, student, no one
On-task behaviors
    Attending, volunteering, asking academic question, asking procedural ques-
    tion, answering academic question, answering procedural question, story,
    choral responding, individual reading aloud, group reading aloud, seatwork,
    other
Off-task behavior
    Out-of-seat inappropriate activity, inappropriate peer interaction, other in-
    appropriate activity
Evaluative feedback
    Academic: praise, criticism, correct, incorrect, no feedback
    Behavioral: praise, criticism, punishment

example, the observations would be inaccurate if we failed to include a variable such as choral reading that occurs in one culture but not in another. We were able to determine what these variables might be only after we had visited many elementary school classrooms in each country. Second, we wanted to develop a method that could be easily understood and applied in a consistent fashion by observers from the three cultures. In order to do this, it was necessary to develop categories that required minimal interpretation by the observer.

Observers were guided through the sequences of observation and recording through taped cues, which they listened to through earphones. The categories of behavior included in the student and teacher coding schemes were defined in great detail.

A description of each category and of the general procedure can be found in Appendix A. The results of the study can be understood, however, by referring to the general outline of the observational categories presented in Table 4.1. Our major purpose was to describe what was being taught, how the classroom was organized, who was in charge of the classroom, the kinds of on-task and off-task behavior that were being displayed, and the types of evaluative feedback that were being offered.

B. Observers and Observer Training

A team of 10 to 20 residents of each city acted as observers. All were carefully trained in the use of the coding system. In Minneapolis, the observers, all women, were former teachers and others who had worked professionally with children. In Sendai, they were students in psychology and social work, and in Taipei, they were students in educational psychology and teacher training programs. The majority in both countries were women.

Training generally lasted from 1 to 2 weeks. A general orientation meeting was held in which the coding systems and the observational procedures were described. Each observer was given a coding manual written in Chinese, Japanese or English which gave detailed descriptions of every step of the procedure and many examples. Observers were given several days in which to study and memorize the behavioral categories. The group then met several times to go over examples and to discuss questions.

After observers had familiarized themselves with the coding system, they practiced applying the coding schemes in classrooms that were not used in the study. They practiced in pairs, using two earphones connected to a single tape recorder, and changed partners after each session. At the end of each day they met to resolve any disagreements that had arisen in coding.

The observer's reliability in using the observational scheme was tested and mastery was assumed when 80% agreement with an experienced observer was reached. The actual observations began only after the observer had spent at least two classroom periods in an assigned classroom and was familiar with the children and the teacher.

C. Analyses of the Data

The data were transcribed from the observational sheets and entered into the computer. The frequency with which each of the 41 categories was coded for each child was determined. (These categories are described in Appendix A.) A summary variable for each child, reported as a percentage, was computed by dividing the frequency with which the category was checked by the number of 10-second observations made of the child during adademic activities. In addition, summary variables were constructed for each classroom by obtaining the averages of the summary variables for the 12 children in the class.

Summary variables also were made for each classroom for the 21 categories coded in the observations of the teachers. (See Appendix A.) These summary variables were obtained by dividing the frequency with which the category was checked by the number of 15-second observations made of the teacher.

Three major types of analyses of the data were conducted. The first consisted of analyses of variance of the data from the observations of the children and the teachers. In the former case, the independent variables were culture, grade, and sex; in the latter case, they were culture and grade. In the second type of analyses, comparisons were made of the observations conducted when reading and math were being taught. Finally, correlations were computed between the children's summary scores for the observational categories and their achievement scores in reading and mathematics.

Data obtained from the observations of the children were analyzed by means of a repeated measure analysis of variance. Classroom (N = 120) was the basic unit of analysis and was defined as a random factor nested within country and grade. Sex was a repeated measure within each classroom. These analyses enabled us to determine whether the observational data differed significantly (1) among the three countries, (2) between the two grades, and (3) between boys and girls. Observations of the teachers were analyzed using a country by grade analysis of variance, again with classroom as the unit of analysis. Scheffé contrasts were used to determine which differences between pairs of countries were statistically significant.

Because of the large number of analyses, we thought it would be distracting to present the results of the statistical analyses in the discussion of the results. We chose, therefore, to consolidate these analyses in the tables that appear in Appendices B and C, which summarize the results of the observations of children and of teachers. When differences are described in the text, it can be assumed that they are statistically significant. Few references are made to sex differences, because the summary variables for boys and girls seldom differed significantly. Those that did appear are discussed in a separate section.

IV. RESULTS: A PROFILE OF CROSS-CULTURAL DIFFERENCES

Cross-cultural differences are emphasized in the presentation of the results. It is important to note from the beginning, however, that there were pervasive differences in the frequencies with which the various observational categories were coded among the 20 classrooms at each grade in all three countries. This should be the case. We purposely chose a diverse, but representative array of classrooms in each country for our study. The differences among the means for the classrooms at each grade failed to be significant only for a few infrequently coded categories. It is important to acknowledge, therefore, that descriptions of a country do not necessarily apply with equal validity to all of the classrooms within a country.

A. Classroom Organization and Behavior

The observer sometimes found that it was impossible to code a child's behavior, even when the child was in school. This situation was relatively frequent in Minneapolis and very rare in the other two cities—the child was at school but was not in the classroom during the time of the observation. For example, the child might be in the school office, on an errand for the teacher, or in the library. Such activities were not necessarily unrelated to adademic work, but many of them did take the child away from the classroom for nonacademic purposes. The category was nearly meaningless in Sendai and Taipei. If a child was at school, the child was in the classroom during academic activities. The category was never coded in Taipei and occurred with an extremely low frequency in Sendai— less than .2% of the time. In Minneapolis, however, this category was coded 13.1% of the time in first grade and 18.4% of the time in fifth grade. It was impossible to assess what a child was doing outside the classroom, for the observer remained in the classroom with the other children. It is doubtful, however, that a large percentage of this time was spent in the library or in other activities related to academic work.

Academic Activities and Transitions.   The first thing coded was the type of activity in which the child was engaged. Because observations were made only during the academic portion of the school day, the children were either involved in an academic activity or were in transition from one academic activity to another. The time spent in transition, therefore, was the complement of the time spent in academic activities. More time spent in transition necessarily meant that less time was spent in academic activities. When the child was coded as being in a transitional activity, no other categories were coded. Thus, all data derived from the observational categories are reported as percentages of the total time the child spent in academic activities.

The first clues about possible bases for differences in academic achievement in the three countries may lie in the fact that American children spent the lowest percentage of time engaged in academic activities. The percentages in the American, Chinese, and Japanese first-grade classrooms were, respectively, 69.8%, 85.1%, and 79.2%. In the fifth-grade classrooms, the corresponding percentages were 64.5%, 91.5% and 87.4%. Not only were the percentages lower in the American classrooms, but the American fifth graders actually spent a lower percentage of their time in academic activities than did the first graders. The percentage of time spent in academic activities increased between first and fifth grades in the Chinese and Japanese classrooms.

Differences among the three countries in instructional time are amplified when the amount of time children spent in school is considered. At fifth grade, for example, we estimate that 19.6 hours per week were devoted to academic activities in the Minneapolis classrooms. This estimate was made by multiplying the percentage of time the children spent in academic activities (64.5%) by the average number of hours the children were in school each week (30.4). This is a dramatic contrast to the estimated 40.4 hours (91.5% times 44.1 hours) spent in fifth-grade Chinese classrooms, and 32.6 hours (87.4% times 37.3 hours) in the Japanese classrooms. Estimates for the first graders in the three countries are more similar: 20.9, 23.4, and 24.3 hours for the American, Chinese, and Japanese classrooms. The potential impact of the differences in instructional time on what children learn in school become even more profound when we take into consideration that the school year in Japan and Taiwan is approximately 2 months longer than the American school year.

Examples of time spent in transition are when the child is putting away a workbook and getting out a reader, when there is a change in the organization of the classroom, or when the child is waiting in line to show the teacher a drawing. In all three countries—as would be expected—more time was devoted to transitional activities in first than in fifth grade, as shown in Figure 4.2. Even so, American children spent more time in transition at both grades than did the Japanese and Chinese children. There were many reasons for this. The organization of the American classrooms changed more frequently, routines were less clearly established, and American children were more likely to be working as individuals without direct supervision. Chinese and Japanese children are given more frequent and explicit instruction in carrying out classroom routines. Perhaps the greatest reason is that the class periods are clearly defined and are usually of constant length in the Chinese and Japanese schools, which increases children's awareness of when one activity has ended and another is about to begin. As a result of these factors, transitions occurred more frequently and more slowly in the American classrooms.

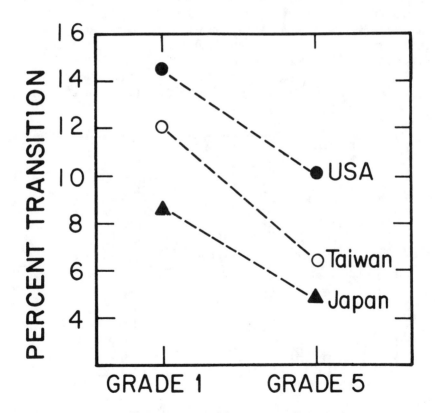

FIG. 4.2.   Percentage of time spent in transitional activities.

Subject being Taught. The subject matter that target children were being taught or on which they were working was coded for each observational interval. Six subjects were considered: language arts (reading, writing, and spelling), mathematics, social science, music, art, and moral education. (For purposes of convenience the term *reading* is sometimes used in place of the term *language arts.*) Physical and biological sciences were seldom taught in the elementary schools we visited. When they were taught, they were coded under "other," along with other subjects that were infrequently included in the curricula. An eighth category was "study period," which was coded when children were allowed to work independently on the subject matter of their choice. Coding the subject being taught would seem to be an easy task. This was not always the case, especially in the loosely organized American classrooms. When the observers could not decide how to code this category, they asked the teacher to describe the subject in which the children presumably were engaged.

The percentages of time children spent working in each subject, broken down by country and grade, are presented in Fig. 4.3. Distributions appear to be generally similar in the three countries and at the two grades. Language arts and mathematics, as expected, were given the largest percentages of classroom time, and more time was spent on language arts during the first than during the fifth grade. These similarities are only superficial. A closer look at the figures indicates important differences. With samples of children as large as those involved in this study and with so many hours of observation, what appear to be relatively small differences turn out to be highly significant statistically. Moreover, small

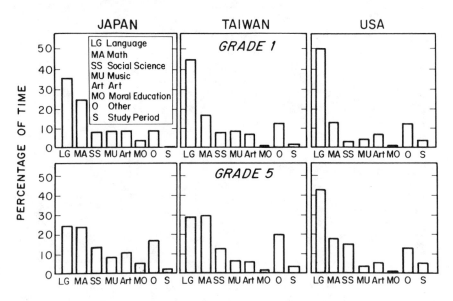

FIG. 4.3.   Percentage of classroom time spent on various subjects.

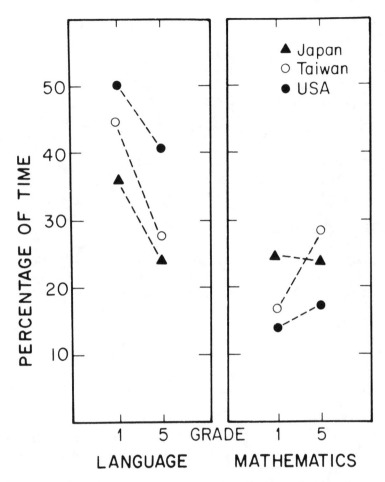

FIG. 4.4. Percentage of classroom time spent on language and mathematics.

differences occurring during 40 hours of observation may have important practical effects when they are translated into the total amounts of time children
spend in school each year.

In order to make it easier to compare the means for language arts and mathematics, the data for these two subjects are presented separately in Fig. 4.4. It is
clear that American children spent a greater percentage of time studying language arts than Chinese children, who, in turn, spent a greater percentage of time
than Japanese children. Differences among the countries were particularly
marked at the fifth grade. Language arts occupied 41.6% of the time devoted to
academic matters in the American classrooms, but only 24% of the time in the
Japanese classrooms and little more than that in the Chinese classrooms.

There was a different pattern for mathematics. At neither grade did American children spend as much as 20% of their time studying mathematics. This was lower than the percentage for either Chinese or Japanese children. At the fifth grade, reading and mathematics occupied approximately equal percentages of time for the Chinese and Japanese children, but the American children spent more than twice as much time on reading as on mathematics.

Percentages of time were converted into estimates of the number of hours spent on language arts and mathematics. The estimates in Table 4.2 were obtained by multiplying the average percentage of time children spent on each subject by the average amount of time the children were estimated to be engaged in instructional activities each week. The American children were estimated to spend 3 hours a week in mathematics. The Chinese and Japanese children, especially at the fifth grade, were estimated to spend over twice that amount of time. The poor performance of American children may be traced, in part, to this large difference in the time they were engaged in activities related to mathematics. Estimates of the amounts of time spent in language arts were more similar among the three countries. Again, however, it seems likely that the greater number of hours the Chinese children received instruction in reading may be related to their greater reading skill.

Chinese and Japanese schools did not emphasize reading and mathematics to so great a degree that time was unavailable for subjects such as art, music, and moral education. In fact, the American schools spent the smallest proportion of time on these subjects. Differences were significant for the percentage of time devoted to art (Japan > Taiwan and the U.S.); music (Japan > Taiwan > U.S.); and moral education (Japan > Taiwan > U.S.). Moral education was used to describe discussions of such things as manners, national heroes and holidays, and social customs of the society. These values can be seen in Fig. 4.3. Teachers in the three countries devoted similar proportions of time to social studies and to other academic subjects, but the American classrooms exceeded those of the

TABLE 4.2
Estimates of the Number of Hours Spent
Each Week in Language Arts and Mathematics

	Country		
	American	Chinese	Japanese
Grade 1			
Language Arts	10.5	10.4	8.7
Mathematics	2.7	4.0	5.8
Grade 5			
Language Arts	7.9	11.1	8.0
Mathematics	3.4	11.7	7.8

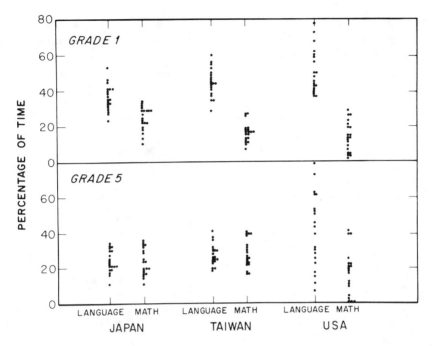

FIG. 4.5.   Proportion of time spent on language and mathematics in each classroom.

other two countries in the proportion of time spent in study periods (U.S. > Taiwan > Japan).

The data related to reading and mathematics are illustrated in still another way in Fig. 4.5. Here, the time devoted to each subject is plotted according to the mean percentage for each classroom. Variability among Minneapolis classrooms was much greater than among those in Taipei or Sendai. This can be readily explained. There are precisely defined national curricula in Taiwan and Japan, and teachers are expected to adhere closely to these curricula. American teachers, especially in elementary schools, are allowed to organize their classrooms according to their own desires—as long as they adhere to the general policies of the schools in which they teach. Guidelines published by American state and local school districts typically define general goals for elementary school education, rather than how time is to be organized or what curriculum is to be followed.

The ranges among the classrooms in Taipei and Sendai in percentage of time spent working on language arts and mathematics were very similar. In Minneapolis, however, the range was greater for language arts than mathematics. The time spent in the fifth-grade American classroom on language arts ranged from 4% to 80%. For mathematics, the range was smaller. Although some teachers spent as much as 40% of their time in activities related to mathematics, others spent practically no time at all. In the first grade, children in one third of the American classrooms spent less than 10% of their time on mathematics. At the fifth grade, children in three classrooms were never observed to be engaged in mathematics during the many days observers were present.

These data lead to the obvious conclusion that American children do less well in mathematics than do Chinese and Japanese children because they spend less time studying mathematics. Although time differences alone do not sufficiently explain the poor performance of American children in mathematics, a partial explanation for differences in achievement arises when they are accompanied by behavioral differences such as those that will be described in later sections.

B. Organization of the Classroom

Classroom organization was reflected in both the observations of the children and of the teachers. Three types of classroom organization were considered: the whole class working as a unit ("class"); the classroom divided into smaller groups ("group"); or children working by themselves ("individual"). The mean percentages of time children spent in each type appear in Fig. 4.6. Because there were no differences in the values obtained for first- and fifth-grade classrooms, results for the two grades were combined. Data from the observations of the

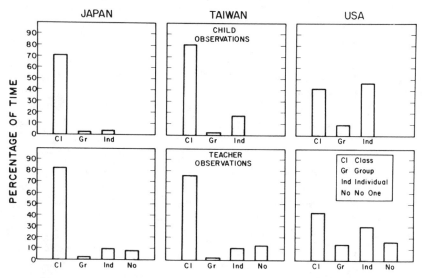

FIG. 4.6.   Percentage of time spent in various classroom organizations, obtained from observations of the children and of the teacher.

children are in the top of Fig. 4.6, and the data from the observations of the teachers are in the bottom.

Japanese and Chinese children spent most of their time at school working, watching, and listening together as a class; they were rarely divided into smaller groups. American children, on the other hand, spent as much time working alone as they did working together as a class. American children worked on individual activities 47% of the time. This percentage was much greater than that for Taipei (18%) or Sendai (28%).

The teachers were coded according to whom, if anyone, they were interacting with. The teacher was considered to be interacting with no one when she was by herself, sitting at her desk writing, talking to another teacher, or setting up materials while the children were working at their desks. Teachers were busier with the children in Grade 1 than in Grade 5. Whereas the overall percentage of time the teachers were not working with children was 10% at the first grade, it rose to 15% at fifth grade. American teachers spent more time interacting with no one (17%) than did Chinese (13%) or Japanese (8%) teachers. Thus, even though American teachers spent as much time in their classrooms as did their Asian counterparts, nearly one fifth of that time was spent in activities that did not involve teaching or working directly with children.

Because American teachers were coded as working with no one 17% of the time, we conclude they were interacting with someone 83% of the time. However, children were coded as being in a teacher-led activity only 48% of the time. Obviously, the amount of time an individual child spends in a teacher-led activity is a function not only of the amount of time the teacher spends teaching, but also of the number of students a teacher works with at one time. Because teachers in Minneapolis spent more time working with small groups and individuals, each child spent less time in activities led by the teacher.

Leader.   The leader of an activity in which a child was engaged could be the teacher, another adult, such as a teacher's aide, or a child. There also were times when no one was responsible for leading or supervising the children's work. This happened when the target child was working alone or was part of a group working by itself. In our observational system a "class" organization required a leader, thus "no one" could be coded as the leader only when there was a "group" or "individual" organization. The percentages of time represented by each type are presented in Fig. 4.7.

Asian and American classrooms had strikingly different patterns of leadership. Children in both grades in Taipei were led by the teacher nearly 90% of the time; in Sendai, over 70% of the time. Children in Minneapolis, in contrast, spent less than half of their time in classrooms led by their teacher. Because teaching responsibilities were seldom assumed by another adult or a child, children in Minneapolis classrooms spent nearly half of their time engaged in ac-

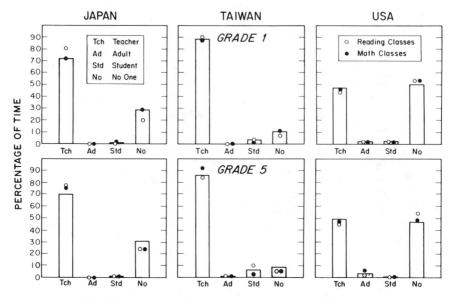

FIG. 4.7.   Percentage of time spent with different types of leaders.

tivities where there was no leader. In Sendai, the percentage of time when there was no discernible leader was 29%, and in Taipei, 9%.

The lack of leadership in the American classrooms may be another factor related to lower levels of achievement. Children can learn without a teacher. Nevertheless, it seems likely that they could profit from having their teacher as a leader more than half of the time. One might argue that skill in subjects such as reading are highly dependent on practice and that children benefit from reading by themselves or in small groups. It is more difficult to summon this argument for mathematics, where more information and demonstrations about definitions and operations may be necessary before practice can lead to improved skills. There was little difference, however, in the percentage of time children worked without a leader in reading and in mathematics.

D. Teaching

What do teachers do when they are teaching? Among the most important functions are imparting information, giving directions, and asking questions related to academic work and classroom procedures. The percentages of time teachers spent in these activities are summarized in Fig. 4.8.

American teachers spent much less time imparting information (21%) than did the Chinese (58%) or Japanese (33%) teachers. These are sobering results. American children were in school approximately 30 hours a week. This means that they were receiving information from the teacher approximately 6 hours a

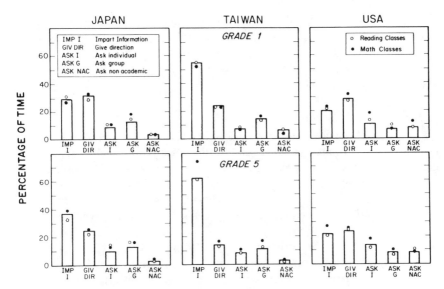

FIG. 4.8.   Percentage of time teachers spent in imparting information, giving directions, and asking questions.

week (.21 times 30). Computing the estimates for Chinese and Japanese classrooms in a similar fashion, the values for Chinese children (26 hours) and Japanese children (12 hours) reveal that they received much more information than the American children. Increasing the length of the school day and year in America—commonly suggested solutions for improving academic achievement—seem to be less efficient means for aiding learning than would efforts to increase the amount of time teachers impart information.

American teachers actually spent somewhat more time giving directions than in imparting information (26% vs. 21%). Children need directions in order to know how to proceed in their academic work, and this may be especially important when, as was the case with the American children, they are expected to work individually on their assignments with little further guidance. The distribution of effort by Chinese teachers was radically different. Teachers spent much more time imparting information than in giving directions. This was also true for the Japanese fifth-grade teachers; the first-grade teachers spent similar amounts of time giving directions and imparting information.

American and Asian teachers used different techniques for asking questions. American teachers spent more time directing questions to individual children; Chinese and Japanese teachers were more likely to direct questions to the entire class. American teachers asked individuals questions 12% of the time, in contrast to 10% and 8% for Japanese and Chinese teachers, respectively. Conversely, the Japanese and Chinese teachers asked the class questions 13% of the time, and the American teachers, 8%.

American teachers asked nonacademic questions about procedures nearly twice the proportion of time (8%) as Chinese (4%) or Japanese (3%) teachers. The looser organization of the American classrooms may make it necessary for American teachers to ask procedural questions in order to evaluate whether children understand what they should be doing.

E. Children's Behavior

The children's behavior could be described in terms of whether it was appropriate (on-task) or inappropriate (off-task) for the situation in which the child was engaged. The observer was required to code one of these categories during each 10-second interval.

Twelve categories described on-task behavior. Some were general and were coded frequently. For example, attending could be coded in a wide range of situations. Other categories, such as asking an academic question, were less commonly used. The countries differed on 10 of the 12 categories. The two exceptions were volunteering and answering procedural questions. These categories had a low frequency of occurrence: 2.4% for volunteering and .4% for answering procedural questions.

Attending.   Attending to the teacher or to the leader of the activity was coded frequently (see Fig. 4.9). If no leader was present and the child was attending to his own work, only "seatwork" was coded. Children in Minneapolis were coded

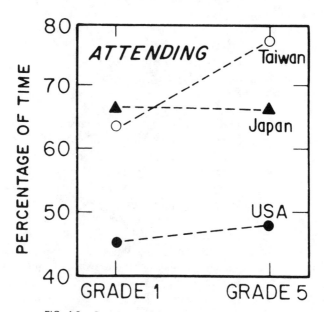

FIG. 4.9.   Percentage of time children were attending.

as attending 46% of the time, children in Taipei, 71% of the time, and children in Sendai, 65% of the time. The percentages were similar at the two grade levels for the American and Japanese children, but the Chinese children displayed a large increase between first and fifth grades.

These results are related to differences in the classroom organization in the three countries. Attending could be coded only when there was a person to whom the child could attend. The American children more frequently worked as individuals where there was no leader to whom attention could be directed. When they were in a class or group organization, however, the American children were appropriately attentive. In the "class" organization at first grade, for example, American children were judged to be attentive 88% of the time, Chinese children, 77% of the time, and Japanese children 87% of the time. At fifth grade the corresponding percentages were 88%, 86%, and 89%. A "group" organization was infrequent in the Chinese and Japanese classrooms, but when it occurred in the American classrooms, the children were coded as being attentive 70% of the time in first grade and 86% of the time in fifth grade.

Data for the category of attending are presented in a different fashion in Fig. 4.10. A word of explanation about this graph is needed. In this and in several other graphs that are presented, the data are plotted according to standard scores (z-scores). The following example clarifies how the z scores were computed. Attention scores for all first graders were combined into one distribution. A z-score was computed for each child by calculating the degree of departure, expressed in standard deviation units, of the child's score from the mean of the total distribution. The z-scores were then regrouped according to classroom in each country. Interpreting the figure is straightforward. The height of a line represents the average z-score for a classroom and the length of a line represents the range of scores in each classroom covered by the mean $\pm$ 3 standard deviations. The 0 point on the vertical axis represents the mean for all classrooms. If the mean for a classroom was above the mean for all three countries, the z-score was positive; if it was below the average, the z-score was negative. The same procedure was repeated for the fifth graders.

Children spent a greater percentage of time attending to the teacher in some classrooms than in others. Even so, there were large cultural differences in the percentages for different classrooms. Most American classrooms were below the mean of all three countries at both Grades 1 and 5.

Seatwork.   A second frequently occurring category of behavior was seatwork, which was coded for any on-task behavior that occurred when the child was working as an individual. Seatwork was also coded when the child was required to attend to the teacher and at the same time take notes or work on problems in "group" or "class" situations. American children were engaged in seatwork 44% of the time, the Chinese children, 34%, and the Japanese children, 33%. Only the differences according to country were significant.

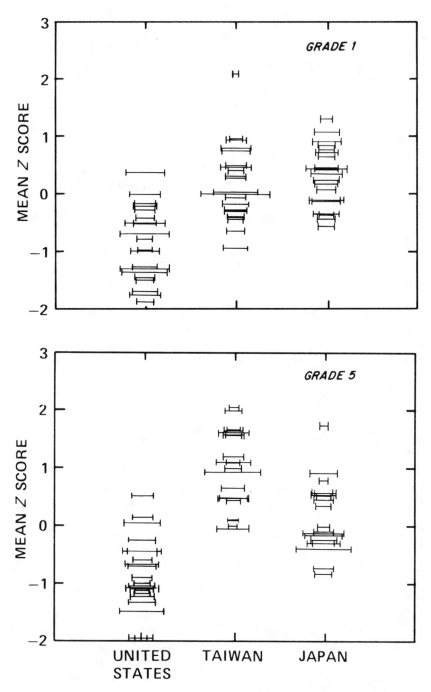

FIG. 4.10. Mean z-score for level of attention shown by children in each classroom.

Questions.   The percentage of time children asked questions related to academic or procedural matters or answered academic questions appear in Fig. 4.11. Children answered questions more frequently than they asked them, but in neither case was a large percentage of spent in these activities. Japanese children rarely asked questions about either academic or procedural matters. Chinese children asked more questions about academic matters than did either the Japanese or American children but asked few questions about procedure. American children asked few questions about either academic matters or procedures.

Group Response.   Choral responding and reading stories aloud in unison were introduced into the coding scheme because they were frequently seen during our preliminary observations in Chinese classrooms. As we expected, therefore, the major cultural difference, evident in Fig. 4.12, is between Chinese and the American and Japanese classrooms. Children in Taipei were more than three times as likely to respond in unison than were children in either Sendai or Minneapolis.

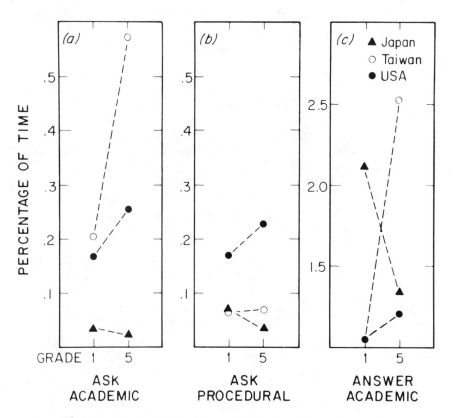

FIG. 4.11.   Percentage of time children spent in asking and answering questions.

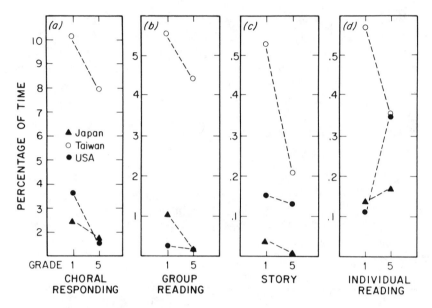

FIG. 4.12.   Percentage of time spent in various types of verbal response.

Stories.   The last two categories of on-task activities involved a child's telling a story or reading aloud to other children. Both occurred infrequently (see Fig. 4.12). Chinese first graders were most frequently observed to be telling a story or reading aloud to other children. Japanese children spent the least amount of time in these activities. Overall, then, the Japanese children showed the least amount of verbalization, and Chinese children the most.

Other Activities.   There is a final category of on-task behaviors, those that were placed in the category "other". In one sense this category is of limited value, for we cannot determine what a child was doing when this category was coded. However, by looking at the percentage of time it was necessary to use this category, we can get some idea about the comprehensiveness of our coding system. The largest percentage of time relevant behaviors could not be coded was found in Minneapolis: 18.6% at the first grade and 8.6% at the fifth grade. Corresponding percentages for Taipei were 3.3% and 1.1%, and for Sendai, 3.9% and 3.6%. We conclude that our coding system better described children's behavior in Chinese and Japanese than in American schools because of differences in degree of structure existing in the classrooms. During regular academic periods, there was a broader variety of behavior in American classrooms than was found in Chinese and Japanese classrooms. This does not mean that behavior in Chinese and Japanese schools was restricted and stereotyped, but that more diverse behaviors tended to take place outside of the classroom during

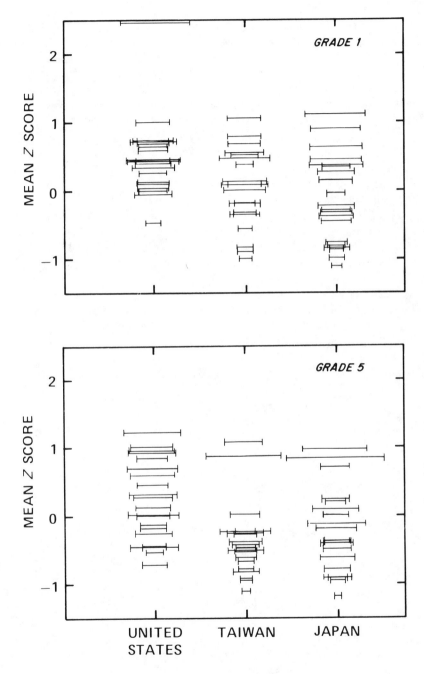

FIG. 4.13.   Mean *z*-score for inappropriate activities shown by children in each classroom.

periods we did not observe, such as recess and physical education, or during lunch and clean-up time.

Inappropriate Behaviors.   Inappropriate activities were observed in every classroom, but they were much more likely to be found in American classrooms than in those of the other two countries. The z-scores based on the total percentage of time spent in inappropriate activites are plotted for each classroom in Fig. 4.13. Because the activities described are inappropriate ones, z-scores below rather than above the mean are more desirable. Many more American than Chinese or Japanese first-grade classrooms were above the overall mean for the three countries. The situation did not improve at fifth grade. An even greater proportion of American classrooms with z-scores above the mean was found at Grade 5 than at Grade 1. The range of scores within the Chinese and Japanese classrooms tended to be higher for values above the mean than for those below the mean, indicating that the high scores may be due to a few unruly children in each of these classrooms, rather than to more widespread inappropriate behavior.

The percentages of time children displayed various types of inappropriate behavior separately by country and grade in Fig. 4.14. The percentages varied between 10% and 20%. It also can be seen in Fig. 4.14 that American children engaged in inappropriate activity to a greater degree than did the Chinese and Japanese children, whether the behavior took place in or out of their seats, with a peer, or by themselves.

American children were frequently out of their seats: 39% of the time in first

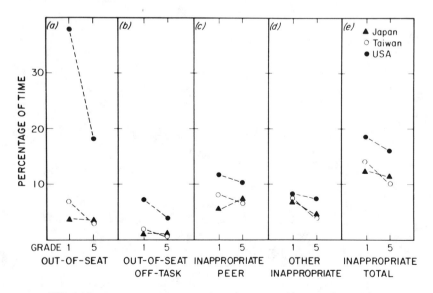

FIG. 4.14.   Percentage of time spent in various types of inappropriate activities.

grade and 20% of the time in fifth grade. Such high percentages were never found in Chinese or Japanese classrooms. What may be tolerable in Minneapolis classrooms with 20–25 children would be impossible in Sendai and Taipei, where there were from 35 to 50 children in each classroom. Differences in the frequencies with which children are out of their seats also are partly attributable to the patterns of organization and leadership in the classrooms of the three countries. American children were the least likely to be involved in a classroom activity led by the teacher but were most likely to be working on a task by themselves. Children can leave their seats more easily when there is no direct supervision and they are working on individual tasks. As is evident in the second panel of Fig. 4.14, being out of their seats did not necessarily mean that the children were engaged in irrelevant activities. Less than a quarter of the time the children were out of their seats was coded as being spent in irrelevant activities.

F. Sex Differences

Little evidence was obtained for sex differences in the children's behavior or in the responses of the teachers to the children. The one variable for which differences were found was in the inappropriate activity demonstrated by the child. The total incidence of inappropriate activity for boys was 15.3% and for girls, 12.1%.

G. Teacher's Responses to the Children

Two of the major aspects of the teacher's behavior already have been discussed: the orientation of the teacher's activities (to the class, a group, an individual, or to no one); and the teacher's didactic role in imparting information, asking questions, and giving directions. Another major aspect was to provide feedback to children for their academic performance and classroom behavior.

Before discussing this last aspect, we should note that teachers were often involved in activities other than those included in our coding scheme. The extensiveness of their involvement in such activities is indicated in the percentage of time observations were checked as "other." This category was used when the teacher was not engaged in an evaluative or didactic role. Teachers are able to assume a didactic role and provide direct and personal feedback only when they are interacting with children. Coding of the category "other" is increased, therefore, to the degree that a teacher is not interacting with children.

Teachers in Minneapolis spent the greatest amount of time—42%—in behaviors coded as "other." In Taipei the percentage was 13% and in Sendai, 26%. This high percentage indicates both the lack of comprehensiveness of the coding scheme and the great range of activities in which teachers were engaged in the American classrooms. Some of the behaviors coded as "other" undoubtedly were related to the teachers' functions as educators. Others were not. One of the most common complaints of American teachers is the great number of roles and activities in which they are expected to participate.

Some of the interactions between the teacher and child were ambiguous. In these cases, all the observer could discern was that an interaction between teacher and child (or children) was taking place. The "ambiguous" category was coded 13% of the time in Minneapolis, 4% in Taipei, and 6% in Sendai.

Our observational scheme obviously encompassed a greater proportion of the behaviors of the teachers in Sendai and Taipei than in Minneapolis, as 55% of the observations of the teachers in Minneapolis were coded as "other" or "ambiguous." This occurred in only 17% of the observations in Taipei, and 32% in Sendai. In order to include a greater proportion of the behavior of the Minneapolis teachers, a much more extensive set of categories of behavior would have been necessary—a task beyond the scope of this initial study.

H. Feedback

The overall frequency of feedback was low. Academic feedback occurred less than 1% of the time: .85% in Minneapolis, .74% in Taipei, and .80% in Sendai. Behavioral feedback occurred even less frequently: .75% in Minneapolis, .74% in Taipei, and .42% in Sendai.

Academic Feedback.   Teachers' responses to the children sometimes concerned schoolwork and at other times, the children's behavior. More than half of the evaluative responses concerned academic work, and the percentage increased between Grades 1 and 5 in all three countries. In Sendai, 60.1% of the feedback in first grade and 70.3% of the feedback in fifth grade were related to schoolwork. The American percentages were similar to those in Sendai: 60.9% in first grade and 71.2% in fifth grade. In Taipei the percentages were somewhat lower: 54.2% and 66.0%.

Academic feedback was divided into five types: praise, a statement that a child's response was correct, no feedback, a statement that a child's response was incorrect, and criticism. The types of feedback coded were the same in the observations of the teachers and of the children. In the observations of the children, no significant differences were found in the percentage of time the teachers in the three countries used the various types of academic feedback. Differences were found in the observations of the teachers. Praise, criticism, and information about the correctness of a response were used with different frequencies in the three countries. As can be seen in Table 4.3, the most common type of feedback given to the children was information about the correctness or incorrectness of a response. Praise was given more frequently than criticism, which teachers seldom used. Teachers in the three countries did not differ in the frequency with which they failed to provide feedback in situations where feedback was appropriate, or in making statements that a response was incorrect. Feed-

TABLE 4.3
Percentage of Time Teachers in Each Culture Gave Four Types
of Academic Feedback

| | | *Country* | | | | | |
| | | *American* | | *Chinese* | | *Japanese* | |
Category	*Grade*	*1*	*5*	*1*	*5*	*1*	*5*
Reward		2.7	1.0	2.2	.4	.8	.6
Information		9.8	8.3	5.6	3.9	9.8	9.5
Information (correct)		2.6	2.7	4.1	1.6	3.8	2.7
Criticism (incorrect)		.1	.2	.5	.2	.1	.1

back of all types tended to decrease between the first and fifth grades. The lack of significant effects for academic feedback obtained from the observations of the children seems to have been due to the low frequency with which this behavior occurred. Clearly, the likelihood that a particular child would be receiving academic feedback from the teacher during the 10-second interval in which the child was being observed is very low. The direction of the effects, however, were the same in the observations of the children and of the teachers.

Behavioral Feedback.   As was the case with academic feedback, responses to children's behavior in the classroom were coded more frequently when the teachers rather than the children were the focus of attention. Four types of behavioral feedback from the teacher were coded: praise, reprimand, physical correction, and physical punishment. As can be seen in Fig. 4.15, teachers in all three countries spent similar amounts of time reprimanding their pupils. Reprimands varied from mild suggestions, such as "you should talk louder," to more severe reactions, such as the teacher's criticizing a child's conduct in negative terms in front of the whole class. Children's adaptation to the routines of school is evident in the sharp decline between Grades 1 and 5 in the frequency with which teachers found it necessary to use reprimands.

Chinese teachers were more likely than Japanese or American teachers to use physical correction and physical punishment to alter children's behavior. American teachers rarely used these techniques. Rather, they were the most likely to use praise, especially at the first grade. As can be seen in Fig. 4.14, all of these types of response to children's classroom behavior declined between first and fifth grades.

Teacher's Feedback to Boys and Girls.   No evidence of differential responses by the teacher to boys and girls was found in the analyses of academic feedback. However, boys did receive more feedback about their behavior(.8%) than girls (.5%). Boys received more frequent criticism than girls (.5% vs. .3%)

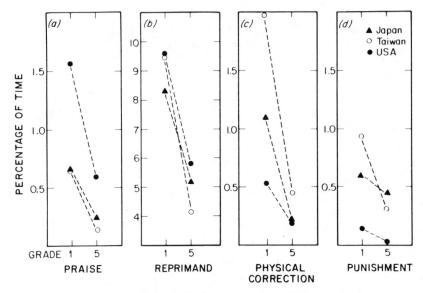

FIG. 4.15. Percentage of time teachers spent in providing various types of response to children's inappropriate behavior.

and nearly twice as much physical punishment (.3% vs. .14%). This was found in all three countries and at both grades. Only one sex difference differed with grade: boys received more praise than girls in the first grade, but the reverse was found in the fifth grade.

I. Observations during Language Arts and Mathematics Classes

The approach of the teachers and the behavior of the children in language arts and mathematics classes can be compared by separating the observational data according to subject matter. Analyses of these data may offer insight into the manner in which the two subjects were taught in these three countries.

The data were analyzed in country by grade analyses of variance in which subject matter was included as a repeated measure. Classroom again was the unit of analysis, and the dependent measure was the percentage of time a category was coded while each subject was being taught. The significant effects are summarized in Appendix B. Of the 33 observational categories, 15 varied significantly as a function of the subject being taught.

The most consistent effects were found for the categories involving the teacher's feedback for the children's academic performance. Comments about the correctness or incorrectness of a response were more likely to occur in mathematics than in language arts classes. There also were more occasions in mathematics than in language arts classes where the teacher did not offer feedback to a child when it was appropriate. Praise and criticism were used as often in one type of class as in the other.

Behavioral, as opposed to academic, feedback was given equally often in the two types of classes, perhaps because inappropriate behavior did not vary as a function of the subject matter on which the children were working. Thus, the teachers had no greater need to provide corrective feedback in one situation than in the other.

American teachers assembled the children into a class more frequently while working on mathematics than on language arts. Chinese and Japanese teachers did not vary their use of the class organization according to what was being taught.

The frequency with which the group form of organization was used varied in a complex manner according to subject matter, country, and grade. Minneapolis teachers were more likely to divide the children into groups for reading than for mathematics instruction, especially at the first grade. In Sendai and Taipei, on the other hand, small groups were organized more often for mathematics than for reading classes. Students were used as leaders more frequently in reading than in mathematics classes in Minneapolis and Taipei, but the opposite trend was found in Sendai.

The percentage of children's on-task behavior was different in language arts and mathematics classes. Volunteering and answering academic questions occurred more frequently in all three countries and in both grades during mathematics classes. The other forms of on-task behavior varied in complex manners. Individual recitation was coded more often in language arts than in mathematics classes in both Chinese and Japanese classrooms but was coded more often in mathematics classes in Minneapolis. Choral responding was found more frequently in mathematics classes, but country and grade influenced its occurrence, making the effect difficult to interpret. Reading aloud necessarily occurred more frequently in reading classes, but the magnitude of the effect varied according to country and grade. Finally, seatwork tended to be coded more often in mathematics than in language arts classes, and the tendency was much greater in Sendai than in the other two cities. The organization and activities that took place in language arts and mathematics classes clearly differed, but analyses of this information according to country were not especially revealing.

J. Relations between Observational Categories and Achievement within Classrooms

Up to this point, we have concentrated our discussion on differences among the three countries and their possible relevance to differences in academic achievement. Another approach to assessing the relation between what goes on in school and children's academic achievement is to compute the within-country correlations between the average frequency of occurrence of various categories of behavior and the average level of achievement in reading and mathematics within each classroom. This was done for each observational category and the achievement scores in reading and mathematics. The achievement scores were obtained several weeks before the observations were begun. Even though the number of classrooms at each grade within each country was only 20, some information emerged from these analyses.

Because the relations differed in the three countries, it is convenient to discuss the results for each country in turn. In the American classrooms, perhaps the most important effect was the negative relation found at fifth grade between the percentage of time the children were left to work alone and achievement in both reading and mathematics, r's $= -.69$ and $-.57$, $p < .01$. The possible importance of classroom organization in explaining differences in achievement among the three countries has been discussed. These data indicate it also is an important factor when differences in achievement among American classrooms are considered.

There were two other consistent effects. First, achievement in reading and mathematics at both grades was negatively related to the frequency with which inappropriate behavior was observed in a classroom, r's $(18) = -.47$ to $-.59$, $p < .05$. Here, again, a factor that differentiated the three countries also was a significant differential factor among American classrooms with different levels of achievement. Second, negative feedback represented by reprimands was consistently related in a negative fashion to achievement, r's $= -.46$ to $-.56$, $p < .05$. In addition, total behavioral feedback and various negative forms of feedback such as punishment, physical forms of correction, and criticism were often negatively related to achievement, r's $= -.46$ to $-.59$. The necessity for behavioral feedback may be another indication of high frequencies of inappropriate behavior in the classroom, rather than a factor, in itself, that may result in low levels of achievement.

It is difficult to see any patterns of significant effects in Taipei and Sendai. Significant correlations were scattered, and in the case of the Japanese first-grade and Chinese fifth-grade classrooms, very sparse. The frequencies of praise, punishment, and total academic feedback were positively related to the first-grade Chinese children's reading scores, r's $= .49$ to $.57$. The frequencies with which a student was a class leader and with which the children told stories in class were also positively related to the first-grade reading scores in Taipei, r's $= .60$ and $.47$.

There were some indications in Sendai that a looser class structure was associated with higher levels of achievement in reading. For example, positive relations with achievement were found for the frequency with which the children worked as individuals and with which no one was in charge of the class, r's $= .45$. A negative correlation, $-.57$, was found for the frequency with which the teachers gave directions in the reading classes. These relations were not significant for the mathematics classes.

It is unfortunate that data for a larger number of classrooms at each grade were not available, for the within-country analyses just described are more tantalizing than they are satisfying. The correlations that were significant were not random, but offered only a minimal outline of the range of effects that may exist.

V. DISCUSSION

The observations offer a clear, if unflattering, picture of ways American elementary school classrooms differ from those in Taiwan and Japan. They also give us important information about possible bases for the differences in achievement among elementary school children in the three countries. Because the levels of achievement in reading and mathematics differed early in the first grade, practices in the homes as well as in the classrooms of the three countries must be involved in the creation of these differences. Data related to the children's everyday lives at home is discussed in another publication. It is our purpose here to concentrate on differences that were observed in the classrooms of the three countries.

We have not described subtle effects. Because the size of our samples was so large and the number of observations was so extensive, even small absolute differences tended to be statistically significant. However, most of the differences we have presented were quite large, and when extended over long periods of time, could have important practical effects.

It would be easy to try to dismiss the significance of the differences in classroom practices by describing certain negative consequences of the educational practices in Taiwan and Japan. Such consequences were not apparent to us. Children in all three countries appear to be cheerful, enthusiastic, vigorous, and responsive. Although some of these characteristics may be more vividly expressed within classrooms in Minneapolis, they are readily apparent to the observer who follows Chinese and Japanese children through their school day. It is possible, of course, that there are negative effects. Children in Asian classrooms are sometimes described as being more burdened by schoolwork and anxious about their progress than are American children. This again was not apparent to us in observing first and fifth graders. Perhaps we would have seen indications of such behavior if we had observed older children. In fact, the reason the study was conducted in the fifth, rather than the sixth grade was related to this possibility. Sixth-grade teachers in Sendai prepare their pupils for the middle-school examinations and we thought it would be difficult to obtain their cooperation. Such intense concern about examinations may lead the teachers to introduce important changes in daily classroom practices. A second complaint often made by Chinese and Japanese teachers and parents is that their system of education deprives children of opportunities for the development and expression of creativity. We have no evidence about either of these possibilities, but they merit further cross-cultural study.

A. Time in Academic Activities

Perhaps the most striking statistic from this study was the low percentage of time American children were engaged in academic activities. At fifth grade, for example, the American children not only spent less time at school than the Chinese and Japanese children, but of the time they were at school, only two thirds was spent in academic activities. What were the children doing the other third of the time? Mainly they were in transition from one activity to another, were out of the room, or were otherwise unavailable for observation. The second situation was especially interesting. In order not to be observed, a child had to be engaged in an activity outside of the classroom, usually alone. Academic activities occupied only part of this time, but we have no data about the activities in which the children were engaged. No provision for obtaining such information was made because we had no idea beforehand that it would be coded so frequently.

We estimated that American children were occupied with academic activities less than half as often as the Chinese children and two thirds as often as the Japanese children. Such data give American educators reason to review the efficiency with which the children's time is used for academic instruction and practice. Large increases in the time children are engaged in academic activities could be accomplished without increasing the amount of time children spend in school.

B. Language Arts versus Mathematics

The emphasis in the American classroom was on literacy. Being an educated young person in America seems to be synonymous with being able to read well. Mathematics is considered to be much less important. This was not the case in Japanese and Chinese classrooms, where more equal attention was given to both subjects. The smaller emphasis on reading in Taipei and Sendai could be explained if it could be argued that learning to read Chinese or Japanese is easier than learning to read English. This is an unlikely argument. During their elementary school years, Chinese children must learn to read and write nearly 3,000 characters and their combinations, and Japanese children must learn to read and write two syllabaries and nearly 1,000 characters. Other subjects, such as art, music, and moral education, also received more attention in Chinese and Japanese classrooms than in American classrooms. Of the traditional three "Rs" in American education, it was the last, arithmetic, that received the least attention and in which the deficiencies of American children were the most blatant.

C. Role of the Teacher

The role of the teacher differs greatly in the three cultures. Chinese and Japanese classrooms were organized so that teachers instructed or supervised the whole class much more frequently than did American teachers. In fact, children in

American classrooms worked as individuals as frequently as they participated in activities together as a class. If the American children had been especially attentive, there might have been great benefits in working individually. But this was not the case. American children were judged to be attending to the teacher much less frequently than were children in Sendai or Taipei. A second justification for allowing the American children to work so often individually would be found if American teachers spent a large amount of time imparting information, thereby enabling the children to work more productively as individuals. This did not occur. The American teachers spent less time imparting information when the children were in the class or a group than did the Chinese and Japanese teachers.

Differences were greatest between Chinese and American classrooms; Japanese classrooms were much more similar to Chinese than to American classrooms. The similarities can be explained in part by the number of children in the classroom. Practices that are tolerable in American classrooms with a small number of children would be impossible in the more populous Chinese and Japanese classrooms. Even with the larger class sizes, however, Chinese and Japanese children spent more time with their teachers than did the American children. Even though American teachers seek to provide individual instruction to their pupils, their division of the class into groups and individuals results in their spending a smaller amount of time instructing any particular child.

A more important factor than size of classes links Chinese and Japanese educational practices. Both cultures ascribe a prestigious role to teachers and important functions to schools in molding children into productive members of society. Teachers whose responsibilities are so highly valued in such societies must perceive their roles differently than do American teachers. As a consequence, their involvement in transmitting information and in developing children's skills must be increased.

D. Inappropriate Behaviors

Not only do American children spend fewer days in school each year, fewer hours in school each day, and a lower percentage of school time participating in academic activities, they also spend more time engaged in inappropriate behaviors. In every category of off-task behavior observed, American children exceeded their Chinese and Japanese counterparts. American children spent more time out of their seats engaged in irrelevant activities, talked more at inappropriate times to their peers, and engaged in other inappropriate activities more frequently than did the Chinese and Japanese children. Boys spent more time than girls in all three cultures in such inappropriate activities.

E. Conclusion

Many proposals have been made recently about how to improve American schools, such as increasing the amount of time children spend in school, reducing class size, and modifying the curriculum. These may be useful, but they are not the types of changes suggested by this study. Rather, the differences that appear to underlie the disparities in achievement in Asian and American classrooms are related to the organization and conduct of the classrooms. Americans appear to expect elementary school children to accomplish much more on their own than they are capable of. At the same time, American teachers may be expected to undertake so many different activities that they are unable to devote appropriate amounts of time to academic teaching. The results of this study suggest that improvement in children's achievement may be obtained by increasing the percentage of time spent in academic activities, by providing more frequent information to the children, by reducing the time children waste at school outside of the classroom and in irrelevant and transitional behavior within the classroom, by distributing the percentage of time spent in subjects such as reading and mathematics more equivalently, and by having the children spend less time working alone.

This is an initial study and more detailed comparative analyses of classroom practices are necessary. Nevertheless, if we assume that the practices observed in the 120 classrooms visited in Minneapolis, Taipei, and Sendai are representative of the classrooms found in each country, suggestions such as those made previously would appear to be worth considering. We cannot import systems of education from countries that differ as greatly from our own as Taiwan and Japan. We can use the comparative data to direct our attention to factors that otherwise might be overlooked or given less emphasis.

ACKNOWLEDGMENTS

This study was supported by National Institute of Mental Health Grant MH 33529. We are grateful to the children, teachers, parents, and school officials who made it possible for us to conduct this study; to the observers who worked so diligently; and to Ai-lan Tsao, our coordinator in Taipei; Elizabeth Clark, our coordinator in Minneapolis; and Susumu Kimura and Tadahisa Kato, our project coordinators in Sendai. We want to express our special thanks to Kirby Heller, who worked closely with us in developing the observational scheme used in this study.

Many others were involved in this research. We especially want to thank Kuniaki Nagai, Max Lummis, Shu-jen Su, and our colleagues at Tohoku Fukushi College and National Taiwan University, who assisted us with criticisms, suggestions, and daily help in this study.

REFERENCES

Azuma, H., Kashiwagi, K., & Hess, R. D. (1981). *Hahaoya no taido kodo to kodomo no chiteki hattatsu.* Tokyo: University of Tokyo Press.
Brophy, J. E. (1983). Fostering student learning and motivation in the elementary school class-

room. In S. G. Paris, G. M. Olson, & H. W. Stevenson (Eds.), *Learning and motivation in the classroom.* Hillsdale, NJ: Lawrence Erlbaum Associates.

Comber, L. C., & Keeves, J. (1973). *Science achievement in nineteen countries.* New York: Wiley.

Crosswhite, F. J., Dossey, J. A., Swafford, J. O., McKnight, C. C., & Cooney, T. J. (1985). *Second International Mathematics Study: Summary Report for the United States.* Urbana: University of Illinois.

Cummings, W. K. (1980). *Education and equality in Japan.* Princeton, NJ: Princeton University Press.

Dallas Times Herald. (1983, December 21). American education: The ABCs of failure.

DeVos, G. A. (1973). *Socialization for achievement.* Berkeley: University of California Press.

Huséu, T. (1967). *International study of achievement in mathematics: A comparison of twelve countries.* New York: Wiley.

Lynn, R. (1982). IQ in Japan and the United States shows a growing disparity. *Nature, 297,* 222–223.

Rohlen, T. P. (1983). *Japan's high schools.* Berkeley: University of California Press.

Stevenson, H. W., & Azuma, H. (1983). IQ in Japan and the United States: Methodological problems in Lynn's analysis. *Nature, 306,* 291–292.

Stevenson, H. W., Stigler, J. W., Lee, S. Y., Lucker, G. W., Kitamura, S., & Hsu, C. C. (1985). Cognitive performance and academic achievement of Japanese, Chinese, and American children. *Child Development.*

Stigler, J. W., Lee, S. Y., Lucker, G. W., & Stevenson, H. W. (1982). Curriculum and achievement in mathematics: A study of elementary school children in Japan, Taiwan, and the United States. *Journal of Educational Psychology, 74,* 315–322.

Wilson, R. W. (1970). *Learning to be Chinese: The political socialization of children in Taiwan.* Cambridge: MIT Press.

Appendices to Chapter 4

APPENDIX 4.A

This appendix is organized into three parts. We first describe the procedure used for scheduling the observations in each classroom and for assigning observers to classrooms; second, the observational scheme developed for coding the children's behavior; and finally, the scheme for coding the behavior of the teachers.

I. SCHEDULING OBSERVATIONS

Two important considerations were kept in mind in scheduling the observations. On the one hand, we sought to obtain a representative sample of each child's behavior in the classroom. On the other hand, we were faced with certain constraints posed by practical needs. A complete set of observations for each child could be gathered during one or two classroom periods. However, data gathered in this way would not necessarily have given us a representative sample of the child's behavior. A random sample of behavior was most desirable, but teachers could not be expected to tolerate observers visiting their classrooms on a random schedule. Obviously, some compromise was necessary between these two considerations. Observations were scheduled, therefore, over 30 (in the case of Sendai) to 40 (in Minneapolis and Taipei) classroom periods spanning a 2- to 4-week interval.

Twelve target children were observed in each of the 20 first-grade and 20 fifth-grade classrooms in which the study was conducted. In each classroom, these target children were divided at random into two subgroups of 6 children each. Each subgroup consisted of 1 boy and 1 girl from each of the three levels of reading achievement. One subgroup was observed during each observational period and the observer alternated observations among the children in the subgroup.

Each subgroup was observed for 20 observational periods. Because each classroom contained two of these subgroups, there were 40 periods of observation in each classroom. For each country, therefore, there were 800 hours of observation at each grade. The sequence in which observations were made of the children and of the teacher is described later.

A. Observational Period

Each observational period lasted approximately 40 minutes. In each period there were 5 cycles of observations of the children and 3 cycles of observations of the teacher. There were rest periods for the observers between cycles.

One cycle of student observations contained twelve 10-second intervals for observation, 2 for each of the 6 children in a subgroup, followed by 10 seconds for coding. Within a cycle, 2 observations were scheduled sequentially for each child to aid the observer in keeping track of the target children. The total number of observations made of each child, therefore, was 200 (5 cycles $\times$ 2 observations per cycle $\times$ 20 observational periods).

One cycle of teacher observations contained four 15-second intervals for observation, each followed by 15 seconds for coding. Each teacher was observed for a total of 480 15-second intervals (3 cycles $\times$ 4 observations per cycle $\times$ 40 observational periods).

Several procedures were instituted to insure that we would avoid bias in sampling observational periods. These included randomizing (1) the order in which observations of child and teacher were conducted; (2) the order in which individual children were observed; and (3) the time in the school day in which observations were made. Observations of teacher and child alternated according to five different random sequences. In addition, the five cycles in each observational period in which the individual children were observed contained five different random orders. Each of the 20 observational periods in which each subgroup of 6 children was observed was unique in the order in which the cycles of child and teacher were intermixed and in the order in which individual children were observed.

Three constraints were placed upon the five sequences of teacher–child observations: (1) Each period always began with a cycle of child observations; (2) no more than two cycles of teacher observations occurred in a row; and (3) two cycles of child observations were scheduled successively twice within each observational period. As a result, a typical observational period might be as follows: C-C-T-C-C-T-T-C, where C = child cycle and T = teacher cycle.

Equal representation of all parts of the school day was insured by distributing the 20 observational periods for each subgroup equally across four time periods. These periods divided the school day into four equal parts, the first and second half of the morning and the first and second half of the afternoon. Within these four time periods, the observer was free to enter the classroom at any time acceptable to the teacher.

B. Daily Procedure

Despite the apparent complexity of the various random procedures introduced, the observer was required only to select an envelope from a pile of 20 that had been organized for each classroom. All the information needed was typed on a label attached to each envelope. The label identified the 6 children in the subgroup and the sequence in which the observations were to be conducted. The coding sheets inside the envelope were printed and assembled in the proper order.

The label also instructed the observer to select one of five cassette tapes that had been made to correspond to the five different sequences of student and teacher observations. Each observer carried a battery-operated tape recorder equipped with an earphone. When the tape was started at the beginning of a 40-minute observational period, the observer heard instructions about when to observe, to code, to move to the next child, to switch from child to teacher observations, and when to rest.

C. Scheduling Observational Periods

Observations were not conducted during certain activities and events. Physical education was the only class in which observations were not scheduled. Other events not coded were recess, assemblies, regularly scheduled snack or lunch periods, classes led by substitute teachers, or periods in which tests were given or there were long films or television programs. Observers were able to avoid such events by obtaining information from the teacher ahead of time.

At least two, and no more than four observers were assigned to a classroom. Two was the minimum necessary to avoid confounding a particular observer with a particular classroom, and we believed that more than four observers would be disruptive of classroom activities. Only one observer was in a classroom at a time. Their observations were divided equally across the two subgroups of children in each classroom and the four time periods. Observations were scheduled in each classroom for a minimum of two and a maximum of four observational periods in a day.

II.   CHILD OBSERVATIONS

A checklist containing 41 categories was used for each 10-second observation. All categories for which behavior occurred were coded, whether the events took place successively or simultaneously.

Coding 41 categories was not as difficult as it might appear. Many categories were not independent and one category often was maintained over a long period of time. For example, 8 of the 41 categories described the subject matter in which the children were engaged, and the subject typically changed no more than once or twice during an observational period.

The 41 categories were organized into eight groups. Four groups described the classroom context: activity type, subject matter, classroom organization, and leader of the activity. Another three groups described behavior of individual children: on-task behaviors, off-task behaviors, and evaluative feedback from the teacher to the child being observed. A final group contained several miscellaneous categories. Each category is described in detail.

A. Activity Type

Activity type was coded first. It consisted of two categories, academic and transitional.

Academic Activity.   The child is working on a specific academic activity, either assigned by the teacher or chosen by the child.

Transitional Activity.   The child is in transition between academic activities. He or she has finished one assignment or task, but has not yet begun the next one. For example, the teacher has handed out homework but has not yet assigned a task; the child is putting away a workbook he/she has been working on and is about to start reading another book; or a child is waiting in line to ask the teacher a question.

One of these two categories was always coded. If the child was in transition from one activity to another, no other category was coded.

B. Subject Matter

The eight categories of subject matter were language, mathematics, social studies, music, art, moral education, study period, and other. The last included subject matter taught infrequently, such as health or religion. Study period was coded when the children were allowed to structure their own time instead of working on an activity prescribed by the teacher. When the child was a member of a small group, the subject matter being studied by the group was coded.

Occasionally, it was difficult for observers in American classrooms to ascertain what subject matter was being taught. Observers were directed in such cases to confer with the teacher after the observational period and code the subject matter according to what the teacher believed she/he was teaching.

C. Classroom Organization

Classroom organization was described by three mutually exclusive categories: class, group, and individual.

Class.   The teacher or classroom leader is working with the class as a whole. Typically, the teacher is lecturing, drilling, giving directions, or directing questions to the entire class. Class is coded even when the teacher interacts with individual students, as long as the whole class still is oriented toward the teacher. Class organization is coded only when there is a leader in the class.

Group.   The teacher has divided the class into small groups that may or may not be working independently of the teacher. For example, the teacher is working with the class. Three children are working together on a separate activity. If the target child (the child being observed during a particular 10-second interval) is part of the larger group, class is coded. If the target child is in the small group, group is coded.

Individual.   Children are working independently and may or may not be working on the same assignment. For example, students are working on their reading workbooks; or the teacher has told a student who has been absent to work independently on an assignment.

D. Leader of the Activity

The leader of an activity in which the child is involved may be the teacher, another adult, a student leader, or no one.

Teacher.   The teacher is involved directly or indirectly with the target child. Examples of direct involvement include talking to or helping the child, and an example of indirect involvement would be lecturing to the class of which the child is a member.

Other Adult.   Another adult, such as the principal, a parent, or a teacher's aid is working with the class, a group, or the individual child.

Student Leader.   Another student has been assigned the responsibility for leading the class or group in which the child is working or directly tutoring the child.

No One.   No one has been assigned the responsibility for working with the class, a group of children, or the individual child.

Our definition of class requires the presence of a leader. Thus, it was impossible to code "no one" as the leader when "class" was coded. If the target child was in a group the leader was coded according to who, if anyone, was leading the group. If "individual" organization was coded, a leader was considered present only if someone was working directly with the target child.

E. On-Task Behavior

The child is doing what is expected by the leader of the class. Any behavior is considered to be on task if it is appropriate, according to the teacher's definition of the situation. There were 12 categories in this group.

Attending.   The child is listening to or watching the teacher, class leader, or another individual. In the last case, the individual must be performing a task defined as appropriate, such as reading to the group. Attending is coded unless the child clearly is engaged in some other activity. Examples of situations where attending is not coded include the following: The teacher is instructing the class and the child is talking with another child; the teacher is writing on the blackboard while lecturing and the child is sitting with his back to the board. The assumption, then, is that unless the child displays clear evidence of not attending, attending is coded.

Volunteering.   The child volunteers to answer an academic question by raising his/her hand or indicating a desire to be chosen.

Asking Academic Question.   The child asks the leader of the class a question about the content of the lesson; for example, "What is the answer to number 4?" or "How do you spell elephant?"

Asking Procedural Question.   The child asks the class leader a question related to procedures to be followed, such as "When is the homework due?" or "Should we use pen or pencil?"

Answering Academic Question.   The child answers a question posed by the class leader. The answer can be verbal or nonverbal, correct or incorrect, and must concern the content of the lesson.

Answering Procedural Question.   The child answers a question about procedures to be followed, directions, or other nonsubstantive matters. For example, the child answers a question posed by the teacher, such as, "What page are you on?" or "Can you see the blackboard?"

Story.   The child recites for an extended period of time. The child could be telling a story, reciting a poem, or giving a show-and-tell presentation.

Choral Responding.   Two or more children respond together in answering a question or reciting. Examples include pledging allegiance to the flag, answering a question in unison, or singing in a group.

Individual Reading Aloud.   The child reads aloud from written material, including letters, numbers, words, or text.

Group Reading Aloud.   Two or more children are reading aloud in unison.

Seatwork.   The child is engaged in a goal-directed activity or task, such as reading silently, working in a notebook, or working on a math problem. If individual organization is coded, all on-task work is coded as seatwork. If the child is listening to the teacher and taking notes, then both attending and seatwork are coded.

Other.   All appropriate, task-relevant behaviors not encompassed in the preceding 11 categories are coded as "other." For example, passing out homework papers at the request of the teacher, tutoring another child, or clapping for another child who gave a good answer would be coded in this category.

F. Off-Task Behaviors

The categories in this group were coded when the child was not doing what he/she was supposed or expected to do. There were two categories in this group.

Inappropriate Peer Interaction.   The child is interacting with a peer rather than engaging in appropriate behaviors. Examples include talking without permission, waving to another child, fighting, or giggling and laughing with other children.

Other Inappropriate Activity.   The child is engaged in off-task behaviors that do not involve peer interaction, such as staring in space while the rest of the class is reading aloud, telling a personal anecdote that is not relevant to the situation, or failing to correct homework with the rest of the class.

G. Evaluative Feedback

The child was given feedback by the teacher about academic work or behavior. Eight categories were in this group, five for coding feedback about academic performance and three for coding feedback about the child's behavior.

Academic Feedback.   The five categories for academic feedback were praise, criticism, correct, incorrect, and no feedback. Praise, criticism, and no feedback conformed to the everyday use of these terms. Correct and incorrect were coded when the teacher indicated to the child only that a response was or was not acceptable.

Behavioral Feedback.   These categories were coded when feedback concerned conduct or behavior of the child. The three categories were praise, criticism, and punishment. Punishment was harsher and more severe than criticism and involved such responses as sending the child from the room or hitting the child.

H. Other Categories

When the observer could not interpret the interaction between the student and the teacher, the category coded was ambiguous teacher–student interaction. Whenever the child was out of his seat, out-of-seat was coded. Because children can be out of their seats for many reasons, it was mandatory that another category also be coded in order to indicate whether the child was engaged in appropriate or inappropriate activity.

Three additional codes should be mentioned. A "9" was coded whenever an observation could not be made due to equipment failure, changes in the class schedule, or other reasons. An "8" indicated that the child was absent from school. A "7" (used only in the American and Japanese classrooms) indicated that the child could not be located, even though he/she was known not to be absent.

III. TEACHER OBSERVATIONS

There were 21 categories in the coding scheme used for teachers. These were divided into four groups: teacher orientation, eliciting response, evaluative feedback, and other.

A. Teacher Orientation

The teacher could be working with the whole class, a smaller group of children, an individual child, or with no one. These were the same categories used to code the child observations, except that they were made from the teacher's point of view rather than the child's. The category "no one" was coded when the teacher was not interacting with any of the children.

B. Eliciting Response

The teacher was considered to be eliciting a response when she was doing something to obtain a response from the children. There were four categories.

Asking an Academic Question to an Individual. The teacher directs a content-related question to a specific student or to a student who is volunteering.

Asking an Academic Question to a Group. A question related to academic content is directed to the class or group as a whole.

Asking a Nonacademic Question. The teacher asks a question that is unrelated to the content of the lesson.

Giving Directions. The teacher gives directions about work to be done or makes statements that are intended to guide the students' behavior in a particular activity.

C. Evaluative Feedback

When the teacher offered feedback concerning a child's academic performance, the coding scheme was the same as that used in observations of the children. Coding for behavioral feedback also followed the scheme used in the observations of children, except that the three categories were expanded to four. Two, praise and punishment, were identical to those used to code behavioral feedback in the observations of children. Two categories, physical correction and reprimand, were substituted for the category "criticism." When the teacher touched a child in order to correct a child's behavior, physical correction was coded. Reprimand, including threats, warnings, and scoldings, was coded when the child was criticized.

D. Other Categories

Four other categories were used in observations of the teacher.

Imparting Academic Information. The teacher transmits academic information to students. Examples include lecturing to the class, explaining class work to individuals or groups, answering students' questions about academic matters, or reading to the class.

Ambiguous Teacher–Student Interaction. This was coded in the same manner as in the observations of children.

Audio-Visual. Use was being made of a television set, movie projector, or another audio-visual device.

Other. This category was coded whenever the teacher's behavior could not be described by any of the preceding categories.

APPENDIX 4.B

Summary of Analyses of Variance of the Observational Data

Category	df	Country (2,114)	Grade (2,114)	Sex (1,1286)	C × G (2,114)
Subject matter					
Language arts		17.43***	35.49***		
Math		11.15***	9.60**		5.79**
Social studies			27.75***		
Music		10.94***	4.58*		
Art					
Moral education		27.22***			
Study period		4.84**			
Other		25.54***	7.81**		4.84**
Percent transitional		13.11***	19.60***		
Organization					
Class		90.22***			
Group		36.94***			5.86**
Individual		62.72***			
Leader					
Teacher		112.68***			
Another adult		12.68***			
Student		23.46***			7.28**
No one		142.06***			
Ambiguous teacher–child relation		36.65***			
Children's behavior (appropriate)					
Attending		56.50***	4.05*	14.33***	5.06**
Volunteering					
Ask academic question		8.82***	4.17*		
Ask procedural question		9.05***			
Answer academic question					5.12**
Answer procedural question					
Tell a story		5.46**			
Choral response		83.17***	11.17**		
Read (individual)		8.26***			4.34*
Read (group)		85.36***	4.50*		
Seatwork		17.04***		31.50***	
Other appropriate behavior		25.54***	7.81***		4.84**
Children's behavior (inappropriate)					
Out-of-seat		87.13***	21.64***		11.95***
Out-of-seat, off-task		58.78***	14.31***	27.63***	5.68**
Peer interaction		13.16***		17.74***	

(*continued*)

Category	df	Variable			
		Country (2,114)	Grade (2,114)	Sex (1,1286)	C × G (2,114)
Other inappropriate behavior		4.72*	14.94***	89.61***	
Total inappropriate behavior		11.55***	6.06*	71.77***	
Teacher's response to children (observations of child)					
Praise				11.80***	
Information (correct)					
Neutral					
Information (incorrect)					
Criticism					
Teacher's response to children (observations of teacher)					
Praise		3.40*			
Criticism		7.48***	4.07*	20.19***	
Punishment				4.77*	
Total behavioral feedback			5.05*	18.80***	

*$p < .05$
**$p < .01$
***$p < .001$

Note: County × Sex interactions were found for the following: Ask academic question ($F = 3.36*$), Other inappropriate ($F = 7.40***$), Inappropriate total ($F = 7.67***$), and Criticism ($F = 4.48**$). Grade × sex interactions were found for Study period ($F = 4.98*$), Choral responding ($F = 6.74**$), Seatwork ($F = 4.91*$), Peer Interaction ($F = 6.07*$), and Praise ($F = 4.43*$). Country × grade × sex interactions were found for Study period ($F = 3.92*$), Other subject matter ($F = 3.23*$), and Other appropriate activities ($F = 3.23*$).

APPENDIX 4.C

Summary of Analyses of Variance of Categories
Showing Significant Effects Associated with Subject Matter
(Language Arts vs. Math) (Subject Matter = S, Culture = C, Grade = G)

		Variable			
Category	df	S (1,112)	SC (2,112)	CG (2,112)	SCG (2,112)
Organization					
Class			4.24*		
Group		4.07*	5.31*		5.74**
Leader					
Student		15.37***	14.12***	5.51*	4.48*
Children's behavior (appropriate)					
Volunteering		7.83**			
Answering academic question		11.52***			
Tell a story		6.37*	7.54***		
Choral response		8.66**	3.48*	8.51**	8.40***
Read (individual)		35.28***			3.43*
Read (group)		54.11***	39.93***		
Seatwork		6.95**	4.86**		
Children's behavior (inappropriate)					
Out-of-seat			3.84*		6.15**
Teacher's response to children (observations of children)					
Information (correct)		5.30*			
Neutral		4.15*			
Information (incorrect)		4.54*			
Total academic feedback		11.50***			

*p < .05
**p < .01
***p < .001

Author Index

Subject Index

A

Ability (*see also* Individual differences)
  crystalized, 98, 104, 140
Academic activities and transitions, cross-cultural differences in, 164–166
  and leadership, 171–172, 174, 185, 197–198
  time-on-task, 174–178, 188, 198
  teacher feedback, 182–185
Achievement
  comparative studies of, xxiii, 153–154, 156 (*see also* Classroom processes, cross-cultural observational studies)
  within classrooms, 185–187
Adaptive instruction, in reading, 8
Algorithm, subtraction, 44, 46 (*see also* Bugs and Procedures)
Automaticity, x–xi
  in arithmetic performances, xxi, xxii, 91–3
  in decoding skills, xv–xvi, 2–3, 5–6, 8, 10, 23–24
  in discourse processing, 30, 140
  in high-performance skills, xvi–xvii

B

Bugs, subtraction, xxi–xxii, 43–47
  categories of, 47–48

instruction to remediate, 72, 82–84 (*see also* Mapping and Prohibition instruction)
theory of the origins of, 44

C

Children's behavior (*see* Student behavior)
Classroom processes
  studies of, vii–viii, xix–xx, 155
    cross-cultural observational, xxiii–xxiv, 154–156 (*see also* Academic activities, Student behavior, Subject-matter treatment, Teaching)
    data analysis, 162–163, 193–204
    design of, 159–161
    samples for, 156–159, 187
    scheduling of observations, 193–201
  organization, cross-cultural differences in, 155, 163–164, 170–171, 185, 197
Cognitive theory
  and instructional theory, vii, xii, xviii–xix, xxiv
  of intelligence, 145–146
  of learning and instructional design, xii–xxiv, 1–2
  of procedural skills, 41–42
  and verbal comprehension, 97–98
    alternative approaches to, 98–103